CCENT/CCNA: ICND1 100-105 Certification Guide

Learn computer network essentials and enhance your networking skills by obtaining the CCENT certification

Bekim Dauti

BIRMINGHAM - MUMBAI

CCENT/CCNA: ICND1 100-105 Certification Guide

Commissioning Editor: Vijin Boricha
Acquisition Editor: Rahul Nair
Content Development Editor: Abhishek Jadhav
Technical Editor: Manish Shanbhag
Copy Editors: Safis Editing, Dipti Mankame
Project Coordinator: Judie Jose
Proofreader: Safis Editing
Indexer: Pratik Shirodkar
Graphics: Tom Scaria
Production Coordinator: Shraddha Falebhai

First published: April 2018

Production reference: 1300418

Published by Packt Publishing Ltd.
Livery Place
35 Livery Street
Birmingham
B3 2PB, UK.

ISBN 978-1-78862-143-4

www.packtpub.com

I would like to dedicate this book to the lovely people of Municipality of Gjilan, Kosovo, and Municipality of Lipkovo, Macedonia.

—Bekim Dauti

`mapt.io`

Mapt is an online digital library that gives you full access to over 5,000 books and videos, as well as industry leading tools to help you plan your personal development and advance your career. For more information, please visit our website.

Why subscribe?

- Spend less time learning and more time coding with practical eBooks and Videos from over 4,000 industry professionals

- Improve your learning with Skill Plans built especially for you

- Get a free eBook or video every month

- Mapt is fully searchable

- Copy and paste, print, and bookmark content

PacktPub.com

Did you know that Packt offers eBook versions of every book published, with PDF and ePub files available? You can upgrade to the eBook version at `www.PacktPub.com` and as a print book customer, you are entitled to a discount on the eBook copy. Get in touch with us at `service@packtpub.com` for more details.

At `www.PacktPub.com`, you can also read a collection of free technical articles, sign up for a range of free newsletters, and receive exclusive discounts and offers on Packt books and eBooks.

About the author

Bekim Dauti works mainly with the administration of computer systems and networks, as well as vocational training in Cisco and Microsoft technologies. Bekim has a bachelor's degree from the University of Tirana and a master's from UMUC Europe, both in information technology. Additionally, he holds several IT certifications from vendors such as ECDL, MOS, CompTIA, Cisco, Microsoft, and Sun Microsystems. Bekim has contributed to over 10 computer books and dozens of articles for PC World Albanian and CIO Albania. Currently, he works as a system administrator at Kosovo Telecom JSC.

I thank God for giving me life, health, and the opportunity to contribute with knowledge sharing. May God Almighty reward my family, friends, the folks at Packt Publishing, teammates at Kosovo Telecom JSC Sys Admin team, my colleagues both at InfoTech Kosova and Qendra për Trajnim dhe Zhvillim, and everyone who supported me in writing this book. Last but not least, peace and blessings to every reader.

About the reviewer

Shiva V.N. Parasram is a professional Cyber Security Trainer and the owner of the Computer Forensics and Security Institute (CFSI). He is also a Certified EC-Council Instructor (CEI), and some of his qualifications include an MSc in Network Security (Distinction), CEH, CHFI, ECSA, CCNA, and NSE. He has successfully executed and delivered forensic investigations, penetration tests, and security training for large enterprises, and he is also the author of Digital Forensics with Kali Linux.

> *If you have to be anything, be brave—Indra J. Parasram. Always be patient, son—Harry G. Parasram. To my parents and best friends. The love that stayed, the love I know. Thank you.*

Packt is searching for authors like you

If you're interested in becoming an author for Packt, please visit `authors.packtpub.com` and apply today. We have worked with thousands of developers and tech professionals, just like you, to help them share their insight with the global tech community. You can make a general application, apply for a specific hot topic that we are recruiting an author for, or submit your own idea.

Table of Contents

Preface

CCENT is the entry-level certification for those looking to venture into the networking world. This guide will help you stay up to date with your networking skills. This book starts with the basics and will take you through everything you need to pass the certification exam. It extensively covers IPv4 and IPv6 addressing, IP data networks, switching and routing, network security, and much more—all in some detail. This guide will provide real-world examples with a bunch of hands-on labs to give you immense expertise in important networking tasks, with a practical approach. Each chapter consists of practice questions to help you take up a challenge from what you have procured. This book ends with mock tests with several examples to help you confidently pass the certification. This Certification Guide consists of everything you need to know in order to pass the ICND 1 100-105 exam, thus obtaining a CCENT certification. However, practicing with real switches and routers or a switch or router simulator will help you succeed.

Who this book is for

If you are a Network Administrator, Network Technician, Networking professional, or would simply like to prepare for your CCENT certification, then this book is for you. Some basic understanding of networks and how they work would be helpful. Sufficient information will be provided to those new to this field.

What this book covers

Chapter 1, *Introduction to Computer Networks*, will teach you about the general concepts of computer networks. In addition, the reader will learn how to build a computer network.

Chapter 2, *Communication in Computer Networks*, will help you understand about communication protocols in computer networks. In addition, the reader will learn about OSI and TCP/IP reference models, IP addressing, IP subnetting, and Ethernet communication technology.

Chapter 3, *Introduction to Switching*, will make you familiar with the switch as an intermediary networking device. At the same time, the reader will learn how switches operate and how to connect a switch to a network.

Chapter 4, *Setting Up the Switch*, will provide an explanation of how to configure a switch in a step-by-step manner.

Chapter 5, *Introduction to Routing,* will make you familiar with the router as an intermediary networking device. At the same time, you will learn how routers function and how to connect a router to a network.

Chapter 6, *Setting Up the Router,* will help you understand how to configure a router in a step-by-step manner.

Chapter 7, *Network Services and Maintenance,* will teach you about the network service and how to enable services on a computer network. In addition, you will become familiar with maintenance process, and you will learn how to maintain the computer network's performance.

Chapter 8, *Network Troubleshooting,* will help you understand troubleshooting, and then you will be able to rectify errors and problems in computer networks.

Chapter 9, *Studying and Preparing for the ICND 1(100-105) Exam,* will make you familiar with ICND 1 (100-105) exam and learn how to prepare for and pass it in a simple and convenient way.

Appendix A, *Answers to Chapters Questions,* contains chapter wise answers to the questions mentioned in the chapters.

Appendix B, *Cisco Device Icons,* represents the symbols that are used in Cisco Network Topology.

Appendix C, *Numbering Systems and Conversions,* explains the binary, octal and hexadecimal numbers along with conversions from decimal to binary, octal and hexadecimal.

Appendix D, *Boolean Algebra,* explains the boolean operations.

Appendix E, *Subnetting,* explains the method of subnetting using examples.

Appendix F, *Cisco Packet Tracer,* explains the installation of Cisco Packet Tracer.

Appendix G, *Graphical Network Simulator-3 (GNS-3),* explains installation of GNS-3.

To get the most out of this book

To understand the content of this book, it is recommended that you have basic knowledge in computer networks. If you are certified with CompTIA Network +, that would be a good foundation for you to advance your knowledge about computer networks through this book.

As you know, it does not make sense to learn computer networks without doing any practical work. Therefore, the suggestions are to practice making cables such as straight through, crossover, and roll over. Setting up a LAN with at least a Cisco switch and router. And download emulators and simulators like Putty and Tera Term, Packet Tracer and GNS3, and Wireshark. All the download links are included on the book.

Download the color images

We also provide a PDF file that has color images of the screenshots/diagrams used in this book. You can download it from `https://www.packtpub.com/sites/default/files/downloads/CCENTCCNAICND1100105CertificationGuide_ColorImages.pdf`.

Conventions used

There are a number of text conventions used throughout this book.

`CodeInText`: Indicates code words in text, database table names, folder names, filenames, file extensions, pathnames, dummy URLs, user input, and Twitter handles. Here is an example: "In the privileged EXEC prompt, enter the `show running-config` (or `show startup-config`) command and press *Enter*."

Any command-line input or output is written as follows:

```
C:\>ping 127.0.0.1
```

Bold: Indicates a new term, an important word, or words that you see onscreen. For example, words in menus or dialog boxes appear in the text like this. Here is an example:

In Windows 10, click **Yes** to let the app make changes to your device:

 Warnings or important notes appear like this.

 Tips and tricks appear like this.

Get in touch

Feedback from our readers is always welcome.

General feedback: Email `feedback@packtpub.com` and mention the book title in the subject of your message. If you have questions about any aspect of this book, please email us at `questions@packtpub.com`.

Errata: Although we have taken every care to ensure the accuracy of our content, mistakes do happen. If you have found a mistake in this book, we would be grateful if you would report this to us. Please visit `www.packtpub.com/submit-errata`, selecting your book, clicking on the Errata Submission Form link, and entering the details.

Piracy: If you come across any illegal copies of our works in any form on the Internet, we would be grateful if you would provide us with the location address or website name. Please contact us at copyright@packtpub.com with a link to the material.

If you are interested in becoming an author: If there is a topic that you have expertise in and you are interested in either writing or contributing to a book, please visit authors.packtpub.com.

Reviews

Please leave a review. Once you have read and used this book, why not leave a review on the site that you purchased it from? Potential readers can then see and use your unbiased opinion to make purchase decisions, we at Packt can understand what you think about our products, and our authors can see your feedback on their book. Thank you!

For more information about Packt, please visit packtpub.com.

1
Introduction to Computer Networks

This chapter is designed to provide you with an introduction to computer networks. It begins with the evolution of **Advanced Research Projects Agency Network** (**ARPANET**) to the internet, and then continues with the explanation of the computer network concept. This chapter discusses the types of networks, topologies, components, architectures, **network operating systems** (**NOS**s), and network media where definitions such as **personal area network** (**PAN**), **local area network** (**LAN**), **metropolitan area network** (**MAN**), **wide area network** (**WAN**), bus, ring, star, extended star, hierarchical, mesh, hosts, nodes, peer-to-peer, and clients/servers are explained. The chapter concludes with a discussion about converged networks, and the current and future computer network trends. To facilitate the understanding of the many definitions covered in this chapter, a large part of the definitions are illustrated with relevant figures.

In this chapter, we will cover:

- Understanding ARPANET and the internet
- Understanding computer networks
- Understanding types of computer networks
- Understanding computer network topologies
- Understanding computer network components
- Understanding computer network architectures
- Understanding network operating systems
- Understanding network medium
- Understanding converged networks
- Understanding computer network trends

From ARPANET to internet

No one can explain the history of the internet better than the internet itself! Everything started with the US government's project to build a stable and tolerant-in-defects communication network known as the **Defense Advanced Research Projects Agency (DARPA)**. The involvement of research centers and academic institutions in the DARPA project made this project gradually evolve into the **ARPANET** and the **Military Network (MILNET)**. While the MILNET project was tasked to support operational requirements, the ARPANET project was undertaken to support the need for research (https://www.internetsociety.org/). That said, from 1962 to 1985, the internet already had built its profile. Thus, based on the saying *"every new beginning is some beginning's end"*, the appearance of the internet on the global computer network stage formally marked the end of the ARPANET's golden era.

According to the internetsociety.org, on October 24, 1995, the **Federal Networking Council (FNC)** through a resolution, priory consulted with members of the internet community and intellectual property rights, defined the term **internet**. According to that resolution, the internet refers to the global information system, which:

- Is logically connected by a global unique address space based on the **Internet Protocol (IP)** or its subsequent updates;
- Is able to support the communication through a TCP/IP protocol suite or its subsequent updates and other compatible protocols, and;
- Provides, uses and makes accessible, either publicly or privately, high-level layered services on the communications and related infrastructure described in that document.

Over time, the development and advancement of computer network technologies took place. Thus, the need to connect and interconnect more computers to computer networks, and with it, more geographical locations, created a need for well-defined terms and concepts to describe computer networking. Because of this, types of computer networks, computer network topologies, computer network architectures, and computer network components were born. Certainly, a computer network represents one of the biggest inventions of mankind in the field of communications. Simply, mention the internet and one will immediately understand how huge the benefit of a computer network is to humanity.

 You can learn about the brief history of the internet from https://www.internetsociety.org/internet/history-internet/.

What is a computer network?

Before defining computer network, let's first look at the general term of a network in order to then recognize the computer network definition in particular. If you do a search for the word *network* in the Merriam-Webster dictionary, you'll find the definition that a "*network is a group of people or organizations that are closely linked and that work with each other.*" On the same *Merriam-Webster* dictionary, the phrase *networking* is defined as "*exchange of information or services among individuals, groups or institutions.*" Both of these definitions will serve us in a simple, clear, and concrete way to define *computer network* in the following paragraph.

From what was said in the preceding paragraph, a **computer network** is a group of computers connected to each other in order to share resources. When talking about **resources**, usually the resources can be data, network services, and peripheral devices. So, anyone who has experience with computer networks has seen that it is very easy to share files, applications, printers, and other peripheral devices in computer networks. *Figure 1.1* presents an example of a computer network:

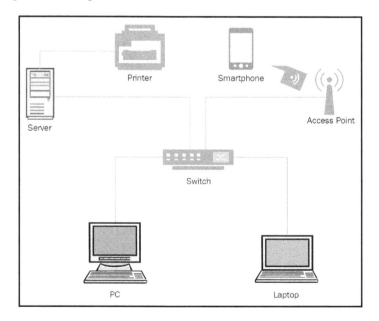

Figure 1.1. Computer network

You can learn more about computer networks at `https://www.computerhope.com/jargon/n/network.htm`.

Requirements for designing a computer network

Of course, the most beautiful part of a computer network is how to design and build one. Computer network design and deployment is Designing and deploying is linked to its definition. Thus, the fundamental requirement for designing a computer network is that there must be two or more computers. Depending on the number of computers on the network and how they access the resources from the same network determines the categorization of computer network types, which will be explained in the following section.

Types of computer networks

Over time, the desire to implement the first computer network, as a result of curiosity, had already been converted to a need that would fulfill the requirements. Precisely, it also led to the development and advancement of computer networking technologies. Thus, the need to connect and interconnect more computers into computer networks, and with it, more locations, in itself resulted as the need to define topologies, architectures, technologies, and computer networking categories. In this way, the types of computer networks like PAN, LAN, MAN, and WAN were born.

You can learn more about types of computer networks at `https://www.lifewire.com/lans-wans-and-other-area-networks-817376`.

Personal area network (PAN)

A **PAN** is defined as a computer network that is used to connect and transmit data among devices located in a personal area, usually over Bluetooth or Wi-Fi to interconnect devices (see *Figure 1.2*). Occasionally, this computer network is called a **home area network** (**HAN**) too:

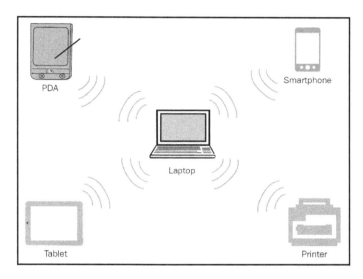

Figure 1.2. Personal Area Network (PAN)

Local area network (LAN)

To understand the **LAN**, let's compare it with the PAN. A PAN is dominated by portable devices (for example, smartphone), while a LAN mainly consists of fixed devices. Both computer networks are covering the local area; however, the LAN has a greater coverage than the PAN, because the LAN usually can cover the floor of the building, several floors of the building, an entire building, or even a few buildings that are close to one another. From that, the main difference is that a PAN is mainly organized around an individual, while a LAN is organized around an organization, business, or legal entity. This then precisely defines the LAN as a computer network that connects two or more computers in a local area for the purpose of sharing resources, as in *Figure 1.1*.

Metropolitan area network (MAN)

From the standpoint of coverage, the **MAN** is bigger than the LAN and smaller than the WAN, whilst from the viewpoint of data transmission speeds, the MAN is faster than both the LAN and WAN. As it was with the PAN and LAN, the reason for the MAN's existence is the need for sharing and accessing the resources in the city or metro. From that, a MAN represents a group of LANs interconnected within the geographical boundary of a town or city, as in *Figure 1.3*:

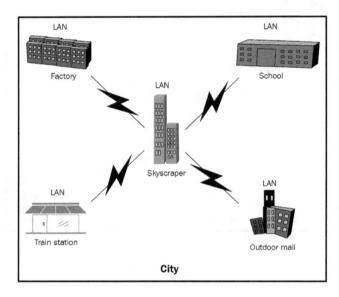

Figure 1.3. Metropolitan Area Network (MAN)

Wide area network (WAN)

Areas that are not covered by a LAN or MAN are covered by a **WAN**. Thus, a WAN is a computer network that covers a wide geographic area using dedicated telecommunication lines such as telephone lines, leased lines, or satellites. That being said, unlike other computer networks which have geographic restrictions of their physical reach, WAN does not. From that, it is obvious that WANs are made up of PANs, LANs, and MANs (see *Figure 1.4*). With that in mind, the best example of a WAN is the internet:

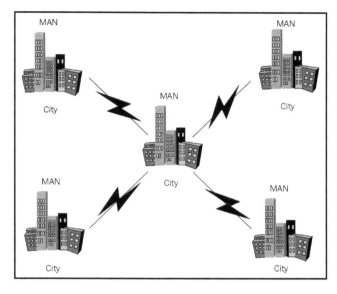

Figure 1.4. Wide Area Network (WAN)

Intranet

The **intranet** is a networking platform primarily designed for employees. That said, it is considered to be the private network of an organization where employees can access network services. The intranet is not just a portal; instead, it is a network that consists of hardware and software too. To better understand it, consider the intranet as an organization's extended LAN, or MAN, or even WAN network. It consists of multiple cables, network devices such as switches, routers, microwave and satellite antennas, access points, servers, computers, and various applications. All that enables employees to communicate, develop content, collaborate in joint projects, and get the job done.

Extranet

In contrast, the **extranet** can be thought of as an intranet with a controlled access. Like the intranet, the extranet is a networking platform too; however, besides employees, the extranet enables controlled access to an organization's intranet for authorized partners, suppliers, customers, or others business-related individuals and organizations outside the company. Specifically, the extranet represents a controlled access method of the organization's intranet using internet infrastructure.

Computer network topologies

Another way to categorize computer networks is by their **topology**, or the way in which hosts and nodes are arranged and connected to one another, and how they communicate. The computer network mainly recognizes two types of topologies: physical, and logical.

 You can learn more about computer network topologies at http://www.certiology.com/computing/computer-networking/network-topology.html.

Physical topology

Physical topology presents ordering, arrangement, and placement of the physical parts of a computer network, such as computers, peripheral devices, cables for data transmission, and network equipment. Thus, the physical topology of the computer network actually represents its physical structure, which is usually presented in the following shapes: bus, ring, star, extended star, hierarchical, and mesh.

Bus

Bus is the physical topology in which computers, peripheral and network devices are connected through the bus that mainly consists of a coaxial cable (see *Figure 1.5*):

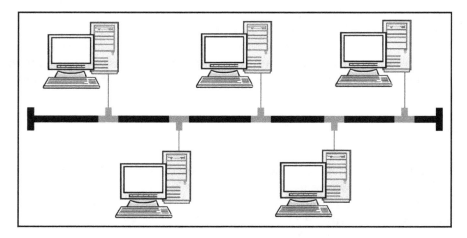

Figure 1.5. Bus physical topology

Ring

Ring is the physical topology in which computers, peripheral and network devices form a closed cycle that takes the shape of a ring network where each device is connected to each other (see *Figure 1.6*). In the past, the coaxial cable was used, but nowadays in dual ring networks, optical fiber is used:

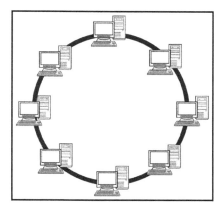

Figure 1.6. Ring physical topology

Star

Star is the physical topology in which computers, peripheral and network devices are connected independently with a central device (see *Figure 1.7*). For this type of topology, mainly a twisted pair cable is used:

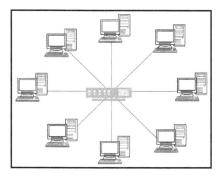

Figure 1.7. Star physical topology

Extended star

Extended star is the physical topology in which computers and peripheral and network devices are connected into two or more star topology networks and then the central components (that is, switches) are interconnected over a bus. In appearance, this type of topology combines star and bus topologies (see *Figure 1.8*). Mainly, a twisted cable pair is used for the star topology, while an optical fiber is used for the bus topology:

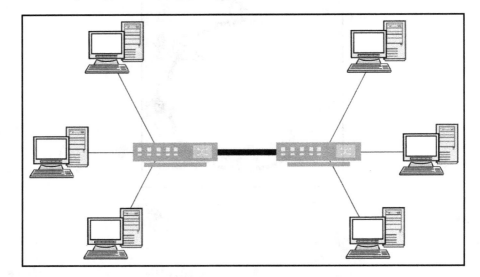

Figure 1.8. Extended star physical topology

Hierarchical

Hierarchical is the physical topology that represents a combination of star and bus topologies. This topology must have at least three levels of hierarchy in which star topologies connect one or more nodes to a single main node, so that all these together are related to the main trunk of the tree (see *Figure 1.9*). As in the case of an extended star topology, this topology uses twisted pair cables and optical fiber:

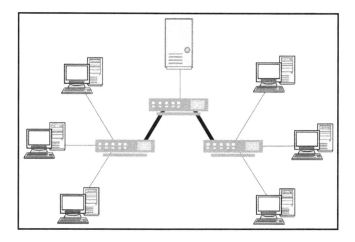

Figure 1.9. Hierarchical physical topology

Mesh

Mesh is the physical topology in which each computer is connected with every computer to form the network (see *Figure 1.10*). Usually, this type of topology is utilized by a WAN to interconnect LANs:

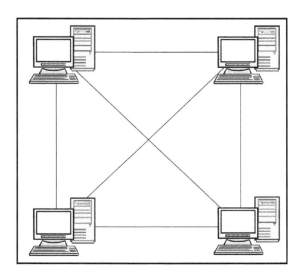

Figure 1.10. Mesh physical topology

Logical topology

Unlike physical topology, **logical topology** represents the logical aspect of the computer network. In logical topology, it is the logical paths that are used to carry electric or light signals from one computer to another, or from one network node to another node. Thus, this topology represents the way in which the data accesses the transmission medium and transmits packets through it. *Figure 1.11* presents the logical topology with its logical components such as computer names, network equipment, network communication technology, and IP addresses:

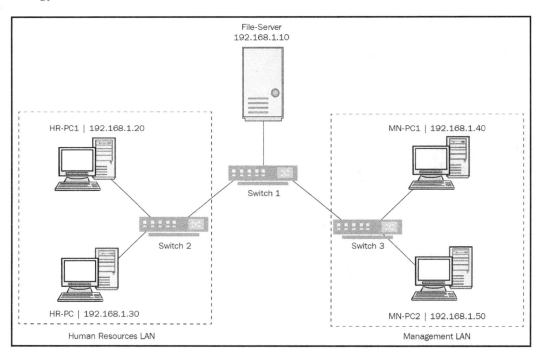

Figure 1.11. Logical topology

Computer network components

Obviously, when talking about computer networks it is essential to mention **components** of a computer network, because computer networks are ultimately composed of their constituent components. Usually, computers and peripheral devices are just some of the computer network components known to most people; however, there are also intermediary devices and network media.

Knowing that the primary purpose of the computer networks has to do with sharing resources, it is very important to understand the process of how the resources are both shared and accessed. Here comes into play the concept of the client and the server, where the client is the one that always requests resources, and the server is the one that provides the requested resources. To better understand clients and servers, as well as the concept of requesting and providing resources, the following sections explain the network components.

You can learn more about computer network components at `https://en.wikiversity.org/wiki/Basic_computer_network_components`.

Clients

Now, going back to the concepts of requesting a resource and providing a resource, actually, that is what is shaping the definition of clients and servers in the computer network. **Clients**, in most cases, are computers that request the resources in a computer network. Clients have an active role in the computer network (see *Figure 1.11*).

Servers

Furthermore, **servers** are network components that provide resources to clients. Servers too have an active role. The following figure, *Figure 1.1*, presents the server with a shared printer in the role of the resource provider, and the PC and laptop in the role of resource requesters.

Hosts and nodes

When talking about hosts and nodes, although their first impression might drive us towards thinking that they are the same thing, in fact they are not! The difference between hosts and nodes is that, while all hosts can be nodes, not every node can act as a host. That way, to every host there is an assigned IP address. So, a **host** is any device with an IP address that requests or provides networking resources to any other host or node on the network; however, there are devices such as hubs, bridges, switches, modems, and access points that have no IP address assigned, but are still used for communications. That said, a **node** is any device that can generate, receive, and transmit the networking resources on the computer network but has no interface with an IP address. Based on that, in *Figure 1.1*, server, smartphone, PC, and laptop are hosts, while switch and **Access Point** (**AP**) act as nodes.

Network interface

A **network interface** is a component-like network card or LAN port on network equipment that enables clients, servers, peripheral devices, and network equipment to get connected and communicate with each other. The network interface has both a passive and an active (manageable network equipment) role in the computer network (see *Figure 1.12*):

Figure 1.12. Network interface card (NIC)

Peripheral devices

Peripheral devices are printers, scanners, **storage area networks** (**SAN**s), and any other peripheral device that provides resources to clients, either through a LAN or as a shared device on a network. These devices play both a passive and an active (like SAN and NAS) role in the computer network:

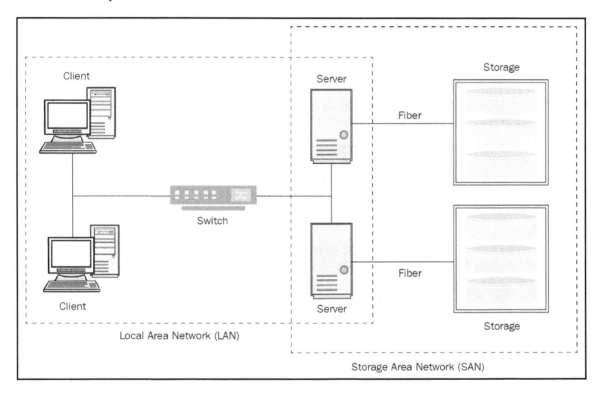

Figure 1.13. Storage area network (SAN)

Applications and shared data

Applications and shared data are virtual network components that represent applications and files shared on the network that are usually provided by servers. These components themselves play a passive role in the computer network, but the server that hosts these services plays an active role in the computer network.

Hubs and switches

Hubs and switches are acting as central components (in Ethernet communication technology) of the computer network to enable interconnection and communication between clients, servers, and peripheral devices, as in *Figure 1.14* . Most hubs are passive devices, while switches play an active role in the computer network:

Figure 1.14. Stack of Cisco switches

Routers

Routers (see *Figure 1.15*) are computer network components that enable routing of the data (that is, packets) from a LAN to the internet, and vice versa. Routers have an active role in the computer network:

Figure 1.15. Stack of Cisco routers

Infrastructure components

Network infrastructure is also the part of the discussion when we discuss about network components. So, of course, the question is, what is network infrastructure? In its simple format the answer would be that **network infrastructure** is any physical and logical network component that enables connection, communication, operation, management, and security of the network.

Firewall

No matter what professional background you might have, it is just enough to get to know the name of the firewall and you will immediately think that there is no joke with such device. Leaving the humor aside, a **firewall** (see *Figure 1.16*) is a network device that provides security to the network infrastructure. It does so by controlling and monitoring both incoming and outgoing traffic based on configured security rules. In a nutshell, the firewall to a network infrastructure is like a security officer at an organization's main gate:

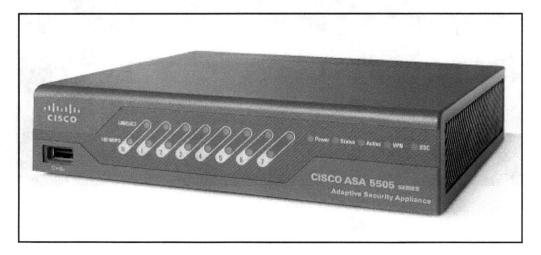

Figure 1.16. Cisco firewall

Wireless access point

Nowadays, we often hear expressions like "*I got connected to the internet with wireless*" or "*I've found an open wireless.*" This and many other similar expressions make us understand that the discussion is about the access point. That said, an AP (see *Figure 1.17*), often known as a **wireless access point**, is a network device that enables access to the wired network. With APs in a network infrastructure, the network becomes more accessible by enabling the access to organization services while on the go. In addition, it enables the support for the new trends like **Bring Your Own Devices (BYOD)**:

Figure 1.17. Stack of access points (APs)

Wireless access controller

Since network infrastructure has many network devices, including APs for the security purposes as well as for the **quality of services** (**QoS**), organizations will employ a **wireless access controller**. It is a networking device that enables organizations to centrally manage APs.

Computer network architectures

When talking about computer networks, actually we are talking about the essential and broader concept of the elements that make up a computer network. In this form of discussion, while the computer network types deal with the area coverage, the physical and logical topologies deal with the physical arrangement and logical structure of the computer network. Having said that, the computer network architecture represents the computer network design that allows the computer network components to communicate with one another.

You can learn more about computer network architectures at `https://it.toolbox.com/blogs/craigborysowich/network-architecture-types-092110`.

Peer-to-peer networking (P2P)

Peer-to-peer is a computer network in which the participating computers do not play the predefined roles in the network, but instead they change roles from client to server, and vice versa, based on the actual activity on the network. For example, if computer A is accessing resources from computer B, then computer A acts as the client, while computer B acts as the server. After some time, if computer B accesses resources from computer A, then computer B becomes a client and computer A becomes a server. As you may notice, they switch roles based on who is requesting and who is providing a resource on the network. *Figure 1.18* presents an example of peer-to-peer networking:

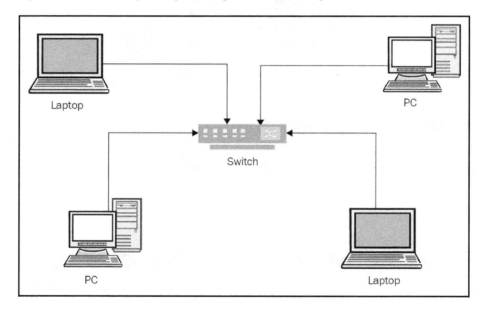

Figure 1.18. Peer-to-peer computer network

Client/server networking

Client/server is a computer network in which participating computers have a predefined role. That means that, in this computer network architecture, computers that access resources act as clients, while computers that provide resources act as servers. In general, this is a computer network architecture with dedicated servers that provide resources on the network. Midsize and enterprise computer networks are the best example of the client/server computer network. *Figure 1.19* presents an example of client/server networking:

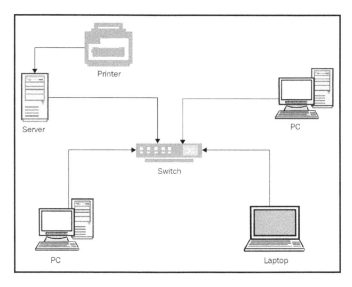

Figure 1.19. Client/server computer network

Network operating system (NOS)

An **NOS** is software that, alongside the execution of common computer programs, enables the provision of network services too. The most common network services are file and print sharing; however, today's NOSs are noticeably more advanced. Thus, NOS enables you to configure network services such as directory services, web server, mail server, database server, proxy server, DHCP server, remote access server, and many more. Just as the services provided by NOS are varied, the NOS itself is different too. So, the most popular NOSs today are Windows Server, Linux Server, and macOS X server.

Windows

The **Windows Server** (see Figure 1.20) is Microsoft's OS designed for servers. It is a **Graphical User Interface (GUI)**-based OS; however, since Windows Server 2008, there is a Server Core option that is based on the **Command Line Interface (CLI)**. As of the Windows Server 2012 R2 version, they are offered only in 64-bit platform. The **New Technology File System (NTFS)** continues to be Microsoft's Windows Server filesystem; however, Windows Server 2012 has introduced the **Resilient File System (ReFS)** as an attempt to succeed the NTFS:

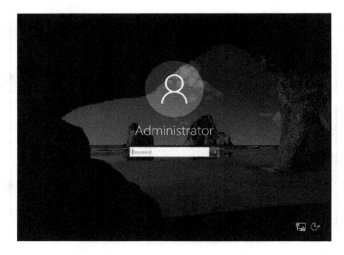

Figure 1.20. Login screen in Windows Server 2016

Linux

If there is something worth mentioning in the world of information technology in general, operating systems in particular, it is unequivocally the **Linux** OS (see *Figure 1.21*). That is because the world of technology knows no innovative initiative to have gathered more volunteers than Linux itself. Unlike Windows Server, known to be proprietary OS, Linux server is licensed under the GNU GPL (free software license) and distributed by several distros such as Red Hat, SUSE, Oracle, Novell, Ubuntu, Debian, Mandrake, Mandriva, and so on. The Linux community is one of the largest communities in the world of volunteer developers from across the globe that would contribute to further Linux development. In essence, Linux is CLI-based, but there are also versions of graphical user interfaces like KDE and GNOME among the most popular. Linux, like Windows Server, is offered in 64-bit platform too:

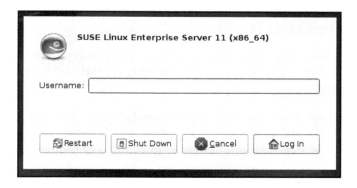

Figure 1.21. Login screen in SUSE Linux Enterprise Server 11

macOS X Server

Perhaps by age, macOS X Server (see *Figure 1.22*) is younger than Windows Server and Linux Server NOSs, but in terms of reliability it is gaining more and more industrial support. In its heart, macOS X Server is basically a version of Unix OS, but has been customized to conform to the familiar GUI of Apple OS for Mac computers. Like Windows Server and Linux Server, macOS X Server is offered in 64-bit too. It is worth mentioning the unique fact that the macOS X Server runs only on Apple's hardware. It is a GUI-based NOS; however, considering the UNIX origin, obviously it can be administered entirely through the CLI as well:

Figure 1.22. Login screen in macOS X Server

Network medium

Depending on whether it is a physical medium (cable) or a wave-based communication (wireless), mainly the following **networking mediums** for data transferring and communication are used:

- **Metallic** mediums, copper wires in twisted pairs and coaxial cables transmit electrical impulses
- **Glass** mediums, fibre optic cable transmit pulses of light
- **Air** mediums, waves and rays from the electromagnetic spectrum transmit signals in different frequencies

 You can learn more about computer network mediums at `https://www.techwalla.com/articles/types-of-media-used-in-computer-networking`.

Twisted pairs

Twisted pairs, as in *Figure 1.23*, is a cable that contains four twisted pairs of copper; a total of eight wires, each with a specified color. The single wires are twisted around each other forming twisted pairs, and then the pairs are twisted around each other forming the cable; and that is done to reduce **electromagnetic interference** (EMI) and cross-talk. Usually, it is available in two types: **unshielded twisted pair** (UTP), and **shielded twisted pair** (STP). Mainly, it is used for designing LANs. The maximum distance that the twisted pairs medium can successfully carry a signal in an Ethernet network is 100 m.

Figure 1.23. UTP cable

Coaxial

Coaxial, as in *Figure 1.24*, is a copper cable presented in two forms: thin coaxial, with a length up to 185 m; and thick coaxial, with a length up to 500 m. In the past, it was used to implement computer networks with the bus and ring physical topologies. Nowadays, it is mainly used by cable **Internet Service Providers** (ISP) for transferring data and video signal:

Figure 1.24. Coaxial cable

Fibre optic

Fibre optic, as in *Figure 1.25*, is a cable made up of glass through which the light is transmitted. Based on the light transmission, it is offered in two modes:

- **Single mode** utilizes only one light, and can reach a length from 40 km to 60 km
- **Multimode** utilizes multiple lights, and can reach a length from 2 km to 3 km.

Apart from its traditional usage in WANs, today fibre optic is used a lot for the implementation of **fiber to the home** (**FTTH**), and MAN networks:

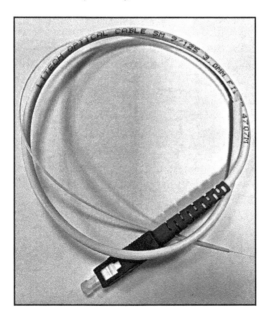

Figure 1.25. Fibre optic cable

Infrared and Bluetooth

Infrared and **Bluetooth** are wireless technologies for transmission of data over short distances. Infrared, as the name explains, uses infrared rays, and requires the line of sight to transmit the infrared signal. On the contrary, Bluetooth operates under 2.4 GHz frequency standard, and it does not suffer from the line of sight communication.

Radio waves

Radio waves, otherwise known as *electromagnetic radiation*, uses electromagnetic waves with a longer spectrum of wavelengths than infrared rays. Since they operate on different frequencies, hence, it makes it possible to cover large areas. Radio waves have found application in WAN's.

Satellite

Whereever the infrared, Bluetooth and radio waves cannot reach the destination, it will be reached by **satellite** signals. Unlike aforementioned wireless technologies, satellite technology uses a wide spectrum of wavelengths and frequencies. Today, it is estimated that there are more than 2,000 satellites in Earth's orbit that enable telecommunications around the globe.

Converged networks

Converged networks, known also as **triple-play services** networks, are networks that have the ability to transmit data, voice, and video, or any combination of these services over the same networks. Converged networks are considered modern networks compared to traditional networks, where only dedicated services were provided on the networks. That has been the reason why we have existing networks such as telephone networks for transmitting voice, broadcast networks for transmitting video, and computer networks for transmitting data.

 You can learn more about converged networks at `https://www.comparebusinessproducts.com/phone-systems/what-is-a-converged-network`.

Growing complexity of networks

To understand the **growing complexity of networks**, let's compare the classic phone devices of many decades ago with today's smartphones. Obviously, the great potential that the smartphones offer compared to the classic phones makes this comparison sound naive; however, it is worth mentioning the fact that while the classic phones have used a dedicated voice communication network that understandably must have been less complex, by contrast the smartphones use a more complex communication network. That is because today's communications networks, from frontend devices to backend devices, are various vendor technologies, resulting in more complexity when it comes to network scaling, upgrading, or patching.

Elements of converged networks

As explained earlier, the **converged network** integrates data, voice, and video into a single network. This is achieved thanks to the technologically advanced equipment and the TCP/IP protocol. Thus, it can be said that the elements of converged networks are a convergent device and a converged service. An example of a **convergent device** is the multiplexer (as in *Figure 1.26*) that, at its input, merges multiple communication signals into a single signal at its output. For the **converged service**, it can be said that it is a service that provides voice, data, and video signals in a single network, thus providing services for all modes of communication:

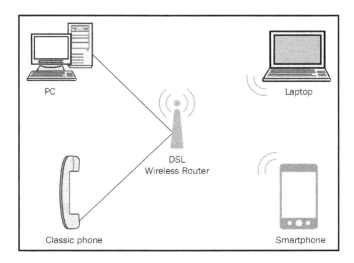

Figure 1.26. Orthogonal Frequency Division Multiplexing (OFDM) multiplexing technique used in DSL Wireless Router

You can learn more about Orthogonal Frequency Division Multiplexing (OFDM) from `http://searchnetworking.techtarget.com/definition/orthogonal-frequency-division-multiplexing`.

Access, distribution, and core layers

Cisco's three-layered architecture helps defining the enterprise networks by simplifying the process of designing a reliable, highly-redundant, and scalable hierarchical inter-network. The three layers of Cisco architecture are as follows:

- **Access layer**, as the name indicates, is the layer in which network services are accessed. This layer mainly consists of computers, servers, hubs, layer 2 switches, access points, and other network end devices. A LAN network can be considered as an access layer analogy.
- **Distribution layer** is the middle layer that plays the role of the bridge by interconnecting the access layer and the core layer. This layer mainly uses layer 3 switches and routers. Extended LANs that form the MAN can be considered as a distribution layer analogy.
- **Core layer** is a fast and highly redundant network that is managed by core switches and routers. It is a backbone of the corporate network that enables the packet's movement between distribution-layer devices in different segments of the network. A WAN network can be considered as a core layer analogy.

Network trends

We live in the **Internet of Things** (**IoT**) era in which the internet dictates the way we live and work. Therefore, things that were only science fiction a few years ago have started to become a reality. Thus, the overwhelming development of technology has transformed our world into an ever-changing environment. This necessarily requires everyone to adapt to this new reality. Some of the current **trends** in computer networks include the following:

- **Improved security** is becoming the topmost priority of enterprise networks. That is due to the fact that the number of users is growing more and more, and with that, more sophisticated have become the cyber criminals attacks.
- **Increased bandwidth** is ranked by analysts as enterprises second priority, right after the security. That is due to continuously increasing demands for traffic, thus putting the networks under pressure as they carry traffic.

- **Software-defined networks** (**SDNs**) continue to increase in popularity, especially by enterprises. That has to do with the convergence nature of SDNs, which multiplex data over multiple physical links, thus providing better performance than dedicated communication networks.
- **Video communication**, besides having made the distance communication between individuals more appealing, has enabled great opportunities for online collaboration and entertainment.
- **Online collaboration**, including video communication, brings people together on a common project. In addition to businesses, more and more of this trend is being embraced by educational institutions and individuals.
- **Bring your own devices (BYODs)** is a network trend that enables users to use their personal equipment to access business data. Obviously, that enables freedom, flexibility, and more opportunities for end users.
- **Cloud computing**, other than changing the way we access and store data, is reshaping the internet too. From businesses to individuals, cloud computing provides on-demand services to any device, anywhere in the world, securely and economically.

Summary

We summarize the chapter with the following points:

- The internet is the network of the networks.
- A computer network is a group of computers connected to each other in order to share resources.
- Usually, the resources can be data, network services, and peripheral devices.
- The fundamental requirement for designing a computer network is that there must be two or more computers:
    - A PAN is defined as a computer network that is used to connect and transmit data among devices located in a personal area, usually utilizing Bluetooth or Wi-Fi to interconnect devices
    - A LAN usually covers the floor of the building, several floors of the building, an entire building, or even a few buildings that are close to one another
    - A MAN represents a group of LANs interconnected within the geographical boundary of the town or city

- A WAN is a computer network that covers a wide geographic area using dedicated telecommunication lines such as telephone lines, leased lines, or satellites
- The intranet is considered to be the private network of an organization where employees can access network services.
- The extranet can be thought of as an intranet with a controlled access.
- Physical topology presents ordering, arrangement, and placement of the physical parts of a computer network, such as computers, peripheral devices, cables for data transmission, and network equipment:
  - Bus is the physical topology in which computers, peripheral and network devices are connected through the bus that mainly consists of coaxial cable.
  - Ring is the physical topology in which computers, peripheral and network devices form a closed cycle that takes the shape of a ring network where each device is connected to each other.
  - Star is the physical topology in which computers and peripheral and network devices are connected independently with a central device.
  - Extended star is the physical topology in which computers, peripheral and network devices are connected into two or more star topology networks, and then the central components (that is switches) are interconnected over a bus.
  - Hierarchical is the physical topology that represents a combination of star and bus topologies.
  - Mesh is the physical topology in which each computer is connected with every computer to form the network.
- Logical topology represents the logical aspect of the computer network.
- In logical topology, it is the logical paths that are used to carry electric or light signals from one computer to another, or from one network node to another node.
- Clients are computers that request the resources in a computer network.
- Servers are network components that provide resources to clients. Servers too have an active role.
- A host is any device with an IP address that requests or provides networking resources to any other host or node on the network.
- A node is any device that can generate, receive, and transmit the networking resources on the computer network.

- A network interface is a component-like network card or LAN port on network equipment that enables clients, servers, peripheral devices, and network equipment to get connected and communicate with each other.
- Peripheral devices are printers, scanners, SAN, and any other peripheral device that provides resources to clients either through a LAN or as a shared device on a network.
- Applications and shared data are virtual network components that represent applications and files shared on the network that are usually provided by servers.
- Hubs and switches are acting as central components (in Ethernet communication technology) of the computer network to enable interconnection and communication between clients, servers, and peripheral devices.
- Routers are a computer network component that enables routing of the data (that is, packets) from an LAN to the internet, and vice versa.
- The computer network architecture represents the computer network design that allows the computer network components to communicate with one another:
    - Peer-to-peer is a computer network in which the participating computers do not play the predefined roles in the network, but instead they change roles from client to server and vice versa, based on the actual activity on the network.
    - Client/server is a computer network in which participating computers have a predefined role. That means that, in this computer network architecture, computers that access resources act as clients, while computers that provide resources act as servers.
- NOSs are software that are capable of managing, maintaining, and providing resources in the network.
- In metallic mediums, copper wires in twisted pairs and coaxial cables transmit electrical impulses.
- In glass mediums, fibre optic cable transmits pulses of light.
- In air mediums, waves and rays from the electromagnetic spectrum transmit signals in different frequencies.
- Twisted pairs is a cable that contains four twisted pairs of copper with a total of eight wires, each with a specified color.
- Coaxial is a copper cable presented in two forms: thin coaxial with the length up to 185 m, and thick coaxial with the length up to 500 m.

- Fibre optic is a cable made up of glass through which the light is transmitted:
    - Single mode utilizes only one light, and can reach the length from 40 km to 60 km
    - Multimode utilizes multiple lights, and can reach the length from 2 km to 3 km
- Infrared and Bluetooth are wireless technologies for transmission of data over short distances.
- Radio waves, or otherwise known as *electromagnetic radiation*, uses electromagnetic waves with the longer spectrum of wavelengths than infrared rays.
- Satellite technology uses a wide spectrum of wavelengths and frequencies.
- The converged networks, known also as triple play services networks, are networks that have the ability to transmit data, voice, and video, or any combination of these services over the same networks:
    - A convergent device is the multiplexer that, at its input, merges multiple communication signals into a single signal at its output
    - A converged service is a service that provides voice, data, and video signals in a single network, thus providing services for all modes of communication
- Cisco's three-layered hierarchical model helps define the enterprise networks by simplifying the process of designing a reliable, highly redundant, and scalable hierarchical internetworks:
    - Access layer, as the name indicates, is the layer in which network services are accessed.
    - Distribution layer is the middle layer that plays the role of the bridge by interconnecting the access layer and the core layer.
    - Core layer is a fast and highly redundant network that is managed by core switches and routers.
- We live in the IoT era in which the internet dictates the way we live and work.

Questions

1. A computer network is a group of computers connected to each other in order to share resources. (True | False)

2. _____ represents a group of LANs interconnected within the geographical boundary of the town or city.

3. Which of the following are the layers of Cisco's three-layered hierarchical model? (Choose two):

    1. Access
    2. Services
    3. Peripheral
    4. Core

4. The converged networks, known also as triple play services networks, are networks that don't have the ability to transmit data, voice, and video, or any combination of these services over the same networks. (True | False)

5. _____ is a cable that contains four twisted pairs of copper with a total of eight wires, each with a specified color.

6. Which of the following are fibre optic modes?

    1. Single
    2. Dual
    3. Triple
    4. Multi

7. The computer network architecture represents the computer network design that allows the computer network components to communicate with one another. (True | False)

8. _____ are a computer network component that enables routing of the data (that is, packets) from LAN to the internet, and vice versa.

9. Which of the following are types of computer networks? (Choose two)

    1. PAN
    2. DAS
    3. NAS
    4. LAN

10. In logical topology, it is the logical paths that are used to carry electric or light signals from one computer to another, or from one network node to another node. (True | False)

11. _____ is the physical topology in which computers and peripheral and network devices are connected independently with a central device.

12. Which of the following represent the physical topologies? (Choose all that apply)
    1. Bus
    2. Ring
    3. Star
    4. All of the above

13. The intranet is considered to be the public network of an organization where employees can access network services. (True | False)

14. _____ is defined as a computer network that is used to connect and transmit data among devices located in a personal area, usually utilizing Bluetooth or Wi-Fi to interconnect devices.

15. Which of the following represent the network architectures? (Choose two)
    1. Peer-to-peer
    2. Client/server
    3. Storage area network (SAN)
    4. Network-attached storage (NAS)

16. The computer network architecture represents the computer network design that allows the computer network components to communicate with one another. (True | False)

17. _____ is the network of the networks.

18. Which of the following are network mediums? (Choose all that apply)
    1. Metallic
    2. Glass
    3. Air
    4. All of the above

2
Communication in Computer Networks

This chapter continues to build the content from the previous chapter. Thus, in this chapter, you will get to know more concepts and definitions about computer networks. We will begin with how computers communicate, where concepts such as message encoding, formatting and encapsulation, and size and timing are explained. Then, message delivery types and types of communication channels will be discussed. Afterwards, we will continue with detailed explanations about communication protocols, OSI and TCP/IP models, and OSI layers and their protocols. The chapter also discusses the Ethernet as the most popular communication technology for LANs, as well as the Ethernet's history, protocols, frame, and **Media Access Control** (**MAC**) addresses. Finally, this chapter will conclude with a discussion about IP addressing technologies such as IPv4 and IPv6, and IPv4 and IPv6 subnetting. To facilitate the understanding of the many concepts and definitions covered in this chapter, a large amount of relevant figures will be included.

In this chapter, we will cover:

- Understanding how computers communicate
- Understanding message delivery types
- Understanding types of communication channels
- Understanding communication protocols
- Understanding OSI and TCP/IP models
- Understanding OSI layers and their protocols
- Understanding Ethernet communication technology
- Understanding IPv4 and IPv6 addresses
- Understanding IPv4 and IPv6 subnetting

How do computers communicate?

In the world of humans, for communication to take place between two individuals, it is required that both sides know the language that they want to communicate in. Similarly, in the world of computers, whenever two computers try to communicate, they must support the communication protocol.

To better understand the communication process between two computers, let's examine the example of communication between two individuals. When two people meet and begin to communicate, the following activities take place:

1. Person A formulates his/her opinion in their mind and utters the words through their mouth.
2. The air then acts as the transmission medium which transfers the words from person A to person B.
3. The transmitted words reach the ears of person B, who then, through the center of knowledge, understands the received words.

This works in almost the same way the communication between two computers occurs:

1. On computer A, an email has been compiled, and when the user clicks the send button, the mail application sends that message out through the computer's network interface.
2. Depending on which connection the computer is using, it is either cable or wireless medium that will transmit the message to the central device (hub or switch).
3. The central device then forwards the message to computer B.
4. The received message by the network interface in computer B is then forwarded through its operating system to the mail application.

 Do you want to know how the internet works? How IP packets travel through a firewall? How a switch and router work? And many other things related to the **Network of Networks**? Then take some time and watch the *Warriors of the Net* movie at: http://www.warriorsofthe.net/.

Message encoding

From the previous example, the sentence *Person A formulates his/her opinion in their mind and utters the words through their mouth* refers to the **encoding** of the message. In the same way, the sentence *the transmitted words reach the ears of person B, who then through the center of knowledge understands the received words* has to do with the **decoding** of the message. From that, we understand that encoding and decoding messages are very important processes of communication since coding converts the information in an acceptable form for the transmission, whilst decoding converts the received message into an intelligible language, as shown in *Figure 2.1*:

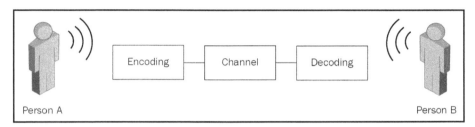

Figure 2.1. Communication between two people

Almost the same process occurs in computers where the message is encoded into electrical impulses, pattern of sounds, or light waves that we (humans) interpret as bits. These bits are then received by computers that decode them into an understandable message such as a text, audio, or a video file.

Message formatting and encapsulation

If you have recently sent a letter to your loved ones via the post office, then you have **formatted** and **encapsulated** the message (see *Figure 2.2*.). That is, in a blank letter, you wrote your message by saluting the recipient of the letter, and that represents the formatting of the letter. Then, inserting the folded letter into an envelope where you will identify the sender and the recipient represents the encapsulation of the letter:

Figure 2.2. Message formatting and encapsulation/de-encapsulation

Similarly, messages are formatted and encapsulated during computer communication, too. The frame is the envelope's equivalent, while the bits are the equivalent of the letter and its contents. Similar to the letter being placed in an envelope, the bits are placed in the frame too, and that represents the **encapsulation process**. When the receiving computer receives the frame and unpacks the frame by taking out the bits from the frame, then that represents the **de-encapsulation** process. Like the envelope, the frame also contains the source address and destination address.

Message size

During the communication of two persons, there is no written standard on how big the **size** of the transmitted message should be. In fact, there is a mutual understanding that the messages that they transmit are usually broken into smaller sentences. This is due to the fact that the person who receives the message is able to process (understand) it. Almost the same happens when two computers communicate. Transmitted messages are broken into small parts, as shown in *Figure 2.3*, so that the receiving computer has time to receive, process, and display the message as comprehensible content.

Unlike communication between people, communication between computers is very strict as far as the size of the message is concerned. This implies that, depending on the communication channel, the size of the messages is different, which means that frames that exceed the standard of the message size by being too long for the defined channel or too short in size are not delivered:

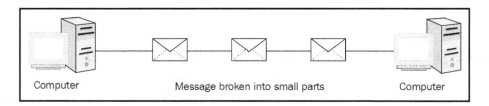

Computer   Message broken into small parts   Computer

Figure 2.3. Message broken into small parts

Message timing

It is obvious that computer communication is very similar to the way humans communicate. The same applies when it comes to the timing of the messages being transmitted. In this sense, we can be impressed by the rules that have been placed to govern the message timing in communication between computers. They are as follows:

- The **access method** enables computers to determine the time when they can begin sending messages. Also, it helps computers know how to react to situations when message collisions occur.
- The **flow control** method enables computers to negotiate the correct timing. Thus, source and destination computers will be able to communicate successfully.
- The **response timeout** method enables computers on the network to wait for responses before beginning to send messages. Also, it helps computers know what action to take if a response timeout occurs.

Message delivery types

Communication preferences are different. Mostly, communication between people occurs in one-to-one, one-to-many, and one-to-all formats. So, depending on the importance of the transmitted message, this is when the sender of a message wants to know if the message has been successfully received by the recipient. Then, it is necessary that the recipient acknowledges the sender of the message.

Unicast transmission

In computer networks, one-to-one communication, as shown in *Figure 2.4*, represents a **unicast** message delivery option. Because in this type of communication, there is only one destination for the message:

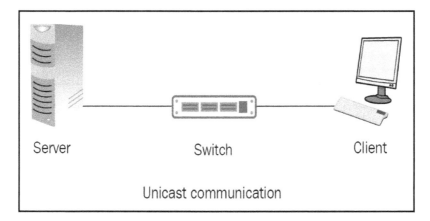

Figure 2.4. Communication between the client and server, which represents unicast communication

Multicast transmission

Similarly, one-to-many communication, as shown in *Figure 2.5*, represents a **multicast** message delivery option. Unlike unicast, in multicast delivery, there are several reachable destinations for the message:

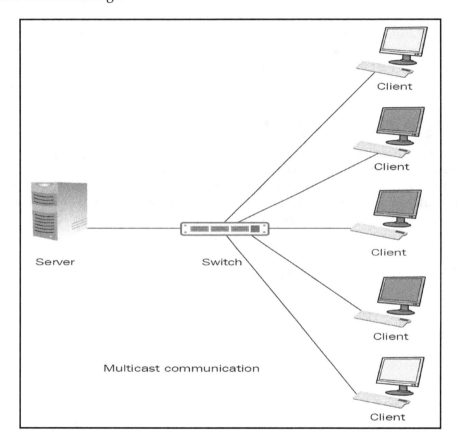

Figure 2.5. Communication between the server and the group of clients, which represents multicast communication

Broadcast transmission

And finally, one-to-all communication, as shown in *Figure 2.6*, represents a **broadcast** message delivery option. In this communication, all computers on the network will receive the message transmitted by the sender computer:

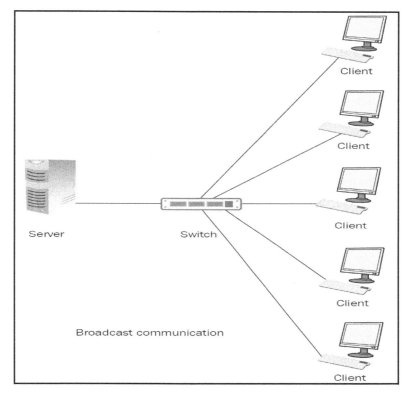

Figure 2.6. Communication between the server and clients, which represents broadcast communication

Types of communication channels

If you have ever tried talking to your friend through a pipe by passing on the voice from your mouth straight to your friend's ear, then you have used a physical communication medium. Other than that, there are logical communication mediums as well. The two together, both the physical and logical mediums, make up the **communication channel** in the telecommunication and computer networks which are commonly used for transmitting information. The communication channel width is measured in **Hertz (Hz)**, while its data rate is measured in **bits per second (bps)**.

Simplex

A simplex communication is often referred to as a one-way communication because the direction of the transmission is predetermined. In this method of communication, the sender is called a **transmitter** because its task is to always transmit messages. Hence, the endpoint where the message arrives is called the **receiver** because its task is to always receive messages. An analogy of simplex communication is the television station that is based on the *structured content* broadcasting method, as shown in *Figure 2.7*:

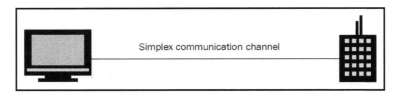

Figure 2.7. TV broadcasting, which represents a simplex communication channel

Half-duplex

In half-duplex communication, both devices can send and receive messages, but not at the same time (simultaneously). This method of communication works in the way that when device A sends the message, device B waits for the message to arrive. This is because the device that is sending the message absorbs the communication channel, thus leaving no space for the other device to send the message at the same time. An analogy of half-duplex communication is radio communication (walkie-talkie), which is based on the *push-to-talk* method, as shown in *Figure 2.8*:

Figure 2.8. Radio communication, which represents a half-duplex communication channel

Full-duplex

Unlike half-duplex, in full-duplex communication, both devices can send and receive messages simultaneously. This means that when device A sends a message to device B, at the same time, device B can send a message to device A, thus eliminating the need to wait for the message to arrive. That way, the communication channel is available for both devices so that they can send and receive messages simultaneously . An analogy of full-duplex communication is the phone communication that is based on the *talk directly* method, as shown in *Figure 2.9*:

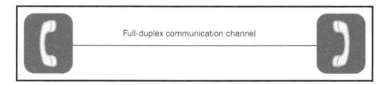

Figure 2.9. Phone communication, which represents the full-duplex communication channel

Communication protocols

The fact that you are able to read and understand this book proves that you know the English language. Like any other language written and spoken around the globe, the English language also has its own rules of grammar, syntax, and spelling. Almost equally, even computers, in order to communicate with one another, must know the communication language. Like human languages, the computer communication language also contain standards and rules, which are called **communication protocols**. In the following sections, you will get acquainted with characteristics of the communication protocols, and will be introduced to some of the well-known communication protocols in computer networks.

Characteristics of communication protocols

The beauty of communication technologies is their variety in every respect. From the message delivery types to the types of communication channels, and from communication protocols to the connection between devices, all of these and many others present the detailed anatomy of the technological communication technology. Thus, the following sections explain the characteristics of communication protocols in terms of the method used for data transmission.

Connection-oriented protocols

Connection-oriented protocols, prior to transferring data, establish an end-to-end logical connection, which is often known as a **virtual link** between two devices. Connection-oriented protocols use the **circuit switching** method of data transmission, where concepts like *handshaking* and *acknowledgment* come into play. Packets follow the same route and reach the destination in the same order as they are delivered, thus making connection-oriented protocols known as **reliable** network services. An example of connection-oriented protocols would be the phone call, as in *Figure 2.9*, in which a logical connection is made before the conversation starts. The most known connection-oriented protocol is the **Transmission Control Protocol** (**TCP**).

Connectionless protocols

Connectionless protocols do not establish an end-to-end logical connection. Instead, each packet contains the destination address of the receiver, and is thus treated as an individual entity. Unlike connection-oriented protocols, packets do not follow the same route, thus the packets do not reach the receiver in the order that they were delivered. Just because of that, connectionless protocols use the *packet switching* method for data transmission and are known to be the **best effort** network services. An example of connectionless protocols would be the postal office system, where each letter contains a destination address. The most known connectionless protocol is the **User Datagram Protocol** (**UDP**).

 You can learn more about connection-oriented protocols vs. connectionless protocols at: https://docs.oracle.com/cd/E19620-01/805-4041/ 6j3r8iu2f/index.html.

Circuit switching versus packet switching

As explained earlier, **circuit-switching** serves as an infrastructure for connection-oriented protocols, while **packet-switching** serves the connectionless protocols. Both methods deal with data transmission. In circuit-switching, when two devices want to communicate, the connection is established to serve the purpose. As long as the transmission is active, the circuit is only available to the communicating devices. Once the transmission is complete, the connection is broken, and the circuit becomes available for other devices to use. The circuit-switching method is traditionally used for voice communication, and thus the best example is the **Public Switched Telephone Network** (**PSTN**), which is still in use worldwide.

Unlike circuit-switching, packet-switching employs a different approach. When two devices want to communicate, no connection is established. Instead, on the sending device, the data is broken into chunks of data known as **packets**. Each packet contains a header. The header contains a destination IP address and the source IP address. In addition, the header contains the number of the packet and the information into how many packets the data has been broken into. All of that information in the header of a packet is handled by the router, which takes care to send packets on their way. Presumably, packets will travel through many routers, each taking its own path. At the destination, based on the number of the packets located in the header, packets are arranged in the right order. The best example of packet-switching is a **computer network**.

Well-known communication protocols

There is a large number of communication protocols that operate under the TCP/IP protocol suite. Each one performs the task that it is assigned with. In the following sections, we will get to know some of them:

- **Hypertext Transfer Protocol** (**HTTP**): It is the protocol used by the browser that carries the **Hypertext Markup Language** (**HTML**) from the server to the client. It operates based on the *request-response* method to access websites.
- **File Transfer Protocol** (**FTP**): It is the protocol tasked to carry files from the source computer to the destination computer.
- **Trivial File Transfer Protocol** (**TFTP**): Unlike FTP, it is a connectionless simple file transfer protocol that utilizes less overhead.
- **Simple Mail Transfer Protocol** (**SMTP**): It is tasked with the responsibility of sending and receiving email from mail server.
- **Post Office Protocol** (**POP**): It is the protocol used by the email client to retrieve emails from the mail server.
- **Internet Message Access Protocol** (**IMAP**): Like POP, IMAP is used by an email app to retrieve emails from the server, however it leaves copies of emails in the mail server too.
- **Domain Name System** (**DNS**): Its responsibility is to locate and translate domain names into IP addresses.
- **Dynamic Host Configuration Protocol** (**DHCP**): It is tasked with the responsibility of dynamically assigning IP addresses to computers in a network.
- **Secure Socket Layer** (**SSL**): It is tasked with enabling a secure channel for data transmission between devices.

- **Transport Layer Security (TLS)**: It is a successor to SSL, and provides privacy and data integrity for data transmission between devices.
- **Telnet**: It is a legacy method that enables administrators to access devices on remote locations.
- **Secure Shell (SSH)**: It is more secure than Telnet, and it enables administrators to access remote devices in a secure way.
- **Point-to-Point Tunneling Protocol (PPTP)**: It is among the first protocols used for **Virtual Private Network (VPN)** implementations with low security.
- **Layer 2 Tunneling Protocol (L2TP)**: It is tasked to extend the functionalities of PPTP by increasing the security of the VPN operation over the internet.
- **Transmission Control protocol (TCP)**: It is a connection-oriented protocol that provides reliable and orderly data transmissions. Error checking of the transmitted data is also included.
- **User Datagram Protocol (UDP)**: It is a connectionless protocol that does the best effort in data transmission.
- **Internet Protocol (IP)**: It is a connectionless protocol tasked to forward packets from the source computer to the destination computer.
- **Network Address Translation (NAT)**: It is responsible for translating private IP addresses into public IP addresses thus enabling a connection to the internet.
- **Routing Information Protocol (RIP)**: It is among the first routing protocols tasked to enable communications between routers by sharing the network topology through the utilization of the **distance-vector** algorithm.
- **Open Shortest Path First (OSPF)**: It is a routing protocol that uses the **link-state routing (LSR)** algorithm to enable the communication between routers by finding the best path.
- **Interior Gateway Routing Protocol (IGRP)**: It is a Cisco proprietary routing protocol that employs the **distance-vector algorithm** to enable communication between routers by exchanging routing information within an autonomous system.
- **Enhanced Interior Gateway Routing Protocol (EIGRP)**: As a successor to IGRP, it is an advanced routing protocol that enables communication between routers by merging the best features from both distance-vector and link-state routing protocols. It is only used in networks with all Cisco networking devices.
- **Internet Control Message Protocol (ICMP)**: It is the protocol used by the active devices in the network to send error messages in order to determine the availability of the service or destination device.
- **Address Resolution Protocol (ARP)**: It is tasked to identify the physical address of a given IP address (that is, a logical address).

- **Reverse Address Resolution Protocol (RARP)**: It is tasked to do the opposite of the ARP by identifying the IP address of a given physical address.
- **Multiprotocol Label Switching (MPLS)**: It is a protocol that operates in between OSI Layer 2 and Layer 3 to enable high performance by forwarding data using labels.
- **Spanning Tree Protocol (STP)**: It is tasked with the responsibility of preventing bridging loops on LANs.
- **Link Layer Discovery Protocol (LLDP)**: It enables network devices to advertise identity, capabilities, and neighbors on LANs.
- **Point-to-Point Protocol (PPP)**: It is tasked with the responsibility of enabling a direct connection between two devices.
- **Neighbor Discovery Protocol (NDP)**: It replaces ARP in IPv6, and thus along with ICMP determines the physical address, reachability, and tracking of neighboring devices.
- **IEEE 802.2**: This standard is responsible for describing the activities of the **Logical Link Control (LLC)** sublayer of the OSI Layer 2.
- **IEEE 802.3**: This standard is responsible for specifying the physical medium and to describe the characteristics of the Ethernet in LANs.
- **IEEE 802.5**: This standard is responsible for specifying a token-passing communication technology in LANs.
- **IEEE 802.11**: This standard specifies the requirements for the implementation of the **Wireless Local Area Networks (WLANs)**.

 You can learn more about *TCP/IP Networking Protocols* by layers and by functions at: `http://www.comptechdoc.org/independent/networking/protocol/protnet.html`.

OSI and TCP/IP model overview

In order to describe the functionality of the network, including communication between computers, a **layered model** is used. These layers facilitate the operating system's work whenever the computer is required to communicate with other computers. This concept dates back to the 1960s, known as the time of internet development. It consisted of two protocols, IP and TCP. At that time, the layered framework called the TCP/IP reference model was designed so that later on, it had set the standard of networking functionality on the internet, enabling computers to communicate through a layered format.

To understand the layered model, let's get familiar with the following concepts:

- The **protocol suite** is a communication protocol stack that is comprised of a set of communications protocols. Some of the most well-known protocol suites in the history of telecommunications and computer networks are IPX/SPX, X.25, AppleTalk, and TCP/IP.
- The **reference model** is a conceptual model that describes what is occurring in each communication layer without giving any description of how that should be accomplished. The most popular reference model is OSI, which is also a protocol model for the OSI protocol suite.
- The **protocol model** is a layered model that describes the protocol functions that are taking place at each layer. Since this model matches the structure of a particular protocol suite, TCP/IP is the most popular protocol model that is also used as a reference model.

TCP/IP protocol model

When considering the fact that communication between two computers consists of certain steps and that these steps in the world of computer networks are known as layers of communications, it will not be that hard to understand the layered nature of the **TCP/IP protocol model**. Named according to two main protocols like IP and TCP, the TCP/IP protocol model consists of four layers known as network access, internet, transport, and application. In addition to IP and TCP protocols, there are other protocols that comprise the TCP/IP protocol suite. So, to not confuse the TCP/IP protocol suite with the TCP/IP protocol model, consider the fact that the TCP/IP protocol suite is a set of protocols where IP and TCP protocols are dominant. Also, the TCP/IP protocol suite is known as the **language** of the internet.

Figure 2.10 represents the communication between PC1 and PC2, as observed by the TCP/IP protocol model. The following takes place in each communication layer in top-down order:

- When the user in PC1 uses a browser to access a certain website on the internet, this enables an interaction between a proper protocol in the application layer and the browser. Once the request of a browser to communicate data over the network has been processed by an HTTP protocol, the request is then forwarded to the next lower layer.
- In the transport layer, TCP protocol is taking care to package the data coming from the HTTP protocol into segments called **datagrams** before then forwarding them to the lower layer.

- In the internet layer, on the received datagrams, the IP protocol adds the source and destination IP addresses, and thus the data is represented by **packets**. Thereafter, packets are transmitted to the lower layer of the TCP/IP protocol model, which is known as network access.
- In the **network access** layer, on the received packets, the **Ethernet protocols** (see section, *Ethernet communication technology*, later in this chapter) are organizing the data into frames by adding the source and destination MAC addresses. Then, these frames are carried over to the network so that they can reach the destination:

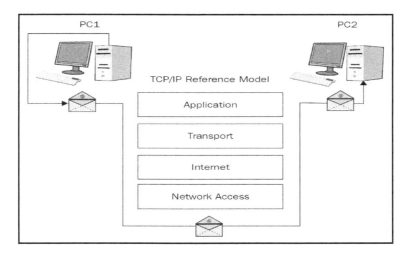

Figure 2.10. TCP/IP protocol model

OSI reference model

Unlike the TCP/IP protocol model, the **Open Systems Interconnection** (**OSI**) reference model consists of seven layers, which are the physical, data link, network, transport, session, presentation, and application layers, and this model was developed by the **International Organization for Standardization** (**ISO**). The OSI reference model is known to be the best layered model, which provides a detailed description about the flow of data from sending to receiving devices involved in the communication process. That is a result of the **strict** approach that the OSI is using in network layers compared to the **lossless** approach that the TCP/IP protocol model is using.

To better understand how the OSI reference model operates, let's look at the assembly line in the automobile factory. Everything starts from the chassis (or frame), which is placed as the first element in the assembly line. At each step of an assembly, one or more elements (or parts) of the vehicle are placed. After a considerable number of steps, at the end of the assembly line, a brand new vehicle comes out which is then sent for testing.

Almost the same happens in the OSI reference model when it comes to describing a communication session between two computers. In each layer of OSI, a certain activity is assigned that prepares the data for the subsequent layer, as shown in *Figure 2.11:*

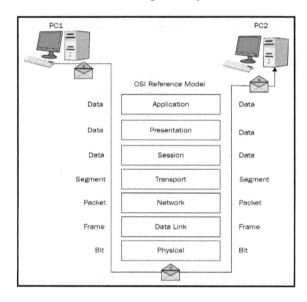

Figure 2.11. The OSI reference model in action

OSI layers and their protocols

As mentioned previously, the OSI reference model consists of seven layers in which certain network functions are performed by their respective **protocols**. In addition to describing the processes that happen within layers, the OSI reference model also describes the interaction of each layer with the neighboring layers above and below. To avoid confusion, you will often encounter situations in the literature where the layers of the OSI reference model are **named with numbers** instead of their respective names (for example, the physical layer as Layer 1).

If you want to easily remember the layers of the OSI reference model, then you can use the following mnemonics where the first letter from each word corresponds to a certain layer of the OSI reference model: **A**ll **P**eople **S**eem **T**o **N**eed **D**ata **P**rocessing, or **P**lease **D**o **N**ot **T**hrow **S**ausage **P**izza **A**way.

Physical layer protocols

The **physical layer** (**Layer 1**) represents both the physical and logical aspects of the computer network. Among the physical components are the **network interface card** (**NIC**), the medium for data transmission, and the network equipment. Among the logical components are electrical signals and the transmission time. In addition, standards such as network medium types, speeds, and distances are integral parts of the physical layer. The terms **electrical signals** and **radio frequencies,** often known as **bits,** are used to represent the **Protocol Data Unit** (**PDU**) at this layer, as shown in *Figure 2.11*. In this layer, the following communication protocols operate:

- IEEE 802.3
- IEEE 802.5
- IEEE 802.11

Data link layer protocols

The **data link layer** (**Layer 2**) is responsible for assigning the physical protocols which are dependable upon the communication technology used in LANs. In addition, it takes care to detect and correct the errors, and getting data to the physical layer so that it can be transmitted. The term **frame** is used to represent the PDU at this layer, as shown in *Figure 2.11*. In this layer, the following communication protocols operate:

- IEEE 802.2
- IEEE 802.3
- ARP
- RARP

Network layer protocols

The **network layer** is responsible for enabling the communication between networks. It provides the routing mechanism, and so logical elements such as IP addressing and routing protocols come into play. The term **packet** is used to represent the PDU at this layer, as shown in *Figure 2.11*. In this layer, the following communication protocols operate:

- IP
- ICMP
- IPSec
- NAT
- RIP operates on port 520
- OSPF

Transport layer protocols

The **transport layer** (**Layer 4**) is responsible for transporting data between network devices. It is interesting since this layer operates the two most well-known protocols, TCP and UDP. While TCP is characterized by reliability, UDP is characterized by the best effort. That said, altogether, the transport layer adds reliability, flow control, transmission error control, and best effort to data transmission. The term **segment** is used to represent the PDU at this layer, as shown in *Figure 2.11*. In this layer, the following communication protocols operate:

- TCP
- UDP

Session layer protocols

Unlike the transport layer, the **session layer** (Layer 5) is responsible for establishing and maintaining the on-demand communication sessions between applications. So, this layer manages and controls the synchronization of data between the applications. The term **data** is used to represent the PDU at this layer, as shown in *Figure 2.11*. In this layer, the following communication protocols operate:

- PPTP operates on port 1723
- L2TP operates on port 1701

Presentation layer protocols

The **presentation layer** (Layer 6) receives data from the application layer and represents it in the format accepted by the subsequent layer. So, in this layer, formats like graphics files, text and data, and sound and video get the meaning. Another important element of this layer is the encryption of data, so it is natural that this layer uses protocols for adding security to data transmission. The term data is used to represent the PDU at this layer, as shown in *Figure 2.11*. In this layer, the following communication protocols operate:

- SSL
- TLS

Application layer protocols

The **application layer** (Layer 7) is responsible for interacting with the operating system or application whenever the user decides to transmit data with their computer over a computer network or the internet. To better understand the functionality of the application layer, instead of thinking about applications, instead try thinking about the processes that enable applications to utilize network services. The term data is used to represent the PDU at this layer, as shown in *Figure 2.11*. In this layer, the following communication protocols operate:

- HTTP operates on port 80
- HTTPS operates on port 443
- SMTP operates on port 25
- POPv3 operates on port 110
- IMAPv4 operates on port 143
- FTP operates on port 21
- DNS operates on port 53
- DHCP operates on port 67 for server, and port 68 for client
- SSH operates on port 22
- Telnet operates on port 23

An application port is a logical endpoint that enables applications from your computer to communicate with applications on other computers. You can learn more about the well-known communication protocols and their corresponding port numbers at: http://www.meridianoutpost.com/resources/articles/well-known-tcpip-ports.php.

Ethernet communication technology

Today, Ethernet is the communication technology that is widely used in LANs. Ethernet operates in the physical layer and data link layer of the OSI reference model. Thus, it defines both Layer 1 technologies and Layer 2 protocols. The data on an Ethernet network is carried on by a frame.

Ethernet history

The merits for the invention of the Ethernet belong to **Dr. Robert Metcalfe**, who in 1973 while working at the Xerox **Palo Alto Research Center** (**PARC**) wrote a memo in which he described his finding. Metcalfe had built an Ethernet network system to interconnect workstations with laser printers, thus making it possible to transfer data up to 1 Mbps. Undoubtedly, being convinced of the potential of the Ethernet network system, he asked DEC, Intel, and Xerox to help promote the Ethernet as the next standard of communication technologies. Thus, ten years later, in 1983, the **Institute of Electrical and Electronics Engineers** (**IEEE**) standardized Ethernet as **IEEE 802.3**. As the years went by, interestingly from the point of view of transmission speeds, Ethernet became increasingly fast. So, in terms of transmission speeds, it evolved from Ethernet to Fast Ethernet, and then to Gigabit Ethernet. Today, it reaches up to 5 Gbps in twisted pairs and up to 100 Gbps in optical fiber.

You can find Dr. Robert Metcalfe's conversation on the first Ethernet LAN at: https://www.youtube.com/watch?v=m_agCPNGOzU.

Ethernet protocols

The Ethernet, as a communication technology that is mostly used in LANs, operates on the first two layers of the OSI reference model. Then, naturally, the protocols like **Logical Link Control (LLC)**, **Media Access Control (MAC)**, and physical (network medium) come into play, as shown in *Figure 2.12*. Let's talk a little bit about these protocols in the following paragraphs:

- The **Logical Link Control (LLC)** sublayer is the upper half of Layer 2 (that is, the Data Link layer). Being placed between Layer 3 (that is, the Network Layer) and the MAC sublayer, means that there are many LLC functions. Thus, the LLC sublayer is responsible for isolating the functions occurring in the MAC sublayer from those occurring on Layer 3. Then, LLC defines the additional error-recovery mechanism from that defined by the MAC sublayer. Furthermore, LLC provides flow control so that the computer on destination is not overwhelmed by the delivery of packets. Last but not least, LLC establishes logical connections between the sender and receiving computers.

- The **Media Access Control (MAC)** sublayer is the lower half of Layer 2. The same as LLC, the MAC sublayer has a considerable number of functions too. When it comes to accessing the network medium by the individual network devices, it is the MAC sublayer that manages it. Another important feature of the MAC sublayer is Layer 2 addressing, which has to do with the process of adding the source and destination MAC addresses to the data packets that are coming from the upper layers, including LLC. Although the Ethernet in its sole nature communicates in the half-duplex channel, it is the responsibility of the MAC sublayer to enable communication in the full duplex channel without causing data loss.

- The **Ethernet Physical** (**Network Medium**) **layer** actually represents Layer 1 of the OSI reference model. From the Ethernet's point of view, in this layer, we are dealing with electrical, optical, and wave properties of physical connections between computers and network devices or between network devices. More precisely, the Ethernet physical layer deals with the physical network mediums such as twisted pair, coaxial, and optical fiber. Also, this layer designates connectors, cable lengths, network devices, topologies, and the number of computers required to form a network:

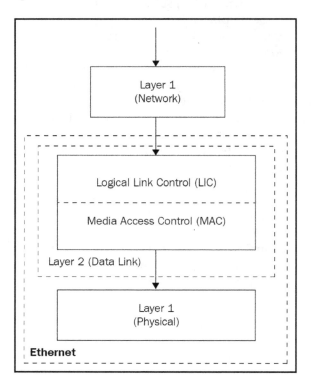

Figure 2.12

Ethernet frame

A data packet that comes from higher layers is entering an Ethernet fabric in Layer 2 (Data Link) which takes care of assembly, and exits through Layer 1 (Physical), which takes care of transmission. That said, an **Ethernet frame** is a Layer 2 and a Layer 1 data packet. Therefore, Ethernet protocols determine the following frame elements:

- The **frame format** consists of six fields (as shown in *Figure 2.13*) such as Preamble and **Start Frame Delimiter** (**SFD**), Destination MAC address, Source MAC address, EtherType, Data, and **Frame Check Sequence** (**FCS**). The Preamble and the SFD together (a total of 8 bytes) form the point of data transmission in the Ethernet frame concept. Destination MAC, a 6-byte field, can be a unicast, multicast, or broadcast address. Like Destination MAC, Source MAC is a 6-byte field that defines the full address of the sender of the frame. The EtherType field (2 bytes) indicates the protocol that is used to encapsulate the data in the frame, and it is often used to indicate the size of the frame. The data field (from 46 bytes to 1500 bytes) is actually the data (also known as the *payload*) that came from the upper layers of the OSI reference model. FCS is a 4-bytes field, which represents the mechanism for error checking in the Ethernet frame.

- The **frame size** is defined from the Destination MAC address field to the FCS field. Thus, the minimum size is 64 bytes, and the maximum size is 1,518 bytes. As you can note, Preamble does not count the size of the frame. The Ethernet is very accurate in terms of frame size. This is observed in frame transmission. If the frame size is smaller than the minimum size, or greater than the maximum frame size, then the receiving device drops the frame. Thus, frames smaller than 64 bytes are called *runt frames* and are the result of collisions, whereas frames larger than 1,500 bytes are called *jumbo frames (or giant)* and are used on LAN networks to support Gigabit Ethernet speeds:

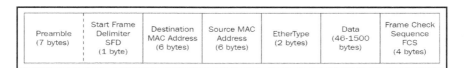

Figure 2.13. Ethernet frame structure

An Ethernet frame II, otherwise known as DIX Ethernet is named according to the first letters of DEC, Intel, and Xerox. It has a maximum size of 1,536 bytes. It is used in TCP/IP networks to support VLAN tagging.

Ethernet MAC addresses

An **Ethernet MAC address**, often known as a physical address, is a unique network address that identifies the network interface on a computer network, and it is used for communication in the Data Link layer. The size of the MAC address is 48 bits expressed in 12 hexadecimal digits, where each digit represents 4 bits. The Ethernet MAC address is burned on the **Read Only Memory (ROM)** of the NIC and is thus often referred to as the **Burned-in Address (BIA)**. It consists of two fields like the **Organizationally Unique Identifier (OUI)** and **Vendor Assigned**, as shown in *Figure 2.14*. Both fields have an identical size of 3 bytes each (or 24 bits) and represent the vendor and the particular device. In literature and elsewhere, you will often see the Ethernet MAC addresses represented in three formats:

- **With dashes**: Usually represented by Windows OS, for example, **00-11-22-AA-BB-CC**
- **With colons**: Usually represented by Mac OS and Linux, for example, **00:11:22:AA:BB:CC**
- **With periods**: Usually represented by Cisco IOS, for example, **0000.1111.AAAA**

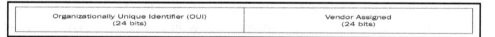

Organizationally Unique Identifier (OUI) (24 bits)	Vendor Assigned (24 bits)

Figure 2.14. Ethernet MAC address structure

To find out the physical address of the NIC on your Windows computer, enter the `ipconfig /all` command in **Command Prompt (CMD)**, or enter the `ifconfig` command on Mac and Linux computers.

Ethernet's CSMA CD vs. Ethernet's CSMA CA

Both **Carrier-sense multiple access with collision detection (CSMA CD)** and **Carrier-sense multiple access with collision avoidance (CSMA CA)** are medium access control methods used on Ethernet communication technologies. The IEEE 802.3 standard is based on the CSMA CD method, while the IEEE 802.11 standard operates on the CSMA CA method. In CSMA CD, when a device intends to transmit data, it senses the medium to see whether it is free. Similarly, any device on the network will act the same way, thus creating opportunities for the collisions to occur. In addition to accessing the medium, CSMA CD also defines the process on how devices must respond after data collision. That said, after **collision is detected (CD)**, devices will retransmit the lost data. Interestingly, CSMA CA uses a proactive approach through **collision avoidance (CA)**. Prior to transmitting data, devices will sense for mediums that are idle, thus avoiding collisions.

The IP addresses and subnets

Nowadays, a lot of effort is being made to advance the development of IP addressing technologies. **IPv6 addressing** is the best example of such an effort. Nevertheless, even though the IPv6 addressing technology is becoming more and more plausible, it still prefers the role of spectator in the great arena of the internet, where **IPv4 addressing** technology continues to be the norm.

IPv4 network addresses

To communicate with a device on the network, it must be equipped with an IP address. Currently, the addressing technology we use is **Internet Protocol version 4 (IPv4) addressing**. The label *v4* represents the fourth version of IP addressing, as specified in IETF publication RCF 791. However, you will often encounter it as simply an IP address. It is a **logical** element that consists of 32 bits and identifies a network interface of a given device. It is organized in 4 octets with 8 bits in each of them, divided by a decimal point for simplicity of interpretation (for example, `192.168.1.1`). If we take into account the fact that 1 byte = 8 bits, then a **32-bit** IP address is 4 bytes (that comes from *32/8 = 4*). Additionally, IETF's RFC 791 document manages IPv4 addresses into prefixes of 8-bit, 16-bit, or 24-bit. This enabled organizing IPv4 addresses into classes of A, B, C, D, and E, which is known as **classful addressing**. Classful addressing defines the bits used for the network portion and bits used for the host portion for a given class. It is obvious then that in the case of IP addresses, everything revolves around the binary numbering system. Thus, the total number of IPv4 addresses is 2^{32} = *4,294,967,296*.

If you compare that number to the number of the world population, it is obvious that nearly three billion IP addresses are missing if an IPv4 address is given to every person.

You can learn more about IPv4 at: `https://blogs.igalia.com/dpino/2017/05/25/ipv4-exhaustion/`.

Public IP addresses

A **public IP address** is considered to be any IP address that enables a device to be accessed from anywhere on the internet. That said, a public IP address uniquely identifies a device on the internet. This is also why a public IP address is often called an **internet address**. In addition, a public IP address is routable. The organization that is responsible for managing both IPv4 and IPv6 addresses is the **Internet Assigned Numbers Authority** (**IANA**), which works under the supervision of the **Internet Architecture Board** (**IAB**). The **Regional Internet Registries** (**RIRs**) are responsible for the allocation of IPv4 and IPv6 addresses to the ISPs. Then, the ISPs allocate IPv4 and IPv6 addresses to organizations.

If you want to learn your public IP address, then run the `show my ip` command on Google or Bing search engines.

Private IP addresses

Unlike a public IP address, a **private IP address** is considered to be any IP address that enables a device to be accessed from anywhere on the intranet. Naturally, a private IP address uniquely identifies a device on the intranet. That is also why a private IP address is often called a **Local IP address**. In addition, a private IP address is a non-routable. The IANA has specified the following IP address ranges for private use:

Class	Address Range
A	`10.0.0.0 - 10.255.255.255`
B	`172.16.0.0 - 172.31.255.255`
C	`192.168.0.0 - 192.168.255.255`

Table 2.1. Private IP address ranges

Loopback IP address

Often when you want to test a TCP/IP protocol suite on your computer's network interface card (NIC), you will run the following command from your computer's Command Prompt:

```
C:\>ping 127.0.0.1
```

The successful reply will look similar to the following:

```
Pinging 127.0.0.1 with 32 bytes of data:
Reply from 127.0.0.1: bytes=32 time<1ms TTL=128
Reply from 127.0.0.1: bytes=32 time<1ms TTL=128
Reply from 127.0.0.1: bytes=32 time<1ms TTL=128
Reply from 127.0.0.1: bytes=32 time<1ms TTL=128

Ping statistics for 127.0.0.1:
    Packets: Sent = 4, Received = 4, Lost = 0 (0% loss)
Approximate round trip times in mili-seconds:
    Minimum = 0ms, Maximum = 0ms, Average = 0ms
```

The 127.0.0.1 address is often called a **loopback IP address**, which comes from the private IP address range **127.0.0.0 - 127.255.255.255**, which is reserved for loopback purposes and diagnostic functions. As such, it is part of the loopback adapter, which is a virtual network card that is isolated from an external network.

Automatic Private IP Addressing (APIPA)

Automatic Private IP Addressing (**APIPA**), supported by Microsoft Windows OS, comes into action when the DHCP on a network is not functional, either permanently or temporarily. APIPA is a private IP address range of 169.254.0.0 - 169.254.255.255, which has been designed for small non-routable networks. It is an **autoconfiguration address**, as shown in *Figure 2.15*, which means that as soon as a DHCP client cannot discover a DHCP server on a given network, Windows automatically assigns an APIPA address to a computer's network interface.

As soon as a DHCP server becomes available, the APIPA address is replaced by the one assigned from the DHCP server:

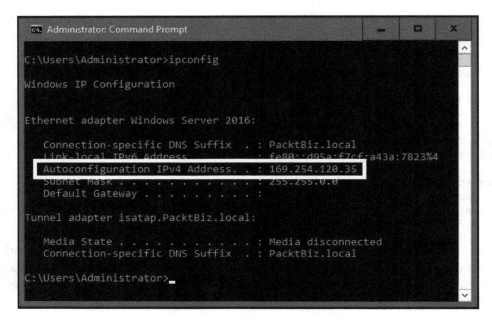

Figure 2.15. An APIPA address assigned by Windows Server 2016

Unicast, multicast, and broadcast addresses

In terms of end-to-end transmission, there's usually the following types of IP addresses:

- A **unicast IP address** is an IP address that identifies a unique host on a network.
- A **multicast IP address** is an IP address that is capable of sending packets to a selected group of hosts, known as a multicast group.
- A **broadcast IP address** is an IP address that is capable of sending packets to all the hosts on a network.

Class A addresses

In **class A**, the first octet (/8 prefix) is used to represent the network portion, and the remaining three octets are used to represent host addresses. It is obvious that in class A, the number of networks is noticeably smaller than the number of hosts per network. For that reason, class A is used to support mostly large organizations that prefer to have a small number of networks and a large number of hosts per network. The following table provides information about class A:

Class	Range	Maximum Number of Networks	Number of Hosts per Network	Leftmost Bit
A	0.0.0.0* - 127.255.255.255**	$2^7 = 128$	$2^{24} - 2 = 16,777,214$	0

* According to the **Internet Engineering Task Force (IETF)**, the IP address 0.0.0.0 is a reserved address *for this host on this network*.

** IP addresses from 127.0.0.1 to 127.255.255.255 are reserved for loopback purposes and diagnostic functions.

Class B addresses

In **class B**, the first two octets (/16 prefix) are used to represent the network portion, and the remaining two octets are used to represent host addresses. It is obvious that in class B, the number of networks is larger than in class A, and the numbers of hosts per network is smaller than in class A. For that reason, class B is designed to support medium-to-large organizations that prefer to have a considerable number of networks with up to 65,534 available host addresses per network. The following table provides information about class B:

Class	Range	Maximum Number of Networks	Number of Hosts per Network	Leftmost Bit
B	128.0.0.0 - 191.255.255.255*	$2^{14} = 16,384$	$2^{16} - 2 = 65,534$	10

* IP addresses from `169.254.0.0` to `169.254.255.255` are reserved for APIPA.

Class C addresses

In **class C**, the first three octets (/24 prefix) are used to represent the network portion, and the remaining octet is used to represent host addresses. It is obvious that in class C, the number of networks is noticeably bigger than the number of hosts per network. For that reason, this class is designed to support mostly small organizations that prefer to have a big number of networks and a small number of hosts per network. The following table provides information about class C:

Class	Range	Maximum Number of Networks	Number of Hosts per Network	Leftmost Bit
C	`192.0.0.0 -` `223.255.255.255`	$2^{21} = 2,097,152$	$2^8 - 2 = 254$	110

Class D addresses

Like classes A, B, and C, class D addresses are 32-bit network addresses too, and are reserved for multicasting. The characteristic of this class is that all of the hosts within a group share the group's receiving IP address. The following table provides information about class D:

Class	Range	Leftmost Bit
D	`224.0.0.0 - 239.255.255.255`	1110

Class E addresses

Class E addresses are reserved for experimental purposes and future development. The following table provides information about class E:

Class	Range	Leftmost Bit
E	240.0.0.0 - 255.255.255.255*	1111

* IP address 255.255.255.255 represents the *global* broadcast IP address.

IPv6 network addresses

If it were not for the lack of IPv4 address space, we would not have IPv6. It is very natural then that **Internet Protocol version 6** (**IPv6**) **addressing** has been introduced to overcome IPv4 address exhaustion. Like IPv4, IPv6 too is a logical element that identifies a device on a computer network. The label *v6* represents the sixth version of IP addressing, as specified in IETF publication RFC 2460. Unlike IPv4, IPv6 is a 128-bit address size organized into 8 groups of hextets (16 bits), each divided by a colon for simplicity of interpretation (for example, 2001:0DB8:85A3:0000:0000:8A2E:0370:7334). In contrast to IPv4, in IPv6, you can omit any leading zeros (0s) in any hextet. Be careful to apply this rule only to leading 0s and not on trailing 0s. In addition, you can omit all zero (0) segments by placing a double colon (::) to replace one or more hextets consisting of all 0s. If we take into account the fact that 1 byte = 8 bits, then a 128-bit IPv6 address is a 16-byte (that comes from *32/8 = 4*) address space. Also, unlike IPv4, which is represented in a decimal format, IPv6 is expressed in a **hexadecimal** format. From that, because in IPv6 addresses everything revolves around the hexadecimal numbering system, the total number of IPv6 addresses is 2^{128} = *340,282,366,920,938,463,463,374,607,431,768,211,456*. This means that there are plenty of IPv6 addresses available for every inhabitant on planet earth!

You can learn more about IPv6 at http://ipng.com/.

Global unicast addresses

The beauty of IPv6 is that there are enough addresses for everyone's devices. So, we do not need to use NAT to connect our devices to the internet, because with IPv6 **global unicast** addresses, they become reachable on the internet. That said, IPv6 global unicast addresses are the equivalent of IPv4 public addresses. Like public IPv4 addresses, IPv6 global unicast addresses are also **routable**, and can be configured statically or assigned dynamically. Currently, only *2000::/3* addresses are assigned by IANA to the global pool. *Figure 2.16* shows the structure of an IPv6 global unicast address:

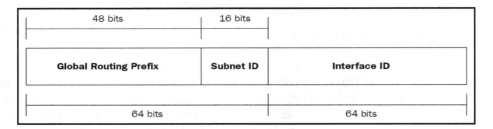

Figure 2.16. Structure of an IPv6 global unicast address

 You can test your computer's IPv6 connectivity at: `https://test-ipv6.com/`.

Link-local addresses

Link-local addresses are similar to APIPA addresses in IPv4. This is because, like APIPA and link-local addresses, they too are **automatically configured** on all interfaces. Link-local addresses use the `FE80::/10` prefix and are not **routable**, meaning that these addresses are only used to communicate between devices on the same local link.

Unique local addresses

Similar to global and link-local addresses, **unique local** addresses also fall in the **unicast group** of IPv6 addresses. Unique local addresses use the FC00::/7 prefix and are only **routable** within a site or between a limited number of sites. This reminds us of the private addresses of IPv4. However, IPv6 unique local addresses should not be routable to the internet (they are not IPv6 global unicast addresses) nor should they be translated to IPv6 global unicast addresses (remember, there is no NAT in IPv6).

Loopback address

A **loopback** address is another unicast IPv6 address that uses the :1/128 prefix and identifies the localhost. This reminds us of the 127.0.0.1 loopback addresses of IPv4. That way, when an application sends a packet to this address, the packet will get returned to the application after being looped back by the IPv6 stack.

"This host, this network" address

An IPv6 address with the ::/128 prefix represents an unspecified address that is the same as the IP address 0.0.0.0 in IPv4. Similar to IPv4, in IPv6, that address is assigned by the OS and acts as the source address until the host has initialized completely and learns its IPv6 address. As such, this address should not be assigned to any host.

Multicast addresses

Similar to IPv4 multicast addresses, in IPv6, **multicast addresses** are also used to send data to a group (multicast). In IPv6 address space, multicast addresses are specified by the FF00::/8 prefix.

Anycast

In IPv6, an **anycast address** represents any IPv6 unicast address that can be assigned to multiple devices. That way, when a packet is sent to an anycast address, it then gets routed to the nearest device that has the address. There is no anycast address in IPv4.

Autoconfiguration

As far as autoconfiguration in IPv6 is concerned, there are two ways to automatically assign an IPv6 global unicast address to devices:

- **Stateless Address Autoconfiguration** (**SLAAC**) enables a router to provide an IPv6 global unicast address to a device without the use of a DHCPv6 server. This method of assigning IPv6 global unicast addresses relies on the local router's ICMPv6 **Router Advertisement** (**RA**) messages. This way, a prefix, prefix length, default gateway address, and other information are obtained by one device. However, it is worth mentioning the Router Advertisement options:
  - SLAAC only,
  - SLAAC and DHCPv6, and
  - DHCPv6 only
- **Stateful DHCPv6** works the same way as DHCP in IPv4. Unlike IPv4, in IPv6, there is a new protocol named DHCPv6 that is used to provide devices on the network with IPv6 addresses, prefixes, and other configuration data.

You can learn more about IPv6 address space at: `https://www.iana.org/assignments/ipv6-address-space/ipv6-address-space.xhtml`.

Subnetting

IP classes contain both network and host portions known as prefixes, which enables the creation of more networks. Obviously, those are logical networks that enable the effective use of IP address ranges. With that in mind, **subnetting** (for more on subnetting, see *Appendix E: Subnetting)* represents a logical division of one large network into multiple smaller networks. In subnetting, a **subnet mask** plays an important role in identifying the network and determining the size of the network. Additionally, subnetting enables you to identify the network address, host addresses, and broadcast address of a given network. By definition, a subnet mask is a **32-bit address** used in combination with an IPv4 address to indicate the network and its computers.

Each class has a default subnet mask. The following table shows the default subnet masks associated with IP address classes:

Class	Subnet Mask
A	255.0.0.0
B	255.255.0.0
C	255.255.255.0

Classful subnetting

Classful subnetting comes from classful addressing in which, as we've learned earlier, IP addresses are organized into classes. Since each class contains a certain prefix, it is the prefix (8-bit, 16-bit, and 24-bit) that determines the portion representing the network ID and the portion representing the host's ID. From that, we understand that it is not a subnet mask that contains the network portion and the host portion of an IPv4 address; instead, it just tells the computer what the IP address actually contains. The following table shows the classful subnetting in IPv4 addressing:

Class	Range	Default Subnet Mask	Network Prefix	Network ID/Host ID
A	0.0.0.0 - 127.255.255.255	255.0.0.0	/8	N.H.H.H
B	128.0.0.0 - 191.255.255.255	255.255.0.0	/16	N.N.H.H
C	192.0.0.0 - 223.255.255.255	255.255.255.0	/24	N.N.N.H

Classless subnetting

Unlike classful subnetting, **classless subnetting**, known formally as **Classless Inter Domain Routing (CIDR)**, works with the principle of bit borrowing. Simply, it borrows bits from the host portion to add them into the network portion for the sake of creating more small networks, thus enabling far more rational usage of IPv4 address spacing. Interestingly, **classless routing protocols** send the subnet mask along with their updates, something that **classful routing protocols** do not:

- **Class A classless subnetting** (see *Figure 2.18*) can borrow from 1 to 8 bits from the second octet, from 1 to 8 bits from the third octet, and from 1 to 6 bits from the fourth octet. In total, it can borrow an additional 22 bits from the host's portion of a class A IPv4 address (N.H.H.H):

Class	Network Prefix	Subnet Mask	Borrowed Bits	Subnets	Hosts per Subnet
	/8	255.0.0.0	0	1	16777214
	/9	255.128.0.0	1	2	8388606
	/10	255.192.0.0	2	4	4194302
	/11	255.224.0.0	3	8	2097150
	/12	255.240.0.0	4	16	1048574
	/13	255.248.0.0	5	32	524286
	/14	255.252.0.0	6	64	262142
	/15	255.254.0.0	7	128	131070
	/16	255.255.0.0	8	256	65534
	/17	255.255.128.0	9	512	32766
	/18	255.255.192.0.	10	1024	16382
A	/19	255.255.224.0	11	2048	8190
	/20	255.255.240.0	12	4096	4094
	/21	255.255.248.0	13	8192	2046
	/22	255.255.252.0	14	16384	1022
	/23	255.255.254.0	15	32768	510
	/24	255.255.255.0	16	65536	254
	/25	255.255.255.128	17	131072	126
	/26	255.255.255.192	18	262144	62
	/27	255.255.255.224	19	524288	30
	/28	255.255.255.240	20	1048576	14
	/29	255.255.255.248	21	2097152	6
	/30	255.255.255.252	22	4194304	2

Figure 2.17. Class A classless subnetting

- **Class B classless subnetting** (see *Figure 2.18*) can borrow from 1 to 8 bits from the third octet, and from 1 to 6 bits from the fourth octet. In total, it can borrow an additional 14 bits from the host's portion of a class B IPv4 address (N.N.H.H):

Class	Network Prefix	Subnet Mask	Borrowed Bits	Subnets	Hosts per Subnet
	/16	255.255.0.0	0	0	65534
	/17	255.255.128.0	1	2	32766
	/18	255.255.192.0.	2	4	16382
	/19	255.255.224.0	3	8	8190
	/20	255.255.240.0	4	16	4094
	/21	255.255.248.0	5	32	2046
	/22	255.255.252.0	6	64	1022
B	/23	255.255.254.0	7	128	510
	/24	255.255.255.0	8	256	254
	/25	255.255.255.128	9	512	126
	/26	255.255.255.192	10	1024	62
	/27	255.255.255.224	11	2048	30
	/28	255.255.255.240	12	4096	14
	/29	255.255.255.248	13	8192	6
	/30	255.255.255.252	14	16384	2

Figure 2.18. Class B classless subnetting

- **Class C classless subnetting** (see *Figure 2.19*) can borrow from 1 to 6 bits from the fourth octet. In total, it can borrow an additional 6 bits from the host's portion of a class C IPv4 address (N.N.N.H):

Class	Network Prefix	Subnet Mask	Borrowed Bits	Subnets	Hosts per Subnet
	/24	255.255.255.0	0	0	254
	/25	255.255.255.128	1	2	126
	/26	255.255.255.192	2	4	62
C	/27	255.255.255.224	3	8	30
	/28	255.255.255.240	4	16	14
	/29	255.255.255.248	5	32	6
	/30	255.255.255.252	6	64	2

Figure 2.19. Class C classless subnetting

In **Fixed-length subnet masks** (**FLSM**), subnets have the same size. That subnetting method is not suitable for situations where subnets of different sizes are required in the subnet hierarchy. To overcome that problem, the IETF in the RFC 1812 document has introduced the **Variable-length subnet mask** (**VLSM**). It enables to subnetting the subnets, thus being able to divide the large subnet into smaller sub-subnets. This way, a smaller network with fewer sets of hosts can be handled.

IPv6 subnetting

Unlike IPv4 subnetting, **IPv6 subnetting** uses a different approach. If we have a look at the structure of an IPv6 global unicast address (as shown in *Figure 2.20*) from the perspective of the IPv4 address structure, then we can understand that the **Global Routing Prefix** and **Subnet ID** represents the network portion, and that the **Interface ID** represents the host portion. As you can note, organizations typically use the **Subnet ID** field to create additional subnets. Starting from the fact that the subnet ID is 16 bits, it matches the Class B of the IPv4 addressing, thus enabling us to create 2^{16} = 65535 subnets. And then, each of these subnets alone will have 2^{64} hosts (the size of the Interface ID). In cases where more subnets are required, additional bits from the Global Routing Prefix field can be borrowed that have a maximum of 48 bits:

48 bits	16 bits	64 bits
Global Routing Prefix	**Subnet ID**	**Interface ID**
Network ID		Host ID

Figure 2.20. Structure of an IPv6 global unicast address

Summary

We can summarize the chapter with the following points:

- Coding and decoding of messages are very important processes of communication:
    - Coding converts the information to an acceptable form for the transmission.
    - Decoding converts the received message into an intelligible language.
- Packing bits into the frame so they can be transmitted represents the encapsulation.
- When the receiving computer receives the frame and unpacks it by taking out the bits, this accomplishes de-encapsulation.
- Communication between computers is very strict as far as the size of the message is concerned.
- Access method, flow control, and response timeout are essential parts of the message timing:
    - In unicast message delivery, there is only one destination for the message
    - In multicast message delivery, there are several reachable destinations for the message.
    - In broadcast message delivery, all computers on the network will receive the message transmitted by the sender computer.
    - Simplex communication is often referred to as one-way communication because the direction of the transmission is predetermined.
    - In half-duplex communication, both devices can send and receive messages, but not at the same time.
    - In full-duplex communication, both devices can send and receive messages simultaneously.

- The computer communication language also contain standards and rules which are called communications protocols:
    - Connection-oriented protocols, prior to beginining transferring data, establish an end-to-end logical connection, often known as virtual links between two devices.
    - Connectionless protocols do not establish an end-to-end logical connection; instead, each packet contains destination address of the receiver and is thus treated as an individual entity.
- The TCP/IP protocol suite is comprised of a large number of communication protocols where each one performs their assigned tasks.
- In order to describe the functionality of the network including communication between computers, a layered model is used.
- The protocol suite is a communication protocol stack that is comprised of a set of communications protocols:
    - The reference model is a conceptual model that describes what is occurring in each communication layer without giving any description of how that should be accomplished.
    - The protocol model is a layered model that describes the protocol functions that are taking place at each layer.
- Named according to two main protocols like IP and TCP, the TCP/IP protocol model consists of four layers, known as network access, internet, transport and application.
- The OSI reference model consists of seven layers such as physical, data link, network, transport, session, presentation and application, and is developed by ISO:
    - The physical layer (Layer 1) represents both the physical and logical aspects of the computer network.
    - The data link layer (Layer 2) is responsible for assigning the physical protocols dependable upon the communication technology used in LANs.
    - The network layer is responsible for enabling the communication between networks.
    - The transport layer (Layer 4) is responsible for transporting data between network devices.
    - The session layer (Layer 5) is responsible for establishing and maintaining the on-demand communication sessions between applications.

- The presentation layer (Layer 6) receives data from the application layer and represents it in the format accepted by the subsequent layer.
- The application layer (Layer 7) is responsible for interacting with the operating system or application whenever the user decides to transmit data with its computer over a computer network or internet.
- Ethernet is the communication technology that is widely used in LANs:
  - The LLC sublayer is the upper half of Layer 2 (that is, the Data Link layer).
  - The MAC sublayer is the lower half of Layer 2.
  - The Ethernet Physical (Network Medium) layer actually represents Layer 1 of the OSI reference model.
- An Ethernet frame is a Layer 2 and Layer 1 data packet:
  - The frame format consists of six fields (as shown in *Figure 2.12*) such as Preamble and SFD, Destination MAC address, Source MAC address, EtherType, Data, and FCS.
  - The frame size is defined from the Destination MAC address field to the FCS field with the minimum size of 64 bytes, and the maximum size of 1,518 bytes.
- The Ethernet MAC address, often known as a physical address, is a unique network address that identifies the network interface on a computer network and is used for communication in the Data Link layer.
- Currently, the addressing technology being used is the IPv4 addressing, as specified in IETF publication RCF 791.
- IPv6 addressing has been introduced to overcome IPv4 limitations where v6 represents the sixth version of IP addressing, as specified in IETF publication RFC 2460.
- Subnetting represents a logical division of one large network into multiple, smaller networks.

Questions

1. Packing bits into the frame so they can be transmitted represents encapsulation. (True | False)
2. In _____ message delivery, there are several reachable destinations for the message.
3. Which of the following are essential parts of the message timing? (Choose three)
   1. Access method
   2. Flow control
   3. Response timeout
   4. Simplex communication
4. The Ethernet MAC address is often known as a logical address, and it used for communication in the Network layer. (True | False)
5. _____ represents a logical division of one large network into multiple smaller networks.
6. Which of the following are fields of an Ethernet frame? (Choose two)
   1. EtherType
   2. FCS
   3. Coding
   4. Decoding
7. The session layer (Layer 5) is responsible for establishing and maintaining the on-demand communication sessions between applications. (True | False)
8. _____ is responsible for interacting with the operating system or application whenever the user decides to transmit data with its computer over a computer network or the internet.
9. Which of the following are layers of the TCP/IP protocol model? (Choose two)
   1. Network Access
   2. The internet
   3. Presentation
   4. Session
10. An Ethernet frame is a Layer 3 data packet. (True | False)
11. _____ addressing has been introduced to overcome IPv4 limitations where *v6* represents the sixth version of IP addressing, as specified in IETF publication RFC 2460.

12. Which of the following are Ethernet protocols? (Choose two)
    1. LLC
    2. MAC
    3. IP
    4. TCP

13. FTP is the protocol tasked to carry files from the source computer to the destination computer. (True | False)

14. _____ is tasked with the responsibility of preventing bridging-loops on LANs.

15. Which of the following communication protocols operate under the TCP/IP protocol suite? (Choose three)
    1. HTTP
    2. UDP
    3. PPP
    4. SFD

16. Connectionless protocols do not establish an end-to-end logical connection; instead, each packet contains the destination address of the receiver, and is thus treated as an individual entity. (True | False)

17. _____, known formally as CIDR, works with the principle of bit borrowing.

18. Which of the following two ways automatically assign IPv6 global unicast addresses? (Choose two)
    1. SLAAC
    2. Stateful DHCPv6
    3. FLSM
    4. MAC

3
Introduction to Switching

This chapter is designed to provide you with a general introduction to switching. It begins with the definition of a switch, a networking device that connects computers and extends networks. In addition, switch essentials—MAC address table, MAC address learning and aging, frame switching, and frame flooding—are covered within the *What is a switch?* section. It then continues with a discussion of more general switching concepts: unicast, multicast, and broadcast addresses, in particular. This chapter also includes switched networks, frame forwarding methods, and an overview of VLANs, accompanied by commands. Due to its extensive use in LANs, Ethernet communication technology is covered in this chapter too. This time, topics like Ethernet frame encapsulation, Ethernet frame fields, and Ethernet frame processing are discussed. The chapter concludes with a discussion of switch security. To facilitate the understanding of the many concepts and definitions covered in this chapter, a large section on relevant figures is included.

In this chapter, we will cover:

- Understanding what a switch is
- Understanding general concepts of switching
- Understanding switched networks
- Understanding switching domains
- Understanding frame forwarding methods
- An overview of VLANs
- Understanding Ethernet's frame
- Understanding switch security

What is switch?

What is switch? Because we are discussing computer networks, naturally, the first and simplest answers to that question are:

- Switch is a hardware
- Switch is a network device

The next question in this line of discussion is: What is switch's function? To which we answer:

- Switch connects devices on a computer network

Finally, how does switch work? Here is the answer:

- Switch uses a packet-switching method to receive, process, and forward data to a destination device

Switch essentials

A switch is a Layer 2 network device, connecting your computer, other computers, and network peripheral devices on your LAN, whether at home or at work. Switch is used to extend networks, too. It contains two or more physical ports, known as **switch ports,** into which the network cables (see the section *Twisted pairs*, in `Chapter 1`, *Introduction to Computer Networks*, for more on network cables) are plugged. This way, the connections are made and the network is created. Switch connects to the star physical topology, while it uses the bus logical topology for communication. There are both unmanaged and managed switches. An unmanaged switch, as shown in *Figure 3.1*, is cheap, can't be configured, and works right out of the box:

Figure 3.1. Unmanaged switch

Unlike an unmanaged switch, a managed switch (see *Figure 3.2*) is expensive, configurable, and can be managed both locally and remotely:

Figure 3.2. Managed switch

 The name switch may have originated from the way a switch works. A switch switches the frames from an incoming port to an outgoing port. Does that remind you of the **Public Switched Telephone Network** (**PSTN**)?

MAC address table

First things first—switch uses physical addresses, known as MAC addresses, to make forwarding decisions. When a frame enters a switch, the switch examines whether the destination MAC address is located in the MAC table (that is, the **Content Addressable Memory** (**CAM**) table). If so, then the switch simply forwards the frame out of the port that connects the destination host. But what happens to the switch if the destination MAC address is not in the MAC table? In that case, the switch acts as a hub by sending the frame out of all the ports (known as **flooding**), in order to reach all of the hosts except the host from which it has received the frame. When a host responds, the switch learns its destination MAC address from its source MAC address. Then, the switch stores the MAC address in a table called a CAM table. That is how the switch learns the MAC addresses of the devices connected to it. Note that in literature, you will quite often encounter the **MAC address table** expression instead of CAM. Namely, that is what differentiates the switch from the hub, by limiting broadcast domains to only the switch port and the NIC.

You can enter the following command to view the content of the MAC address table on your switch (as shown in *Figure 3.3*):

```
Switch# show mac-address-table
```

```
Switch#show mac-address-table
            Mac Address Table
-------------------------------------------

Vlan    Mac Address       Type        Ports
----    -----------       --------    -----

 1      0005.5ed4.c3ab    DYNAMIC     Fa0/1
 1      0006.2ac8.ee32    DYNAMIC     Fa0/3
 1      000a.41d4.1c01    DYNAMIC     Fa0/4
 1      0010.1128.9993    DYNAMIC     Fa0/5
 1      0060.5c2e.d5bc    DYNAMIC     Fa0/2
 1      00e0.f7cc.1413    DYNAMIC     Fa0/6
```

Figure 3.3. MAC address table on Cisco switch

MAC learning and aging

As explained in the preceding section, the first thing that the switch does is to learn the MAC addresses of the devices that are connected to the switch. The most common way to learn MAC addresses is the dynamic approach, having to do with frames that enter the switch as a result of devices communicating with one another on a LAN. That way, the switch examines the frames by learning their source MAC addresses and identifying the ports in which the frames have entered the switch. Then, the switch records that information in the MAC address table.

To keep the entries in the MAC address table up to date, switch uses an aging mechanism. By default, the entries in the MAC address table are stored for a duration of 300 seconds (or five minutes) from the time the MAC address was last used.

You can enter the following command to show the aging-time of the MAC address table entries:

```
Switch# show mac-address-table aging-time
```

In addition, you can enter the following command to modify the default (or preconfigured) aging-time, where the value is any decimal number in the range of 0 to 1,000,000 seconds:

```
Switch(config)# mac-address-table aging-time <value>
```

If you want to disable MAC address aging, enter 0 as the value. Enter the following command to bring back the default aging-time:

```
Switch(configure)# no mac-address-table aging-time
```

Frame switching

Switch is considered to be an intelligent network device, because by monitoring the incoming traffic, it learns the MAC addresses of all of the devices on the network. After a switch learns the MAC addresses, it starts to forward frames to only the switch ports that the destination MAC addresses match, as shown in *Figure 3.4*. In addition to frame switching, switch does frame filtering, too, by forwarding the frames to only the switch ports that should receive the frames:

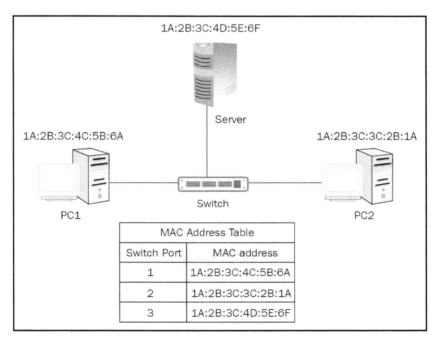

Figure 3.4. Frame switching using entries in the MAC address table

Frame flooding

Other than the dynamic approach, switch uses another method to learn MAC addresses. It does so by **flooding** all of the switch ports of devices connected to the switch, except the receiving port of the frame. Remember that the frame is actually destined for only one device, although it was forwarded to all of the ports. That type of frame forwarding is called an **unknown unicast**, as shown in *Figure 3.5*. The receiving devices will discard the frame, except for the devices that the frame was destined for. This represents the difference from the **broadcast address**, which is destined to all devices in the LAN. The broadcast frame will be processed by all of the receiving devices. That said, the broadcast frame contains all Fs on the frame's destination MAC address (for example, FF:FF:FF:FF:FF:FF):

1A:2B:3C:4D:5E:6F

Server

1A:2B:3C:4C:5B:6A   1A:2B:3C:3C:2B:1A

Switch

PC1   PC2

MAC Address Table	
Switch Port	MAC address
1	1A:2B:3C:4C:5B:6A

Figure 3.5. Learning MAC addresses that are not in the MAC address table

 You can learn more about switches from the tutorial at https://www.lantronix.com/resources/networking-tutorials/network-switching-tutorial/.

Switching general concepts

As explained in the preceding section, the working principle of the switch is based mainly on the MAC address table. So, it is not surprising that the very first thing that a switch does on a given computer network is to populate its MAC address table, as soon as possible. From there on, things seem to be simpler to switch.

Ingress and egress ports

In the switching technique, we encounter frames that enter the switch and frames that exit the switch, based on certain rules. Given the multiport structure of the switch, we can naturally conclude that the ports where the frames enter the switch are called **incoming ports**, and the ports where the frames exit the switch are called **outgoing ports**. In a similar format, the frames that enter the switch in an incoming port are known to be **inbound frames**, while the frames that exit the switch in an outgoing port are known as **outbound frames**. Almost identically, the terms ingress and egress are used. **Ingress** represents a frame entering the switch on a specific port, and **egress** represents a frame leaving the switch through a particular port.

Source and destination MAC addresses

In the section *Ethernet MAC addresses*, in `Chapter 2`, *Communication in Computer Networks*, you learned that an Ethernet MAC address, often known as a physical address, is a unique network address that identifies the device's network interface on a computer network; it is used for communication in the Data Link layer. From there, it can be understood that the **source MAC address** is actually the physical address of the network interface of a device that is sending frames. The **destination MAC address** is the physical address of the network interface of a device that is receiving frames. The following sections illustrate unicast, multicast, and broadcast MAC addresses.

Unicast MAC address

Recalling the definition of unicast transmission from the section *Unicast transmission* in `Chapter 2`, *Communication in Computer Networks*, it can be said that a **unicast MAC address** is the unique destination for a receiving device, which enables the sending device to transmit frames in a one-to-one format to the receiving device, as shown in *Figure 3.6*. Notice that, along with the destination MAC address, part of the Ethernet frame is the source MAC address, which is also unicast. Remember that ARP protocol enables the sending device to determine the destination MAC address of the receiving device:

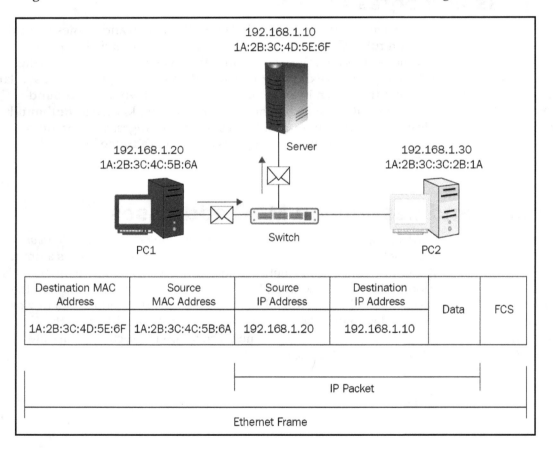

Destination MAC Address	Source MAC Address	Source IP Address	Destination IP Address	Data	FCS
1A:2B:3C:4D:5E:6F	1A:2B:3C:4C:5B:6A	192.168.1.20	192.168.1.10		

Figure 3.6. Unicast MAC address

Multicast MAC address

Recalling the range of multicast IPv4 addresses from the section *Class D addresses* in *Chapter 2, Communication in Computer Networks,* it can be said that a multicast MAC address enables the sending device to transmit frames to a group of devices in a one-to-many format, as shown in *Figure 3.7*. Notice that the sending device uses its unicast MAC address (that is, the server's source MAC address, `1A:2B:3C:4D:5E:6F`), while the group of devices that are subscribed to the multicast membership uses the destination MAC address of `01:00:5E:00:00:FF`. One thing to be considered in the case of multicast MAC addresses in IPv4 is the `01-00-5E` value, which leads the multicast MAC address. The remaining 23 lower bits of the multicast IP address are converted from binary into hexadecimal, in order to complete the string of the multicast MAC address with the six other hexadecimal characters:

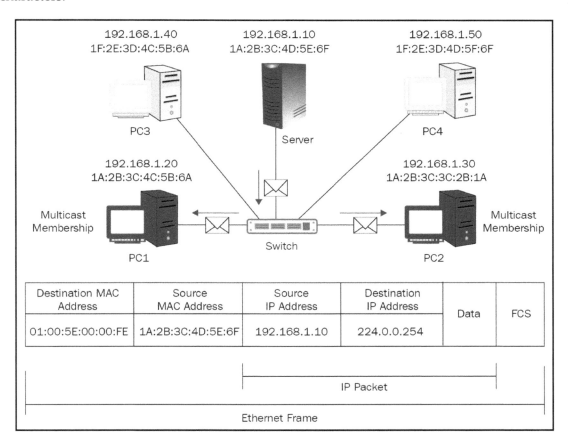

Figure 3.7. Multicast MAC address

Broadcast MAC address

As discussed earlier in this chapter, in the section *Frame flooding*, the destination MAC address becomes a broadcast MAC address when it contains all Fs in the address string (for example, FF:FF:FF:FF:FF:FF). A broadcast MAC address enables the sending device to transmit frames in a one-to-all format to all receiving devices on a LAN, except for the port that the frame entered the switch, as shown in *Figure 3.8*. Similarly, its counterpart, the multicast IPv4 address, contains all 1s in the host portion of the address string:

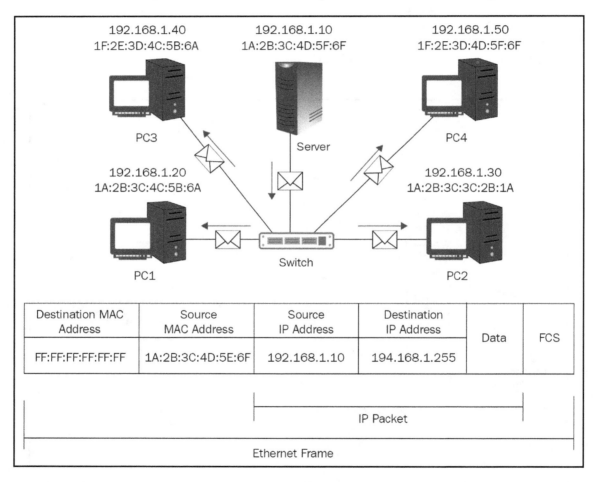

Destination MAC Address	Source MAC Address	Source IP Address	Destination IP Address	Data	FCS
FF:FF:FF:FF:FF:FF	1A:2B:3C:4D:5E:6F	192.168.1.10	194.168.1.255		

Figure 3.8. Broadcast MAC address

If you want to learn more about switches, browse `https://www.lifewire.com/definition-of-network-switch-817588`.

Switched networks

If we compare the networks of the past to networks now, from a design point of view, the changes are obvious. But, if we look at networks from a purpose point of view, then we realize that the networks of the past and the networks today are no different at all. Both share a common goal: sharing of resources. To ensure that these resources are available to users, a large number of network devices are required to seamlessly work together. Among the numerous networking devices out there, switches are the ones that act as connection points, be it on a home network or a corporate network. As the name indicates, a switched network is a computer network that is made up mostly of switches. However, there is also the concept of a fully switched network, which represents a computer network that is solely comprised of switches.

The role of switched networks

First, let's discuss how hosts are connected to the network through the switch. From a physical topology point of view, usually, the switch is placed in the **Main Distribution Facility (MDF)** or **Intermediary Distribution Facility (IDF)**; from there, the cables (usually twisted pairs) are then distributed to the hosts.

The characteristic of the switch is that each host establishes a direct connection with the switch (see *Figure 3.9*), without any interference from other connections. In that way, each host communicates directly with the switch, meaning that the data is transmitted from host to switch, and vice versa, at the same time. This represents the core function of the switch. The simultaneous transmission is known as **full-duplex,** and represents another strong feature of the switch, enabling a network free of collisions.

In addition, it enables effective transmission and an increase in transmission speed:

Figure 3.9. Hosts connected directly to the switch

Features of the switch

Given the importance of switches in computer networks, it is natural to encounter switches in different shapes and sizes. This variety enables the deployment of appropriate switches, based on network requirements. Therefore, the following are some of the features that should be considered in choosing the appropriate switch:

- **Number of ports**: Usually, switches have from 4 to 48 ports. Therefore, how many ports the switch should have depends on the number of devices on the network.
- **Speed per ports:** Nowadays, there may still be FastEthenet switches with 100 Mbps per port on the market. However, it looks like switches with 1 Gbps have become the norm.
- **Storing frames:** There may be situations where certain ports on a switch become overloaded by network traffic, especially the ports that connect the servers. Therefore, switches with the ability to store frames in memory (known as **buffer**) enable high performance in congested situations.
- **Power over Ethernet (PoE)**: Often, for remote devices, it is required to provide a power supply. In order to overcome these unfavorable situations, PoE switches (as shown in *Figure 3.10*) offer the ideal solution:

Figure 3.10. Power over Ethernet (PoE) multi-layer switch

- **Reliability**: Due to the fact that a switch plays the role of a central device that connects almost all of the devices on the network, reliability is a factor that must not be compromised at all.
- **Scalability**: It is normal for networks to expand over time; therefore, switches should be able to support scalability.
- **Cost**: The cost of the switch depends on the features mentioned previously. The more features supported by the switch, the higher the cost of the switch.

Fixed configuration switches

With fixed configuration switches, you get what you pay for. That said, **fixed configuration switches** (as shown in *Figure 3.11*) cannot have features expanded beyond the existing ones that came with the switch. The market offers a great variety of this type of switches, so that they are able to support different network requirements:

Figure 3.11. The rear of the fixed configuration switch

Modular configuration switches

Unlike fixed configuration switches, modular configuration switches (see *Figure 3.12*) are highly flexible. As the name indicates, this type of switch offers the ability to expand features by installing relevant modules. The installation of modules in switches is almost identical to the installation of expansion cards in PC slots. So, the bigger the switch chassis, the more modules can be installed:

Figure 3.12. The empty slots for adding modules with additional features

Stackable configuration switches

Unlike the two previous types of switches, stackable configuration switches (see *Figure 3.13*) enable the increase of switch port number. This is achieved by interconnecting the switches with a special cable, thus stacking them one on top of another using the **uplink port**. Usually, stackable switches use a separate port for uplink, enabling the stack to operate as a single switch. There are stackable switches on the market that support **StackPower** technology, which enables sharing the power among stackable switches:

Figure 3.13. The rear of stackable configuration switches with stack ports

Overview of Circuit Switching and Packet Switching is an article worth reading. You can access it at `http://computernetworkingsimplified.in/physical-layer/overview-circuit-switching-packet-switching/`.

Frame forwarding methods

We now know that switches work on the principle of frame forwarding. As soon as the frame enters the switch through the incoming port, the frame is examined, and then forwarded to the device at the destinations via the outgoing port. However, it cannot be said that there is a single method of **frame forwarding**. A variety of frame forwarding methods are discussed in the following sections.

Store-and-forward switching

Among the features mentioned in brief in the section *Features of the switch*, we discussed *storing frames*. In a meaningful format, the *storing frames* feature is based on **store-and-forward switching**. This switching method means that once the frame enters the switch, its data is stored until the whole frame arrives. During the time that the frame is kept in buffers, it is analyzed for destination information. In addition, using **Cyclic Redundancy Check (CRC)**, the switch checks the frame for errors. If the frame contains errors, then the frame is discarded. Conversely, if the frame does not contain errors, then it is forwarded through the outgoing port to its destination. The store-and-forward switching method has found application in converged networks, enabling **Quality of Services (QoS)** analysis.

Cut-through switching

In contrast to store-and-forward, the cut-through switching method is far more pragmatic. In the **cut-through switching method**, as soon as the frame enters the switch, the examine process upon its data takes place immediately. Thus, there is no waiting for the whole frame to arrive. Interestingly, the switch buffers only the part of the data of the frame from which it can determine the destination MAC address. Recalling the section *Ethernet frame* in Chapter 2, *Communication in Computer Networks*, the destination MAC address comes right after the Preamble and SFD field.

After the switch determines the destination MAC address, it then matches it with the information on the MAC address table so that it can determine the outgoing port. When that is done, the switch forwards the frame to the destination interface over its outgoing port. Notice that no error checking is done on the frame. Although the cut-through switching method is simpler than the store-and-forward switching method, there are two variants of it, described as follows.

Fast-forward switching

If you have heard of **First in First out (FIFO)**, **fast-forward switching** works on that principle, because latency is measured from the first bit received to the first bit transmitted. For that reason, this switching variant is considered to have the lowest level of latency. That said, as soon as the frame enters the switch, its destination MAC address is determined, and the frame is immediately forwarded to its destination. There is no waiting for the entire frame to arrive so that the forwarding can be done. However, this way of handling frames can cause frames to be transmitted to their destinations with errors. Because of that, the receiving devices discard the frames with errors upon receipt.

Fragment-free switching

Unlike fast-forwarding, **fragment-free switching** employs the storing of a certain amount of the frame. Based on that, the switch stores only the first 64 bytes, enabling error checking on these bytes. Once 64 bytes of the frame have been analyzed, the destination MAC address has been determined, and these bytes have been checked for errors, the frame is then forwarded to its destination. Networking has shown that collisions and network errors are likely to occur in the first 64 bytes. That is the reason why only these bytes are stored by the fragment-free switching variant. Also, it can be concluded that fragment-free switching gets frame storing and error checking from the *store-and-forward switching* method, and gets forwarding the frame before it arrives as a whole from the cut-through switching method.

How a Switch Works, presented by TechRepublic, provides a broad overview of switch functions: http://www.dbillings.com/networking/ How_a_Switch_Works.pdf.

Switching domains

You have seen the many strong features of switches that have to do with how a switch works. Viewed from the point of communication, you became acquainted with how a switch enables communication between devices. However, a switch will not always result in successful communication,because each port on a switch is in a separate collision domain, and all ports on a switch are in the same broadcast domain. This can cause **network congestion,** too.

Collision domains

As you now know, in general, collision occurs when two devices attempt to transmit data on the LAN at the same time. When a collision occurs, the devices have to resend the data, which degrades the network performance. Unlike the *hub* which forwards the data in a broadcast form (and, as such, creates conditions for a collision, too), the *switch* uses the MAC address table to forward data, enabling collisions to occur at the port level. From there, a collision domain is a segment (also expressed as a connection from/to the switch port) on the network where data is likely to collide with one another, when sent at the same time.

Broadcast domains

Recalling the definition of broadcast MAC addresses from the section *Broadcast MAC address*, it can be said that the switch broadcasts frames out of all ports to all devices on a LAN, except the port that the frame entered the switch through. This helps us to understand that the switch propagates the broadcast by enabling every device on the network device to reach all of the other devices. Based on that, it can be concluded that the switch, as a whole, is a broadcast domain. Usually, broadcast messages are used to identify devices or services on the network.

Network congestion

Unpredictable situations can occur in computer networks. Despite communication standards that are clearly defined, to some extent, unpredictability comes from a huge diversity of network components. For example, it might be the case that a device transmits more data than the available capacity, or that the data has not reached the destination, or a variety of other situations. All of these situations, some more and some less, cause **network congestion** in computer networks, which in turn causes delays, loss of data, or even an interruption of services.

 You can learn more about collision domains versus broadcast domains at `https://ciscoskills.net/2011/03/30/collision-domains-vs-broadcast-domains/`.

Switch port settings

Each switch port is characterized by features such as duplex speed, bandwidth, auto-configuration, and Auto-MDIX. In the following sections, you will get to know these features.

Duplex and speed settings

Before we talk about duplex and speed settings, let's first get to know two very important computer networking concepts: bandwidth and throughput. To better understand, think of bandwidth as a water pipe, while throughput is the water that passes through the water pipe. In this analogy, the bandwidth represents the total capacity of a communication channel (in other words, the networking medium), whereas the throughput represents the actual data traffic (often measured in Mbps or Gbps).

For each switch port, bandwidth and duplex are two of the most basic settings. Therefore, it is required that the bandwidth and duplex settings on the switch port match with the device's interface. As discussed in the section *Types of communication channels* in `Chapter 2,` *Communication in Computer Networks*, it can be said that there are two types of duplex settings in Ethernet communication technology:

- **Full-duplex**: Both devices can send and receive messages, simultaneously
- **Half-duplex**: Both devices can send and receive messages, but not at the same time

Nowadays, switches and NICs benefit from auto-configuration, which enables switch ports and a device's interfaces to exchange duplex and speed capabilities. So, depending on the port switch and the device's interface support, they can choose full-duplex speed and the highest bandwidth for communication.

Auto-MDIX

When connecting two devices to each other, it is very important to use the correct cables. So, we need to be careful when connecting PCs with PCs, PCs with switches, PCs with routers, switches with switches, switches with routers, and routers with routers. *Figure 3.14* shows the correct connections between these devices:

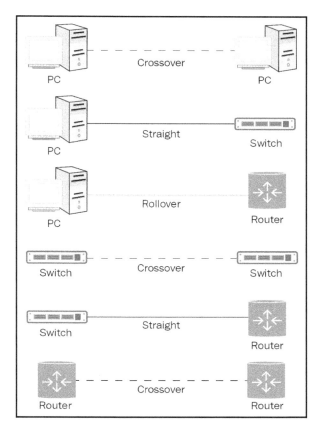

Figure 3.14. Correct cables for connecting devices

However, nowadays, switches are equipped with an **Auto-MDIX feature** that enables them to identify the types of the cables connected between switch ports and device interfaces, and to accomplish the configuration accordingly. That said, whether you are using straight-through or crossover cables to connect switches with any type of devices, the Auto-MDIX feature will take care of the automatic configuration.

Networking cables and connections are explained at `http://cs-study.` `blogspot.com/2012/10/networking-cables-and-connections.html`.

Overview of VLANs

Years ago, when I was attending a Cisco conference, in a conversation with some friends, one of them told us about how he had designed a network and deployed some network devices. As he talked about his solution, my ears caught the expression, *"Set it and forget it."*

There is no doubt that designing a computer network requires proper planning. Planning also includes the configuration of network devices. All of the planning activities contribute to network performance, and that is what matters the most for organizations—knowing that the organization's productivity depends directly upon network performance. Thus, the higher the network performance, the better the business productivity.

Now that we know the advantages and disadvantages of switches, it is very important to get familiar with the technologies that have a positive effect on network performance. One of these technologies is the **Virtual Local Area Network (VLAN)**, which enables the separation of the larger broadcast domains into smaller ones.

VLAN segmentation

First, the concept of VLAN is based on logical connections, rather than physical connections. VLAN enables the grouping of devices in the LAN by creating the impression that all devices are connected to the same cable and own an independent network. Each port of the switch can be assigned a VLAN, so that separate logical networks can be created to forward and flood the unicast, multicast, and broadcast frames. In this way, data that is not intended for devices within a VLAN will be transmitted to other devices in other networks, by devices that support routing, or via routers themselves. As the name suggests, VLANs are virtual networks that do not depend upon the physical locations of users, devices, and networks.

Thus, the network administrator can segment the network according to the network's purpose and function. This enables the implementation of access and security policies by a certain group of users. Some VLAN implementation benefits include performance, security, reduced broadcast domains, cost, improved network management, and others:

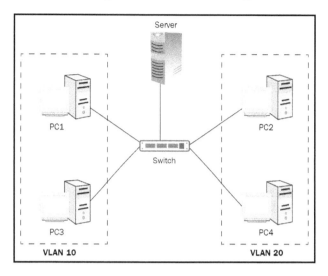

Figure 3.15. VLANs on LAN

Several types of VLANs are used in modern networks. Some of these VLANs are as follows:

- **Default VLAN**: Right after the switch's initial booting and the loading of a default configuration, all of the ports become part of the default VLAN. In Cisco switches, VLAN1 is the default VLAN and cannot be renamed or deleted.
- **Data VLAN**: Often called a user VLAN, data VLAN is a VLAN that is created by the user to segment the network into groups of users or devices. Voice VLAN and management VLAN are not part of this VLAN type.
- **Management VLAN**: This is a VLAN that enables remote access to the switch for management purposes. VLAN1 is an out-of-the-box VLAN that is meant to manage the switch. However, for security reasons, it is recommended to configure another VLAN for managing switch capabilities, and keep it separated from default, data, and native VLANs.
- **Native VLAN**: When configuring a switch port as a trunk, this supports the traffic in a multiswitched environment coming from multiple VLANs (known as tagged traffic). In Cisco switches, VLAN1 is the native VLAN, where the 802.1Q trunk port places untagged traffic.

VLANs in a multiswitched environment

In general, computer networks have one or more switches. The idea behind multiple-switch scenarios in the network has to do with security and network performance. In such multiswitched environments, **VLAN Trunking Protocol** (VTP) is a Cisco proprietary protocol that enables network performance by propagating the VLAN information among all switches.

VLAN trunks

As you know, the purpose of VLANs is to segment switched networks, in order to reduce broadcast domains. However, how can you manage broadcast domains in situations where the hosts of a given VLAN are connected to different switches on a network? In such environments, to take care of network performance, Cisco has introduced the VTP. **VLAN trunks** (see *Figure 3.16*) can be thought of as links that support VLANs beyond single switches. Technically speaking, a VLAN trunk is a point-to-point link between two switches, or between the switch and the router, that propagates the VLAN information among switches and routers. That way, the hosts that are connected on the same VLAN but on different switches can communicate without the need of a router. To implement VLAN trunks, switches and routers should support IEEE 802.1Q, including servers and other hosts with 802.1Q-capable NICs. Like VLANs, VLAN trunks operate in OSI layer 2 (that is, Data Link):

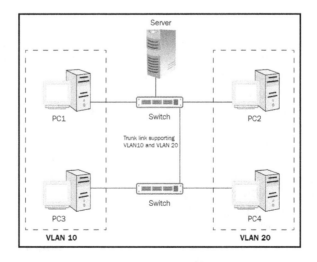

Figure 3.16. Trunk link supporting VLAN 10 and VLAN 20

Inter-VLAN operation

It is estimated that in Cisco switches can be created from 1 to 4,094 VLANs. That sure is a huge number. However, knowing that each VLAN is a broadcast domain, and that switches cannot route traffic like routers do, instantly brings up the question of how VLANs from different networks will communicate? Well, the answer is as simple as adding a router in between! Do you think that will work? It sure will. The concept of **inter-VLAN routing** involves the router that forwards traffic from one VLAN to another VLAN. Inter-VLAN routing is presented with three options:

- **Legacy inter-VLAN routing** is based on a router (see *Figure 3.17*) with multiple physical interfaces connected to different physical switch ports, where each port is set in access mode and assigned to a different VLAN:

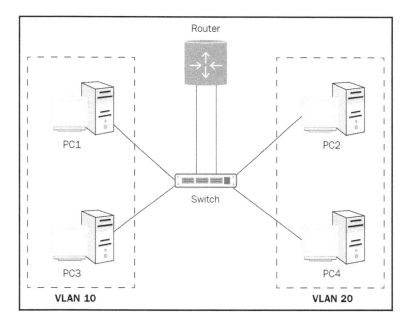

Figure 3.17. Legacy inter-VLAN routing

- **Router-on-a-stick** is based on a router (see *Figure 3.18*) with a single physical interface connected to a physical switch port configured in trunk mode, creating a trunk link to route VLAN-tagged traffic. This option involves subinterfaces on a router—software-based virtual interfaces that are configured with an IP address and VLAN assignment:

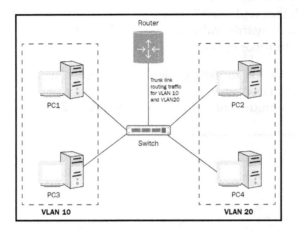

Figure 3.18. Router-on-a-stick inter-VLAN routing

- **Layer 3 switching using SVIs** is based on a multilayer switch (see *Figure 3.19*) with a **Switch Virtual Interface** (**SVI**), where a single SVI is mapped to a VLAN to route traffic among virtual layer 3 interfaces:

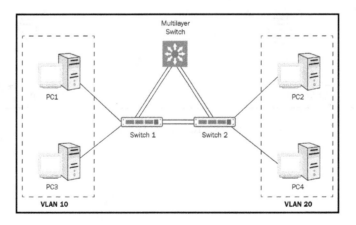

Figure 3.19. Layer 3 switching using SVIs

VLAN basic concepts are explained, with examples, at `https://www.`
`computernetworkingnotes.com/ccna-study-guide/vlan-basic-`
`concepts-explained-with-examples.html`.

Ethernet's frame overview

In the section *Ethernet communication technology*, in `Chapter 2`, *Communication in Computer Networks*, you were introduced to Ethernet history, Ethernet protocols, Ethernet framework, and Ethernet MAC addresses. As a continuation of the second chapter, in the following sections, you will get to know the concepts such as the Ethernet encapsulation frame, Ethernet frame fields, and Ethernet frame processing.

Ethernet frame encapsulation

The **data encapsulation** in the OSI reference model (see *Figure 3.20*) will help you to understand Ethernet frame encapsulation. Note that while data flows from the upper layers to lower layers of the OSI reference model, header information is added. Thus, the Transport layer adds a TCP or UDP header, the Network layer adds an IP header, the Data Link layer adds an Ethernet header, and then, the data gets transmitted. Depending on the medium, the transmission takes the form of electrical, light, or wave signaling, which is expressed in bits for the sake of interpretation. Since Ethernet frame encapsulation is being discussed, let us take a look at the activities that are taking place in the Data Link layer.

As you know the Data Link layer consists of two sublayers: **Logical Link Control** (**LLC**), which represents the upper half of Layer 2, and **Media Access Control** (**MAC**), which represents the lower half of Layer 2. Thus, LLC, being sandwiched by the Network layer and the MAC sublayer, receives the IP packet from the Network layer and prepares it for the MAC sublayer. It does this by isolating the functions occurring in the Network layer from those occurring in the MAC sublayer, defining the additional error-recovery mechanism, providing flow control, and establishing logical connections between the sending and receiving computers. The data is then passed to the MAC sublayer, which adds the **Ethernet header information** (such as the source and destination MAC addresses), manages access to the network medium by devices, and enables full-duplex transmission. While LLC can be considered the NIC's driver software, MAC is implemented by NIC's hardware (that is, NIC's ROM).

At this stage, it is the frame that carries the data from the sending device to the receiving device over the network medium:

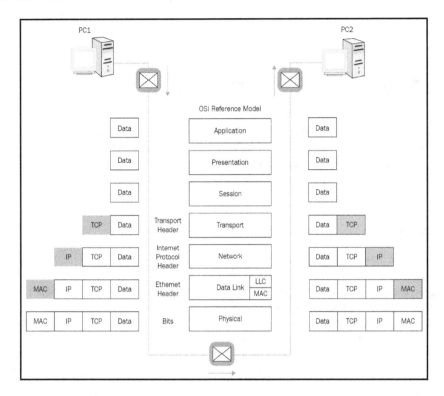

Figure 3.20. Data encapsulation in the OSI reference model

Ethernet frame fields

Based on the IEEE 802.3 standard, an Ethernet frame, as shown in *Figure 3.21*, consists of six fields. These are explained as follows:

- The **Preamble and Start Frame Delimiter** constitutes the first field of the frame, and has a size of 8 bytes. The Preamble size is 7 bytes, and it is used for Ethernet signaling and to avoid transmission speeds to make changes in frame format. SFD has a 1-byte size and is used to indicate to the receiving device that the frame starts right after this field. Both Preamble and SFD are generated by NIC's chipset and contain alternating 0s (zeros) and 1s (ones), which enable the receiving device to synchronize with the Ethernet signaling.

- The **Destination MAC Address** field represents the physical address of the receiving device. This field has a size of 6 bytes, and is mainly displayed in a hexadecimal format. It is usually generated by the NIC driver of the sending device, and may be of unicast, multicast, or broadcast format.
- The **Source MAC Address** field represents the physical address of the sending device. Like the destination MAC address, this field too, has a size of 6 bytes, and is mainly displayed in a hexadecimal format. It is generated by the NIC driver and is of a unicast format only. Note that MAC addresses are static physical addresses assigned by NIC manufacturers.
- The **EtherType** field has a size of 2 bytes and is generated by the NIC's driver. It is used to indicate the length and the protocol that is encapsulated in the Data field. In addition, the EtherType field contains the assigned type values that enable Ethernet products to use the same values for the same frame types.
- The **Data** field, also known as the *payload*, has a size from 46 to 1,500 bytes, and represents the actual data that is about to be transmitted to the receiving device. This data has been generated by OSI Layer 7 and encapsulated by subsequent layers. Note that if the frame size is smaller than the minimum size, or greater than the maximum frame size, then the receiving device drops the frame.
- The **Frame Check Sequence** (**FCS**) field has a size of 4 bytes and contains **Cyclic Redundancy Checksum** (**CRC**), which validates the integrity of the frame once it arrives at the NIC of the receiving device:

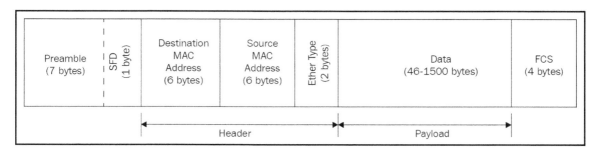

Figure 3.21. IEEE 802.3 Ethernet frame fields

Ethernet frame processing

Let us try to illustrate **Ethernet frame processing** with *Figure 3.22*, assuming that PC1 wants to send a message to PC3. Knowing that the switches operate on OSI Layer 2 and use MAC addresses for communication, all NICs of the PCs in the figure have physical addresses that are **Burned-in-Address (BIA)** on their respective chips (that is, NICs ROM). Interestingly, when the computer boots up, the NIC driver copies the physical address from its respective ROM into the computer's RAM. Thus, when PC1 wants to send a message to PC3 on an Ethernet network (remember, CSMA CD), header information containing the source and destination MAC addresses is attached to a frame. As explained earlier, in the section *Ethernet frame encapsulation*, this represents the **frame encapsulation** process. Shortly, the frame reaches the NIC of PC3, where both the destination MAC address and the payload will be examined. If the destination MAC address of a frame is the same as the physical address stored on the PC3 RAM, then the frame is forwarded to OSI's upper layers; this represents the **frame de-encapsulation** process. Otherwise, the frame is discarded:

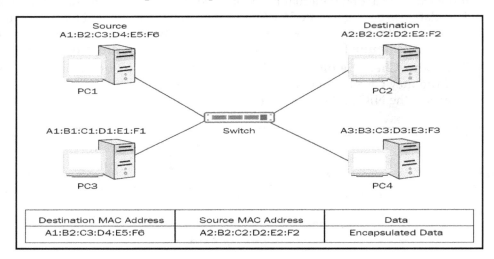

Destination MAC Address	Source MAC Address	Data
A1:B2:C3:D4:E5:F6	A2:B2:C2:D2:E2:F2	Encapsulated Data

Figure 3.22. Switch's frame forwarding process

 An overview of IEEE 802.3 and Ethernet can be found at https://www. saddleback.edu/faculty/msierakowski/frame_types.pdf.

Switch security

As you know, switches are network devices that have multiple ports. This means that there might be situations when a few switch ports might not be used. Unused ports represent the potential for an intruder to gain access to an organization's network. To avoid such situations, **port security** comes into play, by disabling unused ports. In addition, to enable protection against unauthorized access by unplugging a connected device, the MAC address of a device can be associated with a switch port. With that in mind, it can be summarized that port security enables security on **switch ports** by limiting the devices that can connect to ports on the switch.

Secure remote access

The only reason a network administrator would access a switch remotely is to manage it. However, such a connection must be secured, in order to prevent unauthorized access to the switch. Telnet and **Secure Shell** (**SSH**) represent two methods of accessing the switch remotely. While Telnet is considered an older and insecure technology for remote access, SSH is a modern technology that provides secure access to remote devices. That said, let us discuss these two remote access technologies.

Telnet

As described in the section *Well-known communication protocols*, in *Chapter 2, Communication in Computer Networks,* Telnet is considered a pioneering method for accessing devices in remote locations. It is a protocol that operates on OSI Layer 7 and uses TCP port 23, which requires a firewall on your network to permit the Telnet traffic. However, Telnet is insecure, because it transmits credentials (a username and password) in plain text over a communication line.

SSH

Unlike Telnet, SSH is considered a secure technology for accessing remote devices, because it encrypts the connection between the device and the remote device. **Advanced Encryption Standard (AES)** is used to provide security between the switch and the host, while **Standard Hashing Algorithm (SHA-2)** is used to ensure the integrity of the transmitted data. This means that both the username and the password are transmitted in an encrypted format. Like Telnet, SSH operates on OSI Layer 7 and uses TCP port 22, which requires a firewall on your network to permit the SSH traffic. To enable SSH on Cisco switches, the **Internetwork Operating System (IOS)** should support cryptographic features and capabilities.

Port security operation

As mentioned earlier, port security is a method of securing the switch from unauthorized access. This is especially valid for switches in production. Also, note that the MAC address of a device can be associated with a switch port. Thus, only the device with the associated MAC address can access the corresponding port. Also, there are situations where more than one MAC address can be associated with a single port. In those cases, when the maximum number of MAC addresses is reached, the access of devices with unknown MAC addresses will not be allowed. The following are methods to configure port security:

- **Static secure MAC addresses** are manually configured, by being associated to a switch port. These addresses are stored in the switch's MAC address table and are part of the switch's running configuration, too.
- **Dynamic secure MAC addresses** are learned dynamically, and are stored in a MAC address table, but not on a switch's running configuration. If a switch is being restarted, then these addresses are removed from the MAC address table.
- **Sticky secure MAC addresses** are configured manually or learned dynamically, and are stored in a switch's MAC address table. They are part of the switch's running configuration, too.

 To analyze Ethernet traffic, you can use Wireshark, an open source network protocol analyzer. Download Wireshark from `https://www.wireshark.org/#download`.

Summary

We can summarize this chapter with the following points:

- Switch, an OSI Layer 2 device, is used to connect computers and extend networks.
- Switch uses physical addresses, known as MAC addresses, to make forwarding decisions.
- Switch learns MAC addresses dynamically, as they enter the switch.
- Switch does frame filtering by forwarding the frames to only the switch ports that should receive the frames.
- Flooding helps switch learn MAC addresses.
- The ports where the frames enter the switch are called incoming ports.
- The ports where the frames exit the switch are called outgoing ports.
- Ingress represents a frame entering a switch on a specific port.
- Egress represents a frame leaving a switch through a particular port.
- The source MAC address is the physical address of the network interface of a device that is sending frames.
- The destination MAC address is the physical address of the network interface of a device that is receiving the frames:
    - A unicast MAC address is the unique destination MAC address of a receiving device that enables the sending device to transmit frames in a one-to-one format to the receiving device.
    - A multicast MAC address enables the sending device to transmit frames in a one-to-many format to a group of devices.
    - A broadcast MAC address enables the sending device to transmit frames in a one-to-all format to all receiving devices on a LAN, except for the port that the frame entered the switch through.
- A switched network is a computer network that is made up of mostly switches.
- A fully switched network represents a computer network that is solely comprised of switches.
- Fixed configuration switches cannot be expanded in features, other than the existing ones that came with the switch.
- Modular configuration switches offer the ability to expand switch features by installing the relevant modules.

- Stackable configuration switches enable the increase of switch ports.
- Switches use store-and-forward switching and cut-through switching.
- Each port on a switch in in a separate collision domain, and all ports on a switch are in the same broadcast domain.
- Network congestion in computer networks can cause delays, loss of data, or even an interruption of services.
- There are two types of duplex settings on Ethernet communication technology:
    - Full-duplex—Both devices can send and receive messages, simultaneously.
    - Half-duplex—Both devices can send and receive messages, but not at the same time.
- The Auto-MDIX feature enables switches to identify the types of the cables connected between switch ports and a device's interfaces, and to accomplish the configuration accordingly.
- VLANs are virtual networks that do not depend upon the physical locations of users, devices, and networks.
- VLAN trunk is a point-to-point link between two switches, or between a switch and the router that propagates the VLAN information among switches and routers.
- The concept of inter-VLAN routing involves the router forwarding the traffic from one VLAN to another VLAN.
- Port security enables protection against unauthorized access on unused ports by unplugging a connected device.

Questions

1. Port security enables protection against unauthorized access on unused ports or by unplugging a connected device. (True | False)
2. _____ in computer networks causes delays, loss of data, or even an interruption of services.
3. Which of the following are duplex settings on Ethernet communication technology? (Choose two.)
    1. Half-duplex.
    2. Unicast.
    3. Multicast.
    4. Full-duplex.

4. A VLAN trunk is a point-to-multipoint link between two switches, or between a switch and the router that propagates the VLAN information among switches and routers. (True | False)

5. _____ offer the ability to expand the switch features by installing the relevant modules.

6. Which of the following are Application layer protocols for accessing remote switches?

   1. FTP.
   2. TFTP.
   3. Telnet.
   4. SSH.

7. Ingress represents a frame exiting switch on a specific port. (True | False)

8. Switch does _____ by forwarding the frames to only the switch ports that should receive the frames.

9. Which of the following are Ethernet frame fields? (Choose four.)

   1. Inbound frame.
   2. Source MAC address.
   3. Destination MAC address.
   4. Outbound frame.
   5. EtherType.
   6. FCS.

10. Flooding helps the switch to learn MAC addresses. (True | False)

11. _____ are manually configured by being associated to a switch port.

12. Which of the following are inter-Vlan routing options? (Choose two.)

    1. Legacy inter-VLAN routing.
    2. Router-on-a-stick.
    3. Store-and-forward switching.
    4. Cut-through switching.

13. A Data Field, also known as a *payload,* has a size from 46 to 1,500 bytes, and represents the actual data that is about to be transmitted to the receiving device. (True | False)

14. In _____, latency is measured from the first bit received to the first bit transmitted.

15. Which of the following are features that need to be considered when purchasing a switch? (Choose three.)
    1. Number of ports.
    2. Storing frames.
    3. PoE.
    4. Ingress ports.

Setting Up the Switch 4

Unlike the previous three chapters, where concepts such as introduction to computer networks, communication in computer networks, and introduction to switching were discussed, this chapter provides examples about switch configuration. With that in mind, this chapter is designed to provide you with step-by-step, hands-on instructions to configure the main features of the switch in accordance with the objectives of the CCENT certification exam. This chapter starts with the acquaintances of the boot sequence, switch's LED indicators, and how to connect the switch to PC. Next, you will be ready to run the basic switch configuration. Then, this chapter provides more advanced switch configurations, such as how to configure VLANs, VLAN trunks, legacy inter-VLAN routing, router-on-a-stick inter-VLAN routing, and remote access. In the *Configuring remote access* section, in addition to the commands needed to configure Telnet and SSH, you will be presented with the method of accessing the switch remotely from your computer. Finally, the chapter concludes with hands-on examples about switchport security configuration. You will also find a final summary and the questions for this chapter.

In this chapter, we will cover:

- How to run basic configuration
- How to configure Layer 2 protocols
- How to configure VLANs
- How to configure VLAN trunks
- How to configure legacy inter-VLAN routing
- How to configure router-on-a-stick inter-VLAN routing
- How to configure remote access
- How to configure switchport security

Basic switch configuration

In general, the operating system in electronic devices serves to provide hardware functionality. By contrast, network devices use the **Network Operating System** (**NOS**). From that, regardless of whether it is a manageable or unmanageable networking device, it definitely has a NOS. Since this book aims to prepare you for the Cisco CCENT certification exam, it naturally discusses Cisco networking devices, including switches and routers. Both devices support the Cisco **Internetwork Operating System** (**IOS**) which, rewrite, is a NOS that is used by all manageable Cisco devices. The CCENT exam objectives require that a network administrator must have knowledge and skills to configure the Cisco IOS on Cisco switches and routers. At the same time, while their configuration poses a challenge, it's also fun. With that said, this section describes how to run basic configuration on Cisco switches.

Configuration with initial settings

As you might know, an out-of-the box Cisco switch is capable of switching frames between hosts. That is merely due to an IOS on a switch, although at this stage, it is not configured. Regardless, it is a recommended best practice to run an initial configuration on a switch before deploying it in production. There are several ways to access switches for configuration purposes:

- The **console** is a special port on the switch that is used for its management. It is referred to as out-of-band access because it is a direct access to a switch CLI session that does not require preconfiguration on interfaces.
- **Telnet** provides an insecure connection for accessing remote devices. Thus, prior to accessing the switch CLI session, it requires the configuration of an interface with an IP address and enabling Telnet (see the *Configuring Telnet* section later in this chapter).
- The **Secure Shell** (**SSH**) provides an encrypted connection for accessing remote devices. Therefore, prior to accessing the switch CLI session, it requires a configuration of an interface with an IP address and enabling SSH (see the *Configuring SSH* section later in this chapter).

Boot sequence

Just like a PC, a switch is an electronic device made up of hardware and software. See *Figure 4.1* to get familiar with the switch's internal main hardware components:

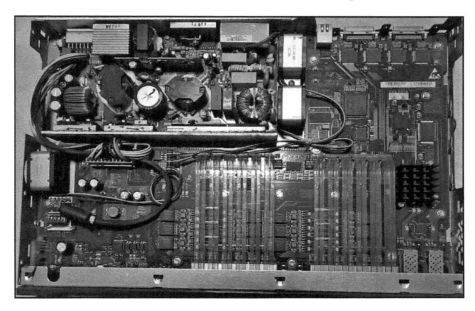

Figure 4.1. Cisco switch internal hardware

When turning on the switch, similar to PC, a switch has its own boot process too. The following steps detail the **switch boot sequence** when it is powered on:

1. First, the **Power-on self-test** (**POST**), a program stored in **Read-Only Memory** (**ROM**), loads to run a hardware check on the **Central Processing Unit** (**CPU**), **Dynamic RAM** (**DRAM**), and the Flash memory.

2. After POST successfully completes its hardware check routine, the **bootloader** is just another program stored in ROM that loads to initialize CPU and Flash memory. It then locates the IOS in Flash memory, and loads it into the DRAM (it holds running-configuration).

3. Finally, the boot loader initializes the **non-volatile RAM** (**NVRAM**) and locates and copies the startup-configuration from NVRAM into DRAM. Afterwards, the startup-configuration file initializes the switch interfaces. By this time, the setup mode prompt is available.

LED indicators

As with any other electronic device, **LED indicators** represent a way to monitor a switch's activity and its performance, as shown in *Figure 4.2*. However, given the fact that switches are available in different models and features, LED indicators may also be different and their placement might vary, too:

Figure 4.2. LED indicators on a switch

 The following article represents the meaning of LED indicators which can be found in almost all the Cisco switches:
www.ciscopress.com/articles/article.asp?p=2181836&seqNum=4.

Connecting to a switch and running initial configuration

Before running a basic switch configuration, you must connect your switch to a PC. To be able to do that, you need a **DB-9** serial port on your PC and a **rollover console cable**, which is the blue cable in *Figure 4.3*. However, these days, it is hard to find a PC with a DB-9 serial port because it is a legacy port. Therefore, to overcome such a situation, a USB-to-DB-9 adapter in combination with a rollover console cable, as shown in *Figure 4.3*, represents an alternative solution:

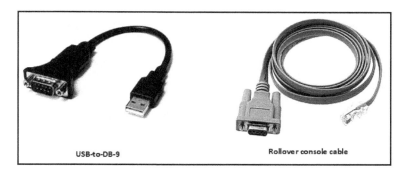

Figure 4.3. USB-to-DB-9 adapter and rollover console cable

Another way of connecting a PC with a switch is by using a DB-9-to-RJ-45 adapter in combination with a custom-built rollover cable (see *Figure 4.4*). This works only if the PC is equipped with the DB-9 male connector:

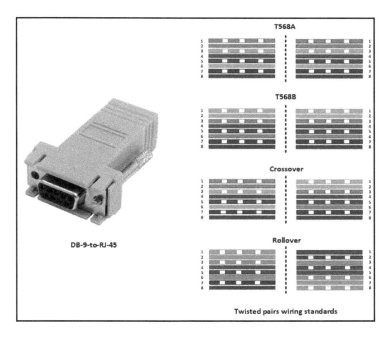

Figure 4.4. DB-9-to-RJ-45 adapter and a custom built roll over cable will enable connecting PC to a switch

After all the cables are connected and both the PC and the switch are turned on, a Terminal emulator program like Putty is required to establish a connection, as in *Figure 4.5*:

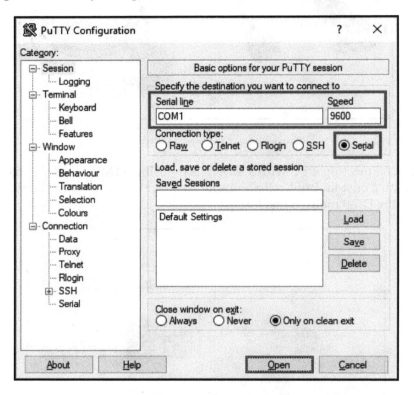

Figure 4.5. Establishing the connection with a switch using Putty

Once the CLI session is established on a switch (see *Figure 4.6*), the setup prompt mode becomes available to run the initial configuration. Mainly, Cisco IOS uses the following command modes:

- **User EXEC Mode** enables access to only a limited number of basic monitoring commands (`Switch`)
- **Privileged EXEC Mode** enables access to all monitoring, configuration, and management commands (`Switch#`):

```
Switch   Ports  Model            SW Version          SW Image
------   -----  -----            ----------          ----------
*    1   26     WS-C2960-24TT    12.2                C2960-LANBASE-M

Cisco IOS Software, C2960 Software (C2960-LANBASE-M), Version 12.2(25)FX,
RELEASE SOFTWARE (fcl)
Copyright (c) 1986-2005 by Cisco Systems, Inc.
Compiled Wed 12-Oct-05 22:05 by pt_team

Press RETURN to get started!


Switch>
```

Figure 4.6. User EXEC Mode on a switch

- **Global Configuration Mode** enables you to configure a switch. The prompt looks like `Switch(config)#`. As the name implies, changes that are made to this mode affect the operation of the switch entirely. Known as **global config** mode too, it includes the following self-descriptive sub-configuration modes:
    - **Line Configuration Mode** enables users to configure management features. The prompt looks like:

      `Switch(config-line)#`

    - **Interface Configuration Mode** enables users to configure switch ports. The prompt looks like:

      `Switch(config-if)#`

The following represents the initial switch configuration. As such, it is recommended to run it every time the switch is taken out of the box, or after the initial startup-configuration has been reloaded on a switch:

- **Accessing Privileged EXEC Mode**: Enter the following command to access Privileged EXEC Mode:

  ```
  Switch# enable
  Switch#
  ```

- **Accessing Configuration Mode**: Enter the following command to access Configuration Mode:

```
Switch# configure terminal
Switch(config)#
```

- **Naming the switch:** Enter the following command to assign a name to the switch:

```
Switch(config)# hostname S1
S1(config)#
```

- **Preventing unwanted DNS lookups:** Enter the following command to prevent the switch from trying to interpret incorrect commands:

```
Switch(configure)# no ip domain-lookup
```

- **Setting up a password for Privileged EXEC Mode:** Enter the following commands to set up a password for Privileged EXEC Mode:

```
Switch(config)# enable secret class
Switch(config)# exit
Switch#
```

- **Setting up the password for Console port:** Enter the following commands to set up a password for the Console port:

```
Switch(config)# line console 0
Switch(config-line)# password cisco
Switch(config-line)# login
Switch(config-line)# exit
Switch(config)#
```

- **Setting up the password for Virtual Terminal Lines (VTY)**: Enter the following commands to set up a password for VTY:

```
Switch(config)# line vty 0 15
Switch(config-line)# password cisco
Switch(config-line)# login
Switch(config-line)# exit
Switch(config)#
```

- **Encrypting the plaintext passwords**: Enter the following commands to encrypt the plaintext passwords in running-configuration:

```
Switch(config)# service password-encryption
Switch(config)# exit
Switch#
```

- **Setting up the login MOTD banner**: Enter the following commands to set up a login **Message of the Day** (**MOTD**):

```
Switch(config)# banner motd # Message of the Day #
Switch(config)# exit
Switch#
```

- **Saving the running-configuration**: Enter the following command to save the running-configuration to the startup-configuration on NVRAM:

```
Switch# copy running-config startup-config
Destination filename [startup-config]?
Building configuration... [OK]
Switch#
```

- **Showing the running-configuration**: Enter the following command to show the running configuration:

```
Switch# show running-config
```

- **Showing switch useful information**: Enter the following command to show the IOS version and other useful information of the switch:

```
Switch# show version
```

- **Showing the status of interfaces**: Enter the following command to show the status of the connected interfaces:

```
Switch# show ip interface brief
```

Configuring basic management access

As the name implies, the **Switch Virtual Interface** (**SVI**) is a virtual interface that enables remote management access to the switch. For the SVI to be operable in LANs, the switch needs to be configured with an IP address and subnet mask, whereas for remote LANs, MANs and WANs, the switch also needs to be configured with a default gateway. In its nature, SVI is equivalent to VLANs knowing that the concept of VLAN is based on logical connections rather than physical connections.

That said, remember that it is the VLAN 1 default configuration that is used for switch remote management access. In that regard, because by default all ports are assigned to VLAN 1, it is a security recommendation to use a VLAN that is not in use by users and peripherals devices for remote management access other than VLAN 1:

- **Configuring the VLAN 1**: Enter the following commands to configure `vlan 1`:

```
Switch(config)# interface vlan 1
Switch(config-if)# ip address 192.168.1.10 255.255.255.0
Switch(config-if)# no shutdown
Switch(config-if)# exit
Switch(config)#
```

- **Creating VLAN 99 for management**: Enter the following commands to create `vlan 99` for management purposes based on security recommendations:

```
Switch(config)# vlan 99
Switch(config-vlan)# exit
Switch(config)# interface vlan99
Switch(config-if)# ip address 192.168.1.15 255.255.255.0
Switch(config-if)# no shutdown
Switch(config-if)# exit
Switch(config)# interface range f0/1 - 24, g0/1 - 2
Switch(config-if-range)# switchport access vlan 99
Switch(config-if-range)# exit
Switch(config)#
```

- **Configuring the default gateway**: Enter the following command to configure the default gateway on a switch:

```
Switch# configure terminal
Switch(config)# ip default-gateway ip-address
Switch(config)# exit
```

The interface range in the preceding example refers to the Cisco Catalyst 2960 switch.

Configuring ports

There is a common standard among net admins, in regard to a switch that relates to the fact that usually just the network cables are connected to the switch and then, the device interface and the switch, negotiate parameters, such as full duplex and speed on ports. However, there are situations when configuration of the switch ports is required. Thus, the following sections will provide the commands that are required to configure duplex, speed, and Auto MDI-X parameters:

- **Configuring duplex communication**: Enter the following commands to configure duplex communication:

```
Switch(config)# interface <interface-ID>
Switch(config-if)# duplex full
Switch(config-if)# exit
Switch(config)#
```

- **Configuring port speed**: Enter the following commands to configure the port speed for communication:

```
Switch(config)# interface   <interface-ID>
Switch(config-if)# duplex full
Switch(config-if)# speed 100
Switch(config-if)# exit
Switch(config)#
```

- **Configuring Auto-MDIX**: Enter the following commands to configure the **Automatic Medium-Dependent Interface Crossover (Auto-MDIX)**:

```
Switch(config)# interface <interface-ID>
Switch(config-if)# duplex auto
Switch(config-if)# speed auto
Switch(config-if)# mdix auto
Switch(config-if)# exit
Switch(config)#
```

- **Verifying port configuration**: Enter the following command to show the interface's status and configuration:

```
Switch# show interfaces   <interface-ID>
```

Putty is a terminal emulation program that allows you to access the Terminal output of the switch and configure the switch. You can download Putty from: `https://www.chiark.greenend.org.uk/~sgtatham/putty/latest.html`.

Configuring VLANs

This section describes how to **configure VLANs** on Cisco switches:

- **Creating a VLAN**: Enter the following commands to create a VLAN:

  ```
  Switch(config)# vlan    <vlan-ID>
  Switch(config-vlan)# exit
  Switch(config)#
  ```

- **Naming the VLAN**: Enter the following commands to name the VLAN:

  ```
  Switch(config)# vlan   <vlan-ID>
  Switch(config-vlan)# name    <vlan name>
  Switch(config-vlan)# exit
  Switch(config)#
  ```

- **Assigning port to VLAN**: Enter the following commands to assign the VLAN to the correct switch interface:

  ```
  Switch(config)# interface    <interface-ID>
  Switch(config-if)# switchport mode access
  Switch(config-if)# switchport access vlan   <vlan-ID>
  Switch(config-if)# exit
  Switch(config)#
  ```

- **Assigning multiple ports to VLAN**: Enter the following commands to assign a VLAN to multiple interfaces:

  ```
  Switch(config)# interface range <interface range-IDs>
  Switch(config-if-range)# switchport mode access
  Switch(config-if-range)# switchport access vlan   <vlan-ID>
  Switch(config-if-range)# exit
  Switch(config)#
  ```

- **Assigning VLAN 99 for switch management**: Enter the following commands to set an IP address for vlan 99 that will be used for management purposes:

  ```
  Switch(config)# interface vlan 1
  Switch(config-if)# no ip address
  Switch(config-if)# interface vlan 99
  Switch(config-if)# ip address 192.168.1.99 255.255.255.0
  Switch(config-if)# exit
  Switch(config)#
  ```

- **Removing VLAN from an interface**: Enter the following commands to remove a VLAN assignment from an interface:

```
Switch(config)# interface <interface-ID>
Switch(config-if)# no switchport access vlan
Switch(config-if)# exit
Switch(config)#
```

- **Removing the VLAN ID from the VLAN database**: Enter the following commands to remove the VLAN ID from the VLAN database:

```
Switch(config)# no vlan <vlan-ID>
Switch(config)# exit
Switch#
```

- **Changing VLAN port membership**: Enter the following commands to change the VLAN port membership:

```
Switch(config)# interface <interface-ID>
Switch(config-if)# no switchport access vlan
Switch(config-if)# exit
Switch(config)# interface <interface-ID>
Switch(config-if)# switchport mode access
Switch(config-if)# switchport access vlan <vlan-ID>
Switch(config-if)# exit
Switch(config)#
```

- **Creating voice VLANs**: Enter the following commands to create a voice VLANs:

```
Switch(config)# vlan    <vlan-ID>
Switch(config-vlan)# name    <vlan name>
Switch(config)# exit
Switch(config)# interface    <interface-ID>
Switch(config-if)# switchport mode access
Switch(config-if)# mls QoS trust CoS
Switch(config-if)# switchport voice vlan  <vlan-ID>
Switch(config-if)# exit
Switch(config)#
```

- **Showing the VLAN information**: Enter the following command to view the list of VLANs:

```
Switch# show vlan
```

- **Showing VLANs assigned to the correct interfaces**: Enter the following command to show that the VLANs are assigned to the correct interfaces:

```
Switch# show vlan brief
```

Configuring VLAN trunks

This section describes how to **configure VLAN trunks** on Cisco switches:

- **Configuring IEEE 802.1Q trunk link**: Enter the following commands to configure a trunk link:

```
Switch(config)# interface   <interface-ID>
Switch(config-if)# switchport mode trunk
Switch(config-if)# exit
Switch(config)#
```

- **Configuring a native VLAN as an IEEE 802.1Q trunk link**: Enter the following commands to configure a native VLAN for untagged 802.1Q frames:

```
Switch(config)# interface   <interface-ID>
Switch(config-if)# switchport trunk native vlan   <vlan-ID>
Switch(config-if)# exit
Switch(config)#
```

- **Configuring VLANs to be allowed on the trunk link**: Enter the following commands to configure the list of VLANs to be allowed on the trunk link:

```
Switch(config)# interface   <interface-ID>
Switch(config-if)# switchport trunk allowed vlan   <vlan list>
Switch(config-if)# exit
Switch(config)#
```

- **Configuring the appropriate trunk mode**: Enter the following commands to set the trunk in the appropriate trunk mode:

```
Switch(config)# interface   <interface-ID>
Switch(config-if)# switchport trunk encapsulation [dot1q | isl]
Switch(config-if)# exit
Switch(config)#
```

- **Configuring the trunk to allow all VLANs**: Enter the following commands to set the trunk to allow all VLANs:

```
Switch(config)# interface    <interface-ID>
Switch(config-if)# no switchport trunk allowed vlan
Switch(config-if)# exit
Switch(config)#
```

- **Showing trunked interfaces**: You can enter the following command to show the trunked interfaces:

```
Switch# show interfaces trunk
```

Configuring legacy inter-VLAN routing

This section describes how to configure legacy inter-VLAN routing on a Cisco switch.

Scenario – Router with multiple interfaces

Referring to the definition about **Legacy inter-VLAN routing** discussed in the *Inter-VLAN operation* section of Chapter 3, *Introduction to Switching*, as well as *Figure 4.7*, it is apparent that in the inter-VLAN routing option, the router has multiple interfaces where each interface connects to a certain VLAN. Thus, after assigning IP addresses both on the PCs and router interfaces where each one belongs to a certain subnet, the router can then perform the inter-VLAN routing:

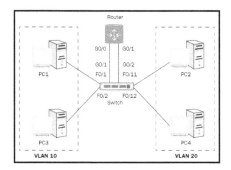

Figure 4.7. Legacy inter-VLAN routing

The following represents the configurations on a switch, and displaying VLAN information on a switch. To configure the router and to display the routing table on a router, see the *Inter-VLAN configuration* section in `Chapter 6`, *Setting up the Router*:

- **Switch configuration**: Enter the following commands to configure legacy inter-VLAN routing on a switch:

```
Switch(config)# vlan 10
Switch(config-vlan)# exit
Switch(config)# vlan 20
Switch(config-vlan)# exit
Switch(config)# interface F0/1
Switch(config-if)# switchport mode access
Switch(config-if)# switchport access vlan 10
Switch(config-if)# exit
Switch(config)# interface F0/2
Switch(config-if)# switchport mode access
Switch(config-if)# switchport access vlan 10
Switch(config-if)# exit
Switch(config)# interface F0/11
Switch(config-if)# switchport mode access
Switch(config-if)# switchport access vlan 20
Switch(config-if)# exit
Switch(config)# interface F0/12
Switch(config-if)# switchport mode access
Switch(config-if)# switchport access vlan 20
Switch(config-if)# end
Switch# copy running-config startup-config
```

Verifying VLAN information on a switch

To verify the VLAN information you can use the following command:

- **Showing VLAN information**: Enter the following command to show the VLAN information on a switch:

```
Switch# show vlan brief
```

Configuring router-on-a-stick inter-VLAN routing

This section describes how to configure **router-on-a-stick inter-VLAN routing** on a Cisco switch.

Scenario – Router with a single interface

Unlike legacy inter-VLAN routing, the router-on-a-stick option (see *Figure 4.8*) of the inter-VLAN routing concept uses a different approach to enable communication among VLANs. In this scenario, the router establishes a trunk link with the switch where the VLANs are configured. Then, on the router side, the subinterfaces are configured with the appropriate IP addresses in a way that each subinterface represents a separate subnet, maps a specific VLAN, and tags the frame for the VLANs. In addition, assigning the IP addresses in a PC's interface as per the corresponding subnets of the subinterfaces, the router can then perform communication among VLANs by traversing the trunk link:

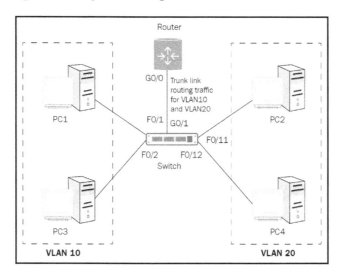

Figure 4.8. Router-in-a-stick inter-VLAN routing

The following represents the configurations on a switch, and displaying VLAN information on a switch. To configure the router and to display the routing table on a router, see the *Router-on-a-stick inter-VLAN configuration*, section in Chapter 6, *Setting up the Router*:

- **Switch configuration**: Enter the following commands to configure the router-on-a-stick inter-VLAN routing on a switch:

```
Switch(config)# vlan 10
Switch(config-vlan)# exit
Switch(config)# vlan 20
Switch(config-vlan)# exit
Switch(config)# interface F0/1
Switch(config-if)# switchport mode access
Switch(config-if)# switchport access vlan 10
Switch(config-if)# exit
Switch(config)# interface F0/2
Switch(config-if)# switchport mode access
Switch(config-if)# switchport access vlan 10
Switch(config-if)# exit
Switch(config)# interface F0/11
Switch(config-if)# switchport mode access
Switch(config-if)# switchport access vlan 20
Switch(config-if)# exit
Switch(config)# interface F0/12
Switch(config-if)# switchport mode access
Switch(config-if)# switchport access vlan 20
Switch(config-if)# end
Switch(config)# interface G0/1
Switch(config-if)# switchport mode trunk
Switch(config-if)# end
Switch# copy running-config startup-config
```

Verifying VLAN information on a switch

To verify the VLAN information you can use the following command.

- **Showing VLAN information**: Enter the following command to show the VLAN information on a switch:

```
Switch# show vlan brief
```

Configuring remote access

This section describes how to configure remote access on Cisco switches.

Configuring Telnet

Enter the following commands to configure *Telnet*:

```
Switch# enable
Switch# configure terminal
Switch(config)# interface vlan 1
Switch(config-if)# ip address 192.168.1.10 255.255.255.0
Switch(config-if)# no shutdown
Switch(config-if)# exit
Switch(config)# line vty 0 15
Switch(config-line)# transport input telnet
Switch(config-line)# password cisco
Switch(config-line)# login
Switch(config-line)# exit
Switch(config)# copy running-config startup-config
```

Open the Command Prompt on your computer and try *telneting* into a remote switch, as shown in *Figure 4.9*. You need to use the `telnet` command accompanied by the IP address of a remote switch:

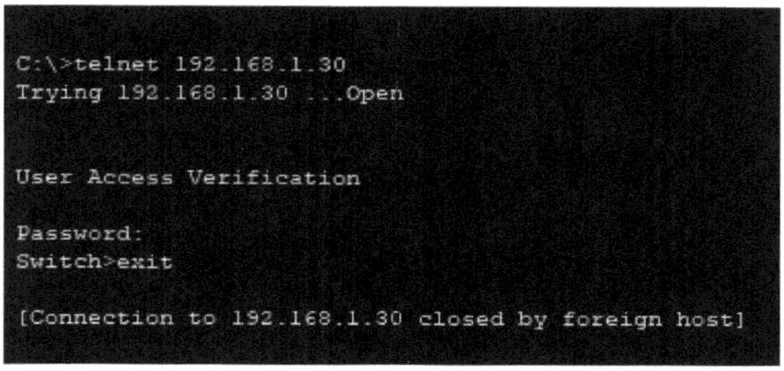

Figure 4.9. Telneting into a switch

Configuring SSH

Enter the following commands to configure SSH:

```
Switch# enable
Switch# configure terminal
Switch(config)# hostname Test
Switch(config)# ip domain-name Test.local
Switch(config)# crypto key generate rsa
How many bits in the modulus [512]: 1024
Switch(config)# interface vlan 1
Switch(config-if)# ip address 192.168.1.20 255.255.255.0
Switch(config-if)# no shutdown
Switch(config-if)# exit
Switch(config)# line vty 0 15
Switch(config-line)# transport input ssh
Switch(config-line)# exit
Switch(config)# username user password cisco
Switch(config)# line vty 0 15
Switch(config-line)# login local
Switch(config-line)# exit
Switch(config)# copy running-config startup-config
```

Open the Command Prompt on your computer and try accessing a remote switch over *SSH*, as shown in *Figure 4.10*. You need to use the `ssh` command followed by a switch, `-l`, the username, and the IP address of a remote switch:

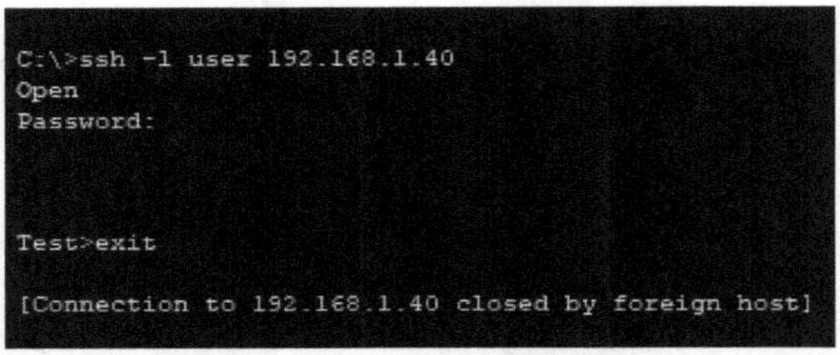

```
C:\>ssh -l user 192.168.1.40
Open
Password:



Test>exit

[Connection to 192.168.1.40 closed by foreign host]
```

Figure 4.10. Remote access to switch over SSH

Other than accessing remote devices through SSH over Command Prompt, you can use a Terminal emulator program like *Tera Term* to log in to a remote switch (see *Figure 4.11*):

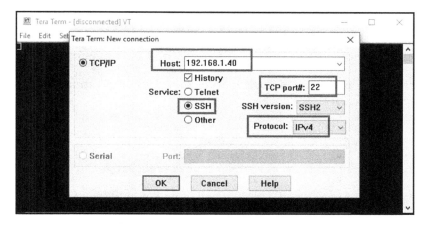

Figure 4.11. Accessing the remote switch with SSH over Tera Term

 Like Putty, Tera Term is a Terminal emulation program that allows you to access the Terminal output of the switch and configure the switch. You can download Tera Term from: `http://logmett.com/tera-term-the-latest-version`.

Use the `show` command, as in the following two formats, to verify the SSH connection on a switch, and to display the version and configuration data for the SSH:

- **Showing SSH status**: Enter the following command to show the status of the SSH connections:

  ```
  Switch# show ssh
  ```

- **Showing version and configuration data for SSH**: Enter the following command to show the version and configuration data for SSH:

  ```
  Switch# show ip ssh
  ```

Configuring switchport security

This section describes how to configure port security on Cisco switches:

- **Configuring basic port security**: Enter the following commands to configure basic port security:

```
Switch(config)# interface    <interface-ID>
Switch(config-if)# no shutdown
Switch(config-if)# switchport mode access
Switch(config-if)# switchport port-security
Switch(config-if)# exit
Switch(config)#
```

- **Configuring a static entry for the MAC address of device**: Enter the following commands to configure a static entry for the MAC address of a device:

```
Switch(config)# interface    <interface-ID>
Switch(config-if)# no shutdown
Switch(config-if)# switchport mode access
Switch(config-if)# switchport port-security mac-address  <mac
address-ID>
Switch(config-if)# exit
Switch(config)#
```

- **Securing single unused port**: Enter the following commands to disable a specific unused port:

```
Switch(config)# interface    <interface-ID>
Switch(config-if)# shutdown
Switch(config-if)# exit
Switch(config)#
```

- **Securing multiple unused ports**: Enter the following commands to disable multiple unused ports:

```
Switch(config)# interface range  <interface range-ID>
Switch(config-if-range)# shutdown
Switch(config-if-range)# exit
Switch(config)#
```

- **Showing port security**: Enter the following command to show the port security settings:

  ```
  Switch# show port-security
  ```

- **Showing port security on interface**: Enter the following command to show the port-security for a specific interface:

```
Switch# show port-security interface    <interface-ID>
```

Summary

We can summarize this chapter with the following points:

- Network devices use the NOS.
- The **Internetwork Operating System (IOS)** is a NOS which is used by the majority of Cisco networking devices.
- The console is a special port on the switch that is used for its management.
- Telnet provides an insecure connection for accessing remote devices.
- SSH provides an encrypted connection for accessing remote devices.
- POST runs a hardware check on the CPU, DRAM, and the portion of the flash drive.
- The boot loader initializes the CPU and flash file system, and then loads an IOS image into DRAM.
- IOS initializes a startup-configuration that is stored in NVRAM, and interfaces from the configuration file.

- LED indicators help monitor switch activity and its performance.
- The DB-9 serial port on the PC and rollover console cable are needed to physically connect the PC with the switch.
- To establish a connection between the PC and the switch, Terminal emulator programs like Putty and Tera Term are required.
- User EXEC Mode enables access to only a limited number of basic monitoring commands `Switch>`.
- Privileged EXEC Mode enables access to all monitoring, configuration, and management commands `Switch#`.
- Line Configuration Mode enable users to configure management features. The prompt looks like `Switch(config-line)#`
- Interface Configuration Mode enable user to configure switch ports. The prompt looks like `Switch(config-if)#`

Questions

1. IOS initializes a startup-configuration which is stored in NVRAM, and interfaces from the configuration file. (True | False)
2. To establish a connection between the PC and the switch, _____ programs like Putty and Tera Term are required.
3. Which of the following commands provides access to Privileged EXEC Mode? (Choose two)
    1. `Switch> enable`
    2. `Switch> en`
    3. `Switch> enable EXEC`
    4. `Switch> en EXEC`
4. LED indicators help monitor switch activity and its performance. (True | False)
5. _____ enables users to configure management features. The prompt looks like Switch(config-line)#.
6. Which of the following commands enables port security?
    1. `Switch(config-if)# switchport mode trunk`
    2. `Switch(config-if)# switchport port-security`
    3. `Switch(config-if)# switchport trunk encapsulation dot1q`
    4. `Switch(config-if)# switchport mode access`

7. Interface Configuration Mode prevents users from configuring switch ports. (True | False)

8. _____ initializes CPU and the flash file system, and then loads an IOS image into DRAM.

9. Which of the following commands provides access to Configuration Mode? (Choose two)

    1. `Switch# configure global`

    2. `Switch# config g`

    3. `Switch# configure terminal`

    4. `Switch# config t`

10. User EXEC Mode enables access to only a limited number of basic monitoring commands (`Switch>`). (True | False)

11. The `Switch(config)#`_____ command is used to create a VLAN.

12. Which of the following commands is used to configure Auto-MDIX?

    1. `Switch(config-if)# mdix enable`

    2. `Switch(config-if)# mdix full`

    3. `Switch(config-if)# mdix dynamic`

    4. `Switch(config-if)# mdix auto`

13. The DB-9 serial port on the PC and rollover console cable are needed to physically connect the PC with the switch. (True | False)

14. _____ Power-on self-test (POST), runs a hardware check on the Central Processing Unit (CPU), Dynamic RAM (DRAM), and the portion of the flash drive.

15. Which of the following commands are used to save running-configuration? (Choose two)

    1. `Switch# copy running-config startup-config`

    2. `Switch# copy run start`

    3. `Switch# copy start run`

    4. `Switch# copy startup-config running-config`

Introduction to Routing 5

So far, you have learned a lot about switches and switching packet technology. It is time for you to learn about routers and packet forwarding technology. This chapter is designed to provide you with an introduction to routing. It beings with a discussion of routing concepts. Then, it continues with explanations of switching packets, sending packets, and path determinations. We then ask the big question: what is a router? After answering the question, it is time to turn the router on. Obviously, POST and bootloader will occupy the stage. No matter what, understanding **Routing Tables** will be the most interesting part of the chapter. The chapter ends with a section on understanding routing types, in which static routing is compared to its counterpart, dynamic routing. The same section provides a brief explanation of dynamic routing protocols, like RIP, OSPF, EIGRP, and others. Last but not least, the chapter provides a summary and questions.

In this chapter, we will cover:

- Understanding routing concepts
- Understanding routing operations
- Understanding what a router is
- Turning a router on
- Understanding routing tables
- Understanding routing types

Routing concepts

Years ago, in one of the videos of the well-known author Kevin Wallace, I heard an interesting statement about routing, that states: *"Educates routers about the best path to reach different networks."* Pay attention to the word *educates*, because you will need it later on in this chapter (and the chapters to follow), now that we are beginning our discussion on routing and routers.

So far, we have discussed both switching and switches. We learned that **switching** (in computer networks) is the change of direction of frames, and we also learned that switches are devices that work on the method of packet switching. That will make it easier for us to discuss routing and routers, because we have a comparative criterion. Whatever we discuss about routing and routers, it will be compared to switching and switches. Routing and routers are communication technologies and devices in a network, respectively, as are switching and switches.

If switches forward frames, routers forward packets, by selecting the path. Switches use **MAC address tables** to forward frames, whereas routers use **routing tables** to forward packets. In addition to that, switches operate on OSI Layer 2, while routers operate on OSI Layer 3. Also, switches have multiple ports, while routers have only a few ports. Remember, Layer 1 devices such as NICs, hubs and bridges contribute in so called collision domains and broadcast domains. However, switches divide collision domains, and routers separate broadcast domains.. And, last but not least, switches connect computers, while routers connect networks.

Understanding host routing

To understand how host routes, we will try to find the answer in switches. Remember that the switch connects hosts, and from those connections, networks are created. Hosts within the same network communicate via switches. But, a challenge comes up when a host (or several hosts on the same network) wants to communicate with a host (or hosts) on another network. Admittedly, that is a job that a switch is not capable of accomplishing. Remember, we are not talking about extended networks via switches, but networks that are connected by routers. See the following screenshot:

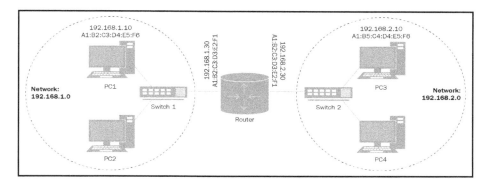

Figure 5.1. LANs interconnected by a router

Figure 5.1 presents networks 192.168.1.0 and 192.168.2.0, connected by a router. Switch 1 connects hosts in the network 192.168.1.0, while switch 2 connects hosts in the network 192.168.2.0. PC1, with the IP address 192.168.1.10, wants to send data to PC3, with the IP address 192.168.2.10. Remember, switches operate in OSI's Layer 2, and use a MAC address table to forward frames. From the figure, we can understand that switch 1 does not contain the MAC address of PC3 in its MAC address table. However, in its MAC address table, the switch does contain the physical address of the router's internal interface, onto which the 192.168.1.0 network is connected. Thus, because PC3 is on a remote network, switch 1 forwards the frame to the router.

Host forwarding decisions

Since the topic of discussion is how the host routes, let us discuss the communication between PC1 and PC3 from *Figure 5.1*—from a host perspective, rather than from a switch, as described in the previous section. As you know, computers use IP addresses to communicate over LAN, MAN, WAN, or the internet, as opposed to switches, which use the MAC address table to forward frames in the LAN. When a host wants to send data to another host, the first thing that a host does is obtain the IP address of the destination host. Remember that besides the IP address, the hostname is another logical element used for communication between computers.

That said, in our example, for the source host to obtain the IP address of the destination host, it uses an address resolution process by referencing its logical name. An example of address resolution is the **Domain Name System (DNS)**, which resolves hostnames into IP addresses. After the host obtains the IP address of the destination host, it then compares the source IP address with a destination IP address, to determine if the host at the destination is in the same, or a remote network. If the destination host is in the LAN, the source host sends the data directly via a switch, by addressing the data to the destination host's MAC address. Conversely, if the destination host is in a remote network, the data is sent to the router via a switch, by addressing the data to the router's MAC address. That router is known as the first hop router, while the data communication is referred to as indirect delivery.

From what has been said so far, the following can be noted:

- In *direct delivery*, the MAC addresses of both the source host and the destination host are used for communication, as in *Figure 5.2*:

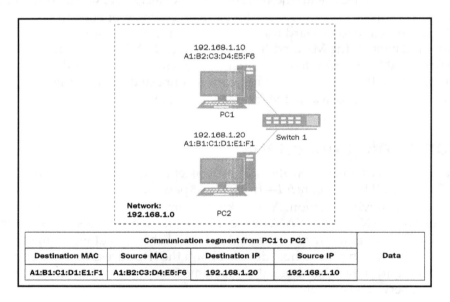

Figure 5.2. Direct delivery (PC1 to PC2)

- In *indirect delivery*, the MAC addresses are used only in the communication segment from the source host to the internal interface of the router, as in *Figure 5.3*. Thereafter, the destination host IP address and the MAC address are used for communication:

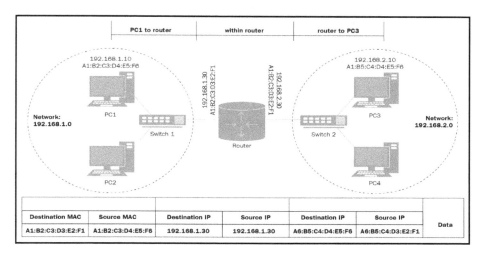

Destination MAC	Source MAC	Destination IP	Source IP	Destination IP	Source IP	Data
A1:B2:C3:D3:E2:F1	A1:B2:C3:D4:E5:F6	192.168.1.30	192.168.1.30	A6:B5:C4:D4:E5:F6	A6:B5:C4:D3:E2:F1	

Figure 5.3. Indirect delivery (PC1 to PC3)

This makes us conclude that the host can send data to:

- Its own interface, by pinging the loopback address of `127.0.0.1`
- A host on the same network, with the same network address (known as a local host)
- A host on a remote network, with a different network address (known as a remote host)

Default gateway

The beauty of technology is that almost every name is self-explanatory. Do you agree with this assessment? The same can be said for the default gateway. If we go back to direct delivery (see *Figure 5.2*), then the IP address and subnet mask are enough for the source host to communicate with each local host. But, in indirect delivery (see *Figure 5.3*), for the source host to be able to communicate with any remote host, the default gateway is required.

From there, the router connected to the local network segment is referred to as the default gateway (as in *Figure 5.4*), while routing protocols help identifying the best path to a destination host so that the data can be delivered. Suffice it to say, the default gateway is a device that connects the local network to remote networks, or to the internet. Expressed through an analogy, the default gateway is the *gate* through which LAN traffic is forwarded to remote networks, and vice versa:

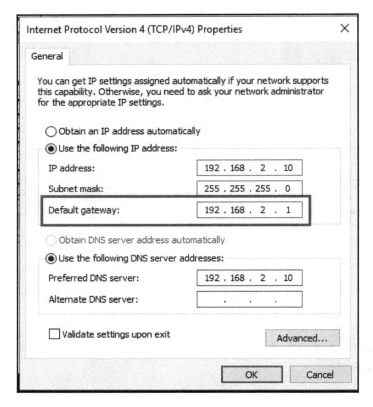

Figure 5.4. Default gateway in Windows-based computer

The default gateway IP address is configured on hosts in two ways:

- Manually, entered by a network administrator or a user with administrative privileges on a local computer
- Dynamically, provided by the **Dynamic Host Configuration Protocol** (**DHCP**) server on a network

Usually, the default gateway on your computer's network interface, acts the IP address of the router's internal interface, that connects the LAN with the outside world (in other words, remote networks or the internet). You can learn more about the default gateway at `https://www.lifewire.com/what-is-a-default-gateway-817771`.

Host routing tables

Interestingly, Windows-based computers have something that is called a routing table, too. Open the Command Prompt and run the `route print` command; as a result, you will get something similar to *Figure 5.5*:

```
C:\Users\Administrator>route print
===========================================================================
Interface List
  5...00 15 5d 3c c9 01 ......Microsoft Hyper-V Network Adapter #3
  1...........................Software Loopback Interface 1
 15...00 00 00 00 00 00 00 e0 Microsoft ISATAP Adapter #3
===========================================================================

IPv4 Route Table
===========================================================================
Active Routes:
Network Destination        Netmask          Gateway       Interface  Metric
          0.0.0.0          0.0.0.0      192.168.2.1    192.168.2.10    271
        127.0.0.0        255.0.0.0         On-link        127.0.0.1    331
        127.0.0.1  255.255.255.255         On-link        127.0.0.1    331
  127.255.255.255  255.255.255.255         On-link        127.0.0.1    331
      192.168.2.0    255.255.255.0         On-link    192.168.2.10    271
     192.168.2.10  255.255.255.255         On-link    192.168.2.10    271
    192.168.2.255  255.255.255.255         On-link    192.168.2.10    271
        224.0.0.0        240.0.0.0         On-link        127.0.0.1    331
        224.0.0.0        240.0.0.0         On-link    192.168.2.10    271
  255.255.255.255  255.255.255.255         On-link        127.0.0.1    331
  255.255.255.255  255.255.255.255         On-link    192.168.2.10    271
===========================================================================
Persistent Routes:
  Network Address          Netmask  Gateway Address  Metric
          0.0.0.0          0.0.0.0      192.168.2.1  Default
          0.0.0.0          0.0.0.0      192.168.1.1  Default
          0.0.0.0          0.0.0.0      172.16.1.1  Default
===========================================================================

IPv6 Route Table
===========================================================================
Active Routes:
 If Metric Network Destination      Gateway
  1    331 ::1/128                  On-link
  5    271 fe80::/64                On-link
  5    271 fe80::fc3a:98f3:88f2:f63f/128
                                    On-link
  1    331 ff00::/8                 On-link
  5    271 ff00::/8                 On-link
===========================================================================
Persistent Routes:
  None

C:\Users\Administrator>_
```

Figure 5.5. Host routing table

As explained in section *Default gateway*, the default gateway is required when hosts need to communicate with remote hosts on remote networks. If you observe *Figure 5.5*, you will notice that this host, the network IP address 0.0.0.0, and the subnet mask 0.0.0.0, uses the default gateway 192.168.2.1. The host routing table contains a default route (that is, 0.0.0.0) that represents the route that is traveled by the data that is destined to be sent on remote networks when no specific route is configured.

Routing operations

As you know, the router is a networking device that connects the networks, while routing is the algorithm that enables the router to select the best path to forward packets to the remote network. The fact that the router connects the networks means that there are not as many ports as there are in switches. Also, the process of determining the best path is based on the routing table, which represents a routing database in which the routes to particular network destinations are stored. So, going back to the word *educates* (mentioned right at the beginning of this chapter), it is the *routing mechanism* that *educates* the router to select the best route for packet delivery to a destination. Thus, the combination of both makes it possible for the data to be delivered efficiently and in a timely manner. This section explains routing operations that may seem simple, which in fact very complex.

Switching packets

Figure 5.1 illustrates the communication of hosts from two different networks. In the *host forwarding decision* section, there is a statement that states that *"Because PC3 is on a remote network, switch 1 forwards the frame to the router."* If switches operate in Layer 2 and use a MAC address table to forward frames, and routers operate in OSI Layer 3 and use a routing table to forward packets, then how do these two network devices communicate with one another?

Let us answer this question with the help of *Figure 5.6*. Obviously, PC1 and PC2 want to exchange data. Both PCs are on different networks, connected to respective routers via respective switches and a WAN link that connects the routers. Now, looking at the communication from the data point of view, it is obvious that the data, in its route from PC1 to PC2, passes through different representations, such as data, segment, packet, frame, and bit, to return to its original format on PC2. This process of data transformation is known as the **encapsulation** from application to NIC, and de-encapsulation from NIC to application. We discussed that in Chapter 3, *Introduction to Switching*. Another thing; because we are discussing routers and routing in this chapter, we will refer to the data as a packet from now on:

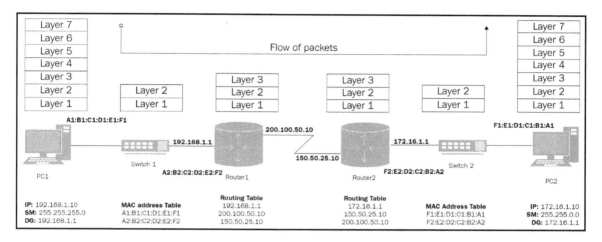

Figure 5.6. Encapsulation and de-encapsulation of packets

Now, we will go back to the question, how do the switch and router communicate? As you know, the primary function of a switch is to forward frames. It does so by switching frames from an ingress port to an egress port, based on information from the MAC address table. On the other hand, the primary function of the router is to forward packets. It does so by moving packets from the local network to a remote network, based on the information from the routing table. Now, pay attention to the term *moving packets*. If we look at it from the perspective of a context, then it is equivalent to switching packets. Do you get the point now? Like switches, routers switch packets from the incoming port to the outgoing port, as per routing information. However, the process of switching packets is not similar to that of switching frames. The following section explains router switching functions.

Router switching functions

If you refer to *Figure 3.20*, the OSI reference model in the section *Ethernet frame encapsulation* in `Chapter 3, Introduction to Switching`, I think you will find it easier to understand the switching function on a router. From the same figure, we can note that when the data moves to any of the OSI lower layers, a *header* and a *trailer* are added. Similarly, from the same figure, it is obvious that when the data moves towards OSI upper layers, then the respective header and trailer are removed.

Now, going back to *Figure 5.6*, when **Router 1** accepts the frame from **Switch 1,** it de-encapsulates the frame by removing the OSI Layer 2 header and trailer, in order to expose the OSI Layer 3 header and trailer. Router 1 will examine the destination IP address, and, based on its routing table, it will switch the packet to **Router 2**. Similarly, Router 2 will examine the destination IP address, and, based on its routing table, it will determine the best path to the destination. For that reason, Router 2 encapsulates the OSI Layer 3 packet into the OSI Layer 2 frame, so that is forwarded to **Switch 2**. Finally, the switch examines the destination MAC address on a frame, and, after matching it with exact information on its MAC address table, forwards the frame to PC2.

Sending packets

In *Figure 5.7*, **PC1** sends a packet to **PC2**. In that process, the very first thing that PC1 does is determining the network that its IP address belongs to, and then determining the network that the IP address of PC2 belongs to. Remember that if the IP address of PC2 (otherwise known as the *destination IP address*) belongs to the same network as PC1, then PC1 does not use the default gateway for sending the packet. Instead, it delivers the packet directly to PC2 via a switch, using MAC addresses. Now, going back to determining its own network, the question is: How PC1 do it? PC1 simply determines its own network by using the AND operator (for more on the AND operator, see *Appendix D, Boolean Algebra*), as follows:

```
PC1 IP address is 192.168.1.10 that in binary(*) is
11000000.10101000.00000001.00001010
PC1 Subnet mask is 255.255.255.0 that in binary is
11111111.11111111.11111111.00000000
Applying AND operator:
11000000.10101000.00000001.00001010
AND
11111111.11111111.11111111.00000000
_____
11000000.10101000.00000001.00000000
PC1 belongs to 11000000.10101000.00000001.00000000 network that in decimal
is 192.168.1.0
```

(*) for more on decimal to binary conversion see *Appendix C, Numbering systems and conversions.*

Next, PC1 will try to determine the PC2 network, in the same format it determined with the use of the AND operator. In this case, PC1 uses the AND operator between the IP address of PC2 and its own subnet mask. However, what if PC1 does not know the IP address of PC2? Suppose that you want to call your friend over the telephone, but you do not know his number. The first thing that you will do is search the number in your phone book. If you do not find it there, you can address the search to the information service of your phone provider. Similarly, PC1 will use address resolution to learn the IP address of PC2, by referencing the logical name of PC2. DNS is an example of address resolution technology, and that is covered in the section *Host forwarding decisions*. So, after PC1 learns the IP address of PC2, it will then try to determine the network in which PC2 belongs. From what is presented in the figure, it is clear that PC1 will determine that PC2 is on a different network.

Furthermore, at this stage, PC1 knows the IP address of PC2, but it does not know its MAC address. This makes PC1 to contact the default gateway, which, in our example, is Router 1. The communication with Router 1 is similar to how PC1 managed to identify the IP address of PC2. Hence, PC1 searches for the Router 1 MAC address in its host ARP table. If it is not there, then PC1 sends an ARP request to Router 1. Shortly after, Router 1 responds back with an ARP reply. Now that PC1 has learned the router's internal interface MAC address (that is, the default gateway MAC address), it encapsulates the packet into an Ethernet frame, with Router 1 MAC address as the *destination MAC address*. The frame is sent to the default gateway via the switch. Remember that the packet sent by PC1 includes the IP address of PC2 as the *destination IP address*:

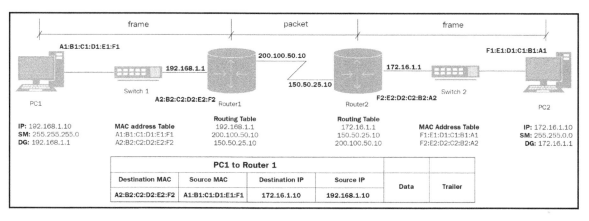

Figure 5.7. Sending a packet from PC1 to Router 1

Packet routing

So, once the frame arrives at Router 1, the Ethernet frame is copied in Router's 1 buffer, and then it is examined by matching the destination MAC address (that is `A2: B2: C2: D2: E2: F2`) with Router 1's MAC address, on the interface where the frame is received. Then, Router 1 examines the `EtherType` field, and learns from the code `0x0800` that there is an IPv4 header in the frame's payload field. In the section *Ethernet frame fields*, in `Chapter 3`, *Introduction to Switching,* we have learned that an *EtherType* field indicates the length and the protocol that is encapsulated in the payload field. Thus, as a result, de-encapsulation is performed, and the destination IP address is matched with any of the Router 1 interfaces. Since the IP address in the destination does not match any of the IP addresses in Router 1 interfaces, Router 1 checks its routing table to forward the packet further. The connection between Router 1 and Router 2, as shown in *Figure 5.8,* happens to be a WAN **Point-to-Point (PPP)** serial link, which means that serial interfaces do not have MAC addresses. That said, the outgoing serial interface in Router 1 encapsulates the frame to the appropriate format, and forwards the same as the broadcast *Address* (`0x8F`) to Router 2, so the packet can reach PC2. In addition, the *control field* (`0x00`) is a 2-byte field that identifies the protocol used in the payload field of PPP encapsulation:

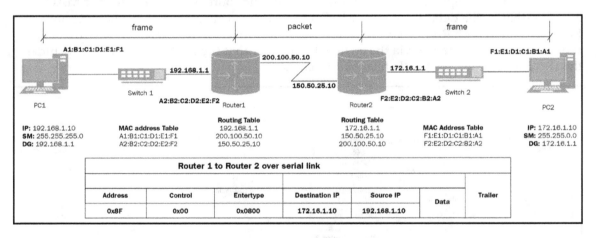

Figure 5.8. Sending a packet from Router 1 to Router 2

Forward to next-hop

If we refer to *Figures 5.7* and *5.8,* Router's 1 and Router 2 are one after the other in the packet's routing path from PC1 to PC2; they are considered to be next-hop forwarding. Although the IP address in the outgoing serial interface in Router 1 belongs to the network 200.100.50.0, and the IP address in the incoming serial interface in Router 2 belongs to the network 150.50.25.0 , they still maintain a direct connection, and, as such, Router 1 and Router 2 are considered to be **directly connected**. This is because the topology provided does not contain any other routers, besides Router 1 and Router 2. Therefore, their routing tables maintain the routing information from Router 1 to Router 2 (and vice versa, from Router 2 to Router 1). The connection between Router 1 and Router 2 is representing the lowest metric in a given topology. In addition, the connection between Router 1 and Router 2 is considered to be Router 1's packet routing path, when it travels from PC1 to PC2.

Reaching the destination

Once the frame arrives at Router 2, the PPP frame is copied into the Router 2 buffer, and then the destination IP address is examined by matching it with the information in the Router's 2 routing table. Since PC2 resides in a network that is directly connected to Router 2, and that information is available in Router 2's routing table, Router 2 can send the packet directly to PC2. However, because the network 172.16.1.0 is an Ethernet network, Router 2 must resolve the destination IP address of PC2 into its MAC address. For that reason, Router's 2 consults its ARP table, in order to match the MAC address for the destination IP address of PC2. If there is no match in Router 2's ARP table, then Router 2 sends an ARP request to PC2. PC2 replies with an ARP reply that contains the PC2 MAC address. Next, Router 2 receives the ARP reply and updates its ARP table with the MAC address information (that is, F1:E1:D1:C1:B1:A1) for the IP address 172.16.1.10. Now that Router 2 has all of the information needed to forward a packet to PC2, it encapsulates the packet into an Ethernet frame and sends it out over its outgoing Ethernet interface (that is, 172.16.1.1) to Switch 2 (as in *Figure 5.9*). As soon as an Ethernet frame arrives at Switch 2, the destination MAC address is matched with the information in the Switch 2 MAC address table, and, if it finds it there, it is forwarded to PC2. Finally, PC2 receives the Ethernet frame that copies it into the buffer, and then examines the destination MAC address with its NIC's MAC address. Once matching is done, the EtherType field indicates that there is an IPv4 header in the Data (that is, payload) Field.

Thus, the Ethernet frame is de-encapsulated, and, from now on, it is forwarded to the upper layers of the OSI reference model by PC2's OS:

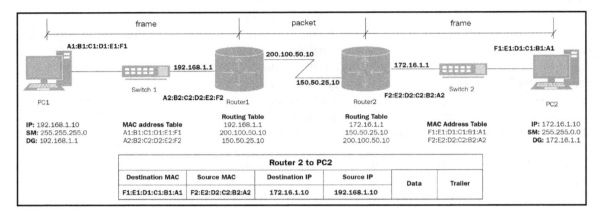

Figure 5.9. Sending a packet from Router 2 to PC2

Path determination

Technically speaking, forwarding packets is not an easy task, because it requires path determination. However, it seems that path determination activity does not pose any trouble to a router, as it accomplishes it in the best possible way. It is important to mention features such as the routing decision, selecting the best path, and load balancing. Each of these includes elements, such as exit interfaces, routing protocols, the routing table, and forwarding processes. We should also mention the specifics of routing protocols, such as the routing algorithm, metrics, and administrative distance, to understand the router components involved in the path determination process.

Routing decision

Earlier, in the section *Routing operations*, you got acquainted with the definition of the router, and what routing is. Also, remember that the router is a network device that is configured, or programmed, to select the best path to forward packets to its destination. In fact, it is the router's routing table that contains all of the possible routes, which are configured either manually or dynamically. Thus, the router will make the routing decision by consulting its routing table for the network address that contains the host for whom the packet is intended. The routing table contains the following possible routes to networks:

- **Direct routes** are usually routes that connect directly to the networks that contain the host for whom the packet is intended and the router over one of the router's interfaces. The host and the internal router's interface belong to the same network address:

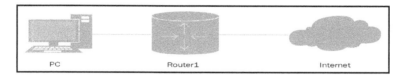

Figure 5.10. Direct routes

- **Remote routes** are routes that connect, through other routers, the networks that contain the hosts for whom the packet is intended. The directly connected router simply forwards the packet to another router, in order to reach the remote network:

Figure 5.11. Remote routes

- **No routes** are routes where the directly connected routers or remotely connected routers lack next-hop information in their routing tables; they forward packets to the *quad zero* 0.0.0.0 0.0.0.0 route, known as a **Gateway of Last Resort**. A Gateway of Last Resort includes a default route, default network, and default gateway, and is either configured manually or learned dynamically, from other routers. However, if the Gateway of Last Resort is missing, then the packet is discarded, and, in turn, an ICMP unreachable message is sent to the source IP address.

Selecting the best path

Earlier in this chapter, we have mentioned that routing is a complex process. So, the question arises: if the routing table contains information about all possible routes to which the router can forward packets, then what enables the router to determine the best path among all of the routes that the router knows? In an attempt to find the answer, let us take a look at the topology as in *Figure 5.12*, where PC1 is sending a packet to PC2:

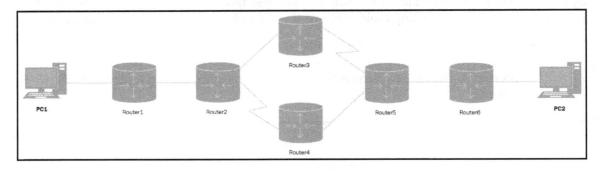

Figure 5.12. Sending packets from PC1 to PC2

Logically, the possible packet routes from PC1 to PC2 are as follows:

- **Route 1:** From PC1 via Router 1 via Router 2 via Router 3 via Router 5 via Router 6 to PC2
- **Route 2:** From PC1 via Router 1 via Router 2 via Router 4 via Router 5 via Router 6 to PC2

In the process of the router determining the best path, there are several factors involved. In general, including the topology from the given figure, the following should be considered:

- **Exit Interfaces:** Routers contain various exit interfaces, to reach remote networks.
- **Routing Protocols:** Each routing protocol has its own specifics, such as a routing algorithm, metric, and administrative distance:
    - A **routing algorithm** is a mathematically formulated operation to select the best route for efficient packet routing.
    - A **metric** represents the cost value assigned to a route, which enables it to calculate the route distance. More precisely, the higher the bandwidth, the lower the distance between the routers. *RIP* uses *hop count* as a metric, *OSPF* uses *link cost* as a metric, and *EIGRP* uses *composite metric* made up of bandwidth, and delay.

- **Routing Table**: A routing table is known as a **Routing Information Base** (**RIB**), is stored in a router, and contains route destinations.
- **Forwarding Process**: This moves the packets from the incoming interface to the outgoing interface by referencing the information on a routing table.

Network Load Balancing (NLB)

Load balancing is a concept that has been widely used in **Information and Communications Technology** (**ICT**). From clients to servers, from networking devices to network applications, load balancing is employed for a more efficient use of resources, so that more work is done within the same amount of time. Obviously, as its name implies, it has to do with the distribution of the load among several processors. In the case of routers, load balancing has to do with the process of routing packets to their destinations, using all of the paths with identical metrics equally. This is possible when the router has many exit interfaces, but a single destination network, in its routing table. This method is called **equal cost load balancing**.

Administrative distance (AD)

The router can be configured with more than one routing protocol. If that happens, the router's routing table will contain more than one route to the same destination network. Instantly, that brings up the question: Which route will the router select? As mentioned in the previous section, each routing protocol has its own specifics, such as a routing algorithm, metric, and administrative distance. It can be understood that each routing protocol will select the best route to reach the destination, depending on the specifics. While the routing algorithm and the metric represent a mathematically formulated operation, respectively, the value assigned to a route to calculate the route distance, the **administrative distance** (**AD**), represents the reliability of the routing protocol. In other words, AD represents the value assigned to a routing protocol in order to select the best path, when there are two or more routes from two or more routing protocols to reach the destination network. *Table 5.1* presents routing protocols and their respective AD values:

Route Source/Routing Protocol	Administrative Distance (AD)
Directly connected route	0
Statically configured route	1

Enhanced Interior Gateway Routing Protocol (EIGRP) summary route	5
External Border Gateway Protocol (BGP)	20
Internal EIGRP	90
Interior Gateway Routing Protocol (IGRP)	100
Open Shortest Path First (OSPF) protocol	110
Intermediate System to Intermediate System (IS-IS) protocol	115
Routing Information Protocol (RIP)	120
External EIGRP	170
Internal BGP	200

What is a router?

As with a switch, a router is:

- A hardware
- A network device

To answer the question, What is the router's function? We can say:

- A router connects networks

The last question is, How does the router work? And the answer is:

- A router uses a packet-forwarding method to route data to a destination network

A router is a computer

As you know, a device is considered to be a computer if it contains the following components:

- Input/output units
- A processing unit
- Memory/storage units
- A communication unit

Then, from what we know about a router, let us compare it with the components just mentioned to conclude whether the router is a computer. *Figure 5.13* presents a Cisco router:

Figure 5.13. Router's front panel

- Unlike computers, routers do not contain input/output units, because the input ports (keyboard and mouse) and output port (VGA) are not available like they are in computers. However, the input/output ports do exist in routers' architecture, and they have to do with the forwarding process.
- Like computers, routers contain processing and memory/storage units. Obviously, you can not expect to see Intel's or AMD's processors in Cisco routers, nor even hard disk drives (HDD). However, Cisco routers utilize CPU chips that are less powerful than PC processors, but sufficient to perform routing operations. In the case of memory, Cisco routers use different types of memory, such as RAM/DRAM, NVRAM, Flash memory, and ROM. RAM/DRAM is a volatile memory that acts as working memory, NVRAM is a non-volatile memory that stores the start up configuration, Flash memory is a type of non-volatile memory that can be deleted and reprogrammed as needed and holds the **router's IOS**, and the ROM, which is a read-only memory, contains the **bootstrap program**.
- Regarding the communication unit, both computers and routers successfully fulfill this component. Cisco routers contain enough ports and interfaces for both management and packet forwarding. Therefore, they are grouped in **in-band** and **management** ports.

Like computers, routers come in all shape and sizes. Cisco manufactures routers for virtually all types of businesses, and their networks. Some of the types of routers that are offered on the market are as follows:

- **Small Office/Home Office** (**SOHO**) routers are mostly non-modular routers, designed for small networks. They include the Cisco **Integrated Services Routers** (**ISR**) 800 series.
- **Branch and mid-range** routers are modular and non-modular routers, intended for small-to-medium businesses. These include the Cisco ISR 1000, ISR 2000, and ISR 4000 series, as well as the Cisco 1000 series **Connected Grid Routers** (**CGR**), and the 2000 series CGR.

- **WAN aggregation** routers are modular routers with multiple slots, designed to satisfy Enterprise network requirements. They include the Cisco **Aggregation Services Routers (ASR)** 1000, and the **Network Convergence System (NCS)** 5000 series.
- **Backbone and service provider core** routers represent the most powerful line of routers that Cisco are manufacturing. These routers are modular, with multiple slots, especially designed to constitute the internet's infrastructure. These include the Cisco NCS 6000 series and ASR 9000 series.

Router's CPU and OS

In the previous section, we confirmed that the router is a form of computer, and that it contains a processor. Unlike computers, which mostly utilize a single processor, Cisco routers use several CPU chips. One reason for that, is that tasks such as routing, forwarding, and switching packets, are shared between the processors. Similar to a computer's processor, the router's CPU chips use **heatsink**, which helps to spread out the heat generated by the CPU chips to the inside of the chassis. Mostly, these chips are manufactured by Cisco. CPU chips produced by manufacturers like Motorola can also be found in Cisco routers. *Figure 5.14* shows heatsink in a Cisco router:

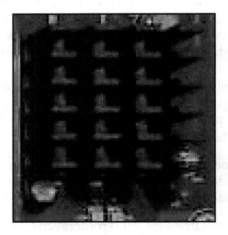

Figure 5.14. CPU chip heatsink

Similar to switches, routers run on **Cisco IOS** that is in fact a NOS for this type of network device. CCENT exam objectives require that a network administrator have the knowledge and skills to configure the Cisco IOS on Cisco routers. Although router configuration may present a challenge, it can be fun at the same time.

Anatomy of a router

Just as routers come in all different shapes and sizes, their internal hardware is also organized in different ways. However, CCENT exam objectives clearly state that the network administrator should be familiar with, and understand the function of, the router's main internal hardware components, like CPU chips, memory, power supply, cooling fan, and heat shields. *Figure 5.15* shows the main internal hardware components of a Cisco router:

Figure 5.15. Router's internal hardware

Connecting to a router

As you know, routers are used to interconnect networks. For that reason, routers contain several types of ports and interfaces that are used for management, configuration, and operations. As we saw in the section, *A router is a computer*, there are routers for networks of all types and sizes. Although they differ in size and purpose, the following ports and interfaces are usually present in each category of routers:

- **Console ports,** including RJ-45 and a new USB type-B (mini-B USB)
- **Auxiliary (AUX),** RJ-45 port considered a legacy port
- **Gigabit Ethernet** interfaces
- **Universal Serial Bus** (**USB**) ports
- **Compact Flash** slots
- **Enhanced high-speed WAN interface card (eHWIC)** slots

LAN and WAN interfaces

Unlike a switch, an out-of-the-box Cisco router is not capable of forwarding frames between networks. Hence, it requires configuration. As explained in the section *A router is a computer*, ports and interfaces (see *Figure 5.16*) on a router are grouped into in-band router interfaces and management ports. LAN and WAN interfaces are known as in-band interfaces, because they require an IP address and a subnet mask. Console and AUX ports are management ports used for configuration, management, and troubleshooting. Similar to a switch, there are several ways to access a router for configuration purposes:

- The **console** is the special port on the router that is used for its management. This is referred to as out-of-band access, because it is a direct access to a router's CLI session that does not require preconfiguration on interfaces.
- **Telnet** provides an insecure connection for accessing remote devices over a network. Thus, prior to accessing the router's CLI session, it requires the configuration of an interface with an IP address and enabling Telnet.
- **Secure Shell** (**SSH**) provides an encrypted connection for accessing remote devices over a network. Hence, prior to accessing a router's CLI session, it requires the configuration of an interface with an IP address and enabling SSH:

Figure 5.16. Router's interfaces and ports

It is also worth noting that in-band interfaces, along with enabling the configuration of the router, can receive and forward packets at the same time. Therefore, to prevent this from happening, two active interfaces on the same router are not allowed (by Cisco IOS) to belong to the same network.

Boot up the router

Just like a PC, a router **boots up** too. The power-on self test (POST) and bootstrap program also run on the router's boot process. Furthermore, hardware components such as CPU chips, RAM/DRAM, NVRAM, and Flash memory are initialized. Finally, the operating system IOS is located and loaded into the RAM/DRAM. That said, this section discusses the router's boot process.

Router's boot up process

Just like a switch, a router has a boot up process. It consists of several phases, and in each phase, significant activities are carried out. The following steps represent the **router's boot process,** when it is powered on:

1. As electricity starts flowing into the router's internal circuitry (more precisely, into the ROM module), the POST performs a hardware check on the CPU, RAM, and the NVRAM. Once the POST is over, the bootstrap program is loaded from ROM to RAM.

2. The bootstrap program initializes the CPU and Flash memory. It then locates the IOS in the Flash memory and copies it into the RAM (it holds running-configuration).

3. Finally, the bootstrap program initializes the NVRAM and copies the start up configuration from it into the RAM. By this time, the setup mode prompt is available.

Bootset files

Switches and routers use various types of memory, like RAM, DRAM, Flash memory, and NVRAM, and it may happen that they are not properly understood. The same applies to the `startup-configuration` file and the `running-configuration` file. Therefore, let us clarify with an illustration in *Figure 5.18*, to better understand the function of these memories and to ensure that each configuration file goes where it should go when the router is powered on:

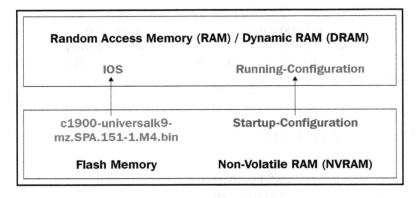

Figure 5.17. Bootset files on Cisco routers

So, IOS is located in Flash memory, whereas `startup-configuration` is located in NVRAM. During power up, after the POST is complete, the bootstrap program (initiated by the ROM) locates the IOS in the Flash memory and loads it into RAM. Similarly, the bootstrap program locates the `startup-configuration` in NVRAM and loads it into RAM, but now, it becomes a `running-configuration` for the current user session, until the `running-configuration` is saved to NVRAM. Does it make sense now?

Router routing tables

The **Routing Information Base** (**RIB**) is a database file stored in RAM that contains all of the information about the routes to directly connected networks and routes to remotely connected networks. As it is explained in this chapter, the routing table plays a decisive role in the router selecting the best path. In addition, other than route information, the routing table may display the metrics of a listed route, too.

Understanding packet forwarding

As you know, each router interface is connected to a particular network. Then, when PC1 sends the packet to PC2, PC1 will consult its routing table; when it determines that PC2 is in the remote network, it sends the packet to the default gateway. In this case, the default gateway is the router that accepts the packet and examines it to learn the destination IP address. Like PC1, the router consults its routing table to know where to forward the newly arrived packet. In contrast to the routing table information at PC1, the router's routing table contains the following information:

- Directly connected routes
- Remotely connected routes
- Manually configured default routes

IPv4 routing table

In Cisco routers, to show the IPv4 routing table (like the one shown in *Figure 5.18*), enter the following command:

```
Router# show ip route
```

The following screenshot depicts the output for the preceding command:

```
SP1>en
SP1#show ip route
Codes: L - local, C - connected, S - static, R - RIP, M - mobile, B - BGP
       D - EIGRP, EX - EIGRP external, O - OSPF, IA - OSPF inter area
       N1 - OSPF NSSA external type 1, N2 - OSPF NSSA external type 2
       E1 - OSPF external type 1, E2 - OSPF external type 2, E - EGP
       i - IS-IS, L1 - IS-IS level-1, L2 - IS-IS level-2, ia - IS-IS inter area
       * - candidate default, U - per-user static route, o - ODR
       P - periodic downloaded static route

Gateway of last resort is not set

      10.0.0.0/16 is subnetted, 1 subnets
S        10.10.0.0/16 [1/0] via 203.0.113.2
      203.0.113.0/24 is variably subnetted, 5 subnets, 2 masks
C        203.0.113.0/30 is directly connected, GigabitEthernet0/0
L        203.0.113.1/32 is directly connected, GigabitEthernet0/0
S        203.0.113.4/30 [1/0] via 203.0.113.10
C        203.0.113.8/30 is directly connected, GigabitEthernet0/1
L        203.0.113.9/32 is directly connected, GigabitEthernet0/1
```

Figure 5.18 Router's routing table

As you can see, other than providing the information on directly connected networks and remotely connected networks, the routing table provides code information, explaining the meaning of each and every letter; additionally, it also provides the information on how the routes have been learned.

Directly connected routing table entries

Remember that the router connects networks. From a communication point of view, this means that each router's interface is equipped with an IP address and a subnet mask. When those interfaces become active, the following entries are automatically added to the routing table:

- **Directly connected** routes are identified by a C code, and are added to the routing table and activated when an interface is equipped with an IP address and subnet mask:

    ```
    C    203.0.113.0/30 is directly connected,    GigabitEthernet0/0
    ```

- **Local interfaces** are identified by an L code, and represent the local interfaces that connect the networks. These interfaces act as default gateways:

    ```
    L    203.0.113.9/32 is directly connected,    GigabitEthernet0/1
    ```

Remote network routing table entries

It is required that a network administrator knows how to interpret the routing table entries. Thus, to understand and be able to interpret a remote network entry, let us examine the following route:

```
D    172.30.32.0/20    [90/4879540]    via    00:00:30    GigabitEthernet0/1
```

- D represents the **route source,** which indicates how the route was learned
- 172.30.32.0/20 represents the **IP address** of a remote network
- 90 represents the **administrative distance** of the route
- 4879540 represents the **metric** to reach the remote network
- 10.1.1.2 represents the **next-hop** IP address to reach the remote network
- 00:00:30 represents the **time elapsed** since the network was learned
- GigabitEthernet0/1 represents the **exit interface** of a router, to reach the remote network

Next-hop IP address

As you may have noticed, in *Figure 5.22*, the IP address 10.1.1.2 represents the next-hop IP address. Based on what was said about next-hop forwarding in the section *Forward to next-hop*, it can be concluded that the next-hop IP address represents the next coming router's interface, where a packet can be forwarded on its way to a remote network.

Routing types

Routers contain interfaces to which networks are connected, and to which packets are forwarded using the routing tables. The routing tables are populated either manually, by entering **static routes**, or dynamically, by using routing protocols. While static routes cannot be updated automatically, **dynamic routes** are updated automatically, by exchanging the routing information among routers. That sure does make dynamic routing more favorable than static routing, particularly in large and complex networks. That said, this section explains static routing and dynamic routing.

Static routing

You may have occasionally heard expressions like a static IP address, a static DNS record, an IP address reserved in DHCP, and so on. As you may know, all of these entries are manually configured by a network administrator or system administrator. Therefore, the same happens with **static routes**. These are entries that are manually configured by the network administrator on the routers, and, as such, represent the routes between two routers. The fact that these routes are manually entered means that they cannot be updated automatically. Therefore, the network administrator needs to update them manually. That can be considered a disadvantage, especially when there is a change in the network topology.

In general, there are two types of static routes in a router's routing table:

- **Static routes** are identified by an S code, and represent the routes to the next router (that is, the next-hop IP address):

      S   203.0.113.0/30   [1/0]   via   203.0.113.9

- **Default static routes** are identified by an S* code, and represent the routes to the Gateway of Last Resort:

      S*   0.0.0.0/0   [1/0]   via   209.165.200.234

Static route applications

As noted in the previous section, static routes are used to provide routes between two routers (or routes to the Gateway of Last Resort, if the routing table lacks information about the route to a specific network). In addition, both IPv4 and IPv6 recognize the following routes as other approaches for using static and default routes:

- **Summary static routes** are identified by an S, too. However, these routes enable reducing advertised routes by summarizing several contiguous networks into single static routes. That said, route summarization is configurable if the destination networks are contiguous, and if multiple static routes are all using the same next-hop IP address. For example, the following summary static route replaces static routes to contiguous networks 192.168.1.0, 192.168.2.0, and 192.168.3.0:

      S   192.168.0.0/22 is directly connected,   Serial0/0/1

- **Floating static routes** are identified by an S*, too. These routes enable creating backup routes when primary routes fail. That said, floating static routes are configurable by specifying a higher administrative distance for the default static routes. For example, for the following default static route, the administrative distance has been set to 5, compared to a value of 1 for the static routes:

      S*   0.0.0.0/0   [5/0]   via   192.168.1.100

 You can learn more about route summarization and floating static routes at http://www.ciscopress.com/articles/article.asp?p=2180209 seqNum=7.

Dynamic routing

Unlike static routing, dynamic routing requires less network administrator interactivity to enter route information into the router's routing table. Dynamic routing protocols are used to propagate the routing information across routers, dynamically updating their routing tables. This approach overcomes the problem of static routing when a change in network topology occurs. Thus, dynamic routing enables routing tables to get adjusted to new route changes more quickly, and with less administrative overhead. Dynamic routing is therefore more scalable, in comparision to static routing.

Dynamic routing protocols

In the section *Communication protocols* in `Chapter 2`, *Communication in Computer Networks*, you were taught that like human languages, computer communication language contains standards and rules that are called *communication protocols*. **Routing protocols** represent the set of rules that assist routers in communicating with one another, by exchanging routing information among themselves. In addition, routing protocols contain routing algorithms that help in selecting the best path, when delivering packets to destination networks. Because of their nature of constant change, routing protocols have received the epithet of being dynamic. Components like data structures, routing protocol messages, and routing algorithms constitute the profile of the **dynamic routing protocols**. *Table 5.2* presents some of the most well-known dynamic routing protocols:

Dynamic routing protocol	Type
RIP	distance vector
RIP version 2 (RIPv2)	distance vector
IGRP	distance vector
EIGRP	distance vector
OSPF	link-state
IS-IS	link-state
BGP	path vector

So, **distance vector** protocols exchange routing information based on *distance* (hop count) and *direction* (next-hop). **Link-state** routing protocols gather information from all other routers, thus creating a complete *map* of network topology. Unlike distance vector and link-state routing protocols, **path vector** routing protocols serve *autonomous systems* by providing next-hop IP addresses, the paths to reach destination networks, and the destination network information in the routing tables. An **autonomous system (AS)**, known differently as a **routing domain**, represents a group of routers that have common administration. That said, in relation to AS, dynamic routing protocols can be categorized into:

- **Internal Gateway Protocols (IGP)**, known as *intra-AS routing*, route packets within AS. RIP, EIGRP, OSPF, and IS-IS are considered to be IGPs.
- **Exterior Gateway Protocols (EGP)**, known as *inter-AS routing*, route packets between ASs. BGP is considered to be EGP.

Another categorization of dynamic routing protocols has to do with subnet masks. They are grouped into:

- **Classful routing protocols**, which do not include the subnet mask when transmitting routing information
- **Classless routing protocols**, which include the subnet mask and network address when transmitting routing information

Routing table terms

Earlier in this chapter, it was mentioned that the routing table is a **Routing Information Base** (**RIB**). From a structural point of view, it has a hierarchical structure. So, unlike a routing table built with the static routing technique, a routing table built with the dynamic routing technique contains far more information. Then, just as the network administrator must know how to interpret the routing table entries, he or she must also understand the output generated by the routing table. That said, the hierarchical structure of a routing table includes the following levels:

- **Ultimate routes** are directly connected routes, dynamically learned routes, and local routes that contain either a next-hop IP address or an exit interface.
- **Level 1 routes** are network routes, supernet routes, and default routes that contain a subnet mask that is equal to or less than the classful mask of the network address.
- **Level 1 parent routes** are subnetted level 1 network routes.
- **Level 2 child routes** are directly connected networks, static routes, or dynamically learned routes that are a subnet of a classful network address. In addition, level 2 child routes are ultimate routes, too.

Summary

We can summarize this chapter with the following points:

- Routers connect networks.
- Routers use routing tables to forward packets.
- Both the IP address and the hostname are logical elements that are used for communication between computers.
- If the destination host is in the LAN, then the source host sends the data directly, via a switch, by addressing the data to the destination host's MAC address.

- If the destination host is in the remote network, the data is sent to the router, via a switch, by addressing the data to the router's MAC address; this refers to an indirect delivery.
- The router connected to the local network segment is referred to as the default gateway.
- Routing is the algorithm that enables the router to select the best path to forward packets to the remote network.
- When the data moves to any of the OSI lower layers, a header and a trailer are added.
- Next-hop forwarding refers to routers being close to one another in the packet's routing path.
- A routing table contains all of the possible routes, which are either manually or dynamically configured.
- A router makes a routing decision by consulting its routing table about the network address that contains the host for which the packet is intended.
- Direct routes are the routes that directly connect the networks that contain the host for which the packet is intended and the router, over one of the router's interfaces.
- Remote routes are the routes that connect the networks that contain the host for which the packet is intended through other routers.
- No routes are usually the routes where the directly connected routers or remotely connected routers lack next-hop information in their routing tables; they then forward packets to a quad zero (`0.0.0.0 0.0.0.0`) route, known as a Gateway of Last Resort.
- Routers contain various exit interfaces to reach remote networks.
- Each routing protocol has its own specifics, such as a routing algorithm, metric, and administrative distance.
- A routing algorithm is a mathematically formulated operation to select the best route for efficient packet routing.
- A metric represents the cost value assigned to a route, which enables it to calculate the route distance.
- The forwarding process moves the packets from the incoming interface to the outgoing interface by referencing the information on a routing table.
- Load balancing, in routers, has to do with the process of routing packets to their destinations using all of the paths with identical metrics equally.
- AD represents the reliability of the routing protocol.

- The RIB is a database file stored in RAM that contains all of the information about the routes to directly connected networks and the routes to remotely connected networks.
- The default gateway is the router that accepts the packet from a host in a directly connected network, and examines it to learn the destination IP address.
- Directly connected routes are identified by a C code, and are added to the routing table when interfaces are equipped with IP addresses and subnet masks, and are activated.
- Local interfaces are identified by an L code, and represent the local interfaces that connect the networks. These interfaces act as default gateways.
- The next-hop IP address represents the next coming router's interface, where a packet can be forwarded on its way to a remote network.
- Static routes are identified by an S code, and represent the routes to the next router (that is, next-hop IP address).
- Default static routes are identified by an S* code, and represent the routes to the Gateway of Last Resort.
- Summary static routes are identified by an S, too, and enable reducing advertised routes by summarizing several contiguous networks into single static routes.
- Floating static routes are identified by an S*, too, and enable creating backup routes when primary routes fail.
- Components like data structures, routing protocol messages, and routing algorithms constitute the profile of the dynamic routing protocols.
- Distance vector protocols exchange routing information based on distance (hop count) and direction (next-hop).
- Link-state routing protocols gather information from all of the other routers, thus creating a complete map of network topology.
- Path vector routing protocols serve autonomous systems by providing next-hop IP addresses, the path to reach destination networks, and the destination network information, in the routing tables.
- An AS, also known as a routing domain, represents a group of routers that have common administration.
- IGP, known as intra-AS routing, routes packets within ASs.
- EGP, known as inter-AS routing, routes packets between ASs.
- Classful routing protocols do not include subnet masks in routing information.
- Classless routing protocols include subnet masks and network addresses in routing information.

- Ultimate routes are directly connected routes, dynamically learned routes, and local routes that contain either a next-hop IP address or an exit interface.
- Level 1 routes are network routes, supernet routes, and default routes that contain a subnet mask that is equal to or less than the classful mask of the network address.
- Level 1 parent routes are subnetted level 1 network routes.
- Level 2 child routes are directly connected networks, static routes, or dynamically learned routes that are a subnet of a classful network address.

Questions

1. Classful routing protocols include subnet masks in routing information. (True | False)
2. _____ protocols exchange routing information based on distance (hop count) and direction (next-hop).
3. Which of the following are specifics of routing protocols? (Choose three.)
    1. Routing algorithm.
    2. Metric.
    3. Administrative distance.
    4. Autonomous system.
4. Directly connected routes are identified by a C code, and are added to the routing table when interfaces are equipped with IP addresses and subnet masks, and are activated. (True | False)
5. _____ is a database file stored in RAM that contains all of the information about the routes to directly connected networks and the routes to remotely connected networks.
6. Which of the following components constitute the profile of the dynamic routing protocol? (Choose three.)
    1. Data structures.
    2. Routing protocol messages.
    3. Routing algorithms.
    4. Next-hop IP address.
7. A metric represents the cost value assigned to a switch, which enables it to calculate the route distance. (True | False)
8. _____ moves the packets from the incoming interface to the outgoing interface by referencing the information on a routing table.

9. Entries on the router's routing table can be configured which way? (Choose two.)
    1. Manually.
    2. Dynamically.
    3. Remotely.
    4. Administratively.

10. If the destination host is in the remote network, the data is sent to the router, via a switch, by addressing the data to the router's MAC address; this refers to an indirect delivery. (True | False)

11. _____ is the algorithm that enables the router to select the best path to forward packets to the remote network.

12. Which of the following are logical elements that are used for communication between computers? (Choose two.)
    1. Hostname.
    2. IP address.
    3. Subnet mask.
    4. Default gateway.

13. Next-hop forwarding refers to routers being close to one another in the packet's routing path. (True | False)

14. _____ are network routes, supernet routes, and default routes that contain a subnet mask that is equal to or less than the classful mask of the network address.

15. Which of the following represent a categorization of dynamic routing protocols? (Choose two.)
    1. Classful routing protocols.
    2. Classless routing protocols.
    3. File transfer protocol (FTP).
    4. Trivial file transfer protocol (TFTP).

16. IOS is located in NVRAM, whereas `startup-configuration` is located in Flash memory. (True | False)

17. _____ are identified by an S, too, and enable reducing advertised routes by summarizing several contiguous networks into single static routes.

18. Which of the following are dynamic routing protocols? (Choose two.)
    1. Transmission Control Protocol (TCP).
    2. User Datagram Protocol (UDP).
    3. Enhanced Interior Gateway Routing Protocol (EIGRP).
    4. Open Shortest Path First (OSPF).

6
Setting up the Router

Like `Chapter 4`, *Setting up the Switch,* this chapter brings to you hands-on examples of the router's configuration. That said, this chapter is designed to provide you with step-by-step instructions of configuring the main features of the router, as outlined in the objectives of the CCENT certification exam. Now that you have become familiar with a router's boot-up process in `Chapter 5`, *Introduction to Routing,* you will be introduced to a router's LED indicators, and how to connect a router to a PC. After that, you will be ready to run the initial configuration on a Cisco router. Then, the chapter provides more advanced router configurations, such as configuring both IPv4 and IPv6 IP addresses on router interfaces, configuring static routes and default static routes, and configuring **Routing Information Protocol** (**RIP**). The legacy interVLAN routing, and router-on-a-stick interVLAN routing, conclude the configuration part of this chapter. At the end, the chapter includes a summary and chapter questions.

In this chapter, we will cover:

- How to turn on the router
- How to run the router's initial configuration
- How to configure static and default routes
- How to configure Routing Information Protocol (RIP)
- How to configure legacy interVLAN
- How to configure router-on-a-stick interVLAN

Connecting the router to a PC and turning it on

Although connecting the router to a PC and turning it on may seem an easy task, it is counted as one of the most important ones when working with routers. To ease that job, this section provides you with the right information on how to connect your router to your PC, turn on the router, and establish an initial session with the router.

Router LED indicators

Like switches, routers also use **LED indicators**, as shown in *Figure 6.1*, to provide a way to monitor their activity and performance. Unlike switches, routers have far more less ports in the front panel (some Cisco router models do not have any at all), and LED indicators in the rear panel are usually placed next to ports and interfaces. Thus, it will not be difficult to identify if an LED is on, indicating an active interface, or if an LED is off, indicating a problem with the interface:

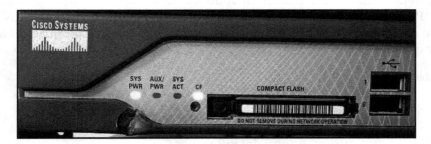

Figure 6.1. LED indicators on router's front panel

Console access

Like a switch, before configuring basic router settings, you must first connect your router to a PC. To be able to do so, you need a DB9 serial port on your PC and a **rollover console cable** (see *Figure 6.2*). However, these days it is hard to find a PC with DB9 serial port, because it is a legacy port. Therefore, to overcome such a situation, a USB-to-DB9 adapter in combination with a rollover console cable, as shown in *Figure 6.2*, represents an alternative solution:

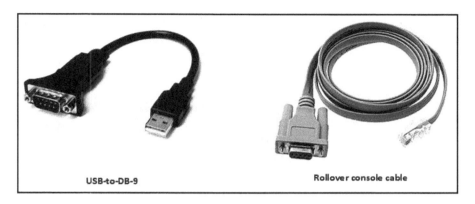

Figure 6.2. USB-to-DB9 adapter and rollover console cable

Turning on the router

When it comes to turning on the router, then undoubtedly that is the easiest thing for a network administrator to do. Simply, just plug in the power cable and turn the switch on, as shown in *Figure 6.3*. Shortly, your router will be turned on:

Figure 6.3. On/off switch to turn on the router

After both the PC and the router are powered on, a terminal emulator program such as **PuTTY** is required for establishing a connection with a router as in *Figure 6.4*:

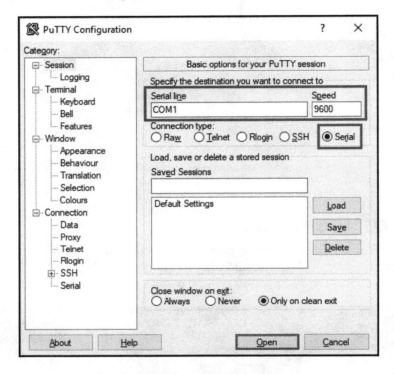

Figure 6.4. Establishing connection with a router using PuTTY

Once the CLI session is established on a router, the setup mode prompt becomes available, as in *Figure 6.5*. As you now know, Cisco IOS uses the following command modes:

- **User EXEC mode** enables access to only a limited number of basic monitoring commands `Router>`.
- **Privileged EXEC mode** enables access to all monitoring, configuration, and management commands `Router#`.

- **Global configuration mode** provides a root access to a router. The prompt looks like `Router(config)#`. As the name implies, in this mode, configurations can be done that affect the overall operation of a router. Also known as **global config mode**, it includes the following self-descriptive subconfiguration modes:

  - **Line configuration mode** enables users to configure management features. The prompt looks like the following:

    ```
    Router(config-line)#
    ```

  - **Interface configuration mode** enables the user to configure the router's interfaces. The prompt looks like the following:

    ```
    Router(config-if)#
    ```

The following screenshot shows the User EXEC mode on a router:

```
Cisco CISCO2901/K9 (revision 1.0) with 491520K/32768K bytes of memory.
Processor board ID FTX152400KS
2 Gigabit Ethernet interfaces
DRAM configuration is 64 bits wide with parity disabled.
255K bytes of non-volatile configuration memory.
249856K bytes of ATA System CompactFlash 0 (Read/Write)


        --- System Configuration Dialog ---

Would you like to enter the initial configuration dialog? [yes/no]: n


Press RETURN to get started!


Router>
```

Figure 6.5. User EXEC mode on a router

Show version output

From what is said in the previous chapters, it is clear that Cisco devices have an operating system. So, for that reason, it is important to know which version of IOS is running on networking devices. That way, we will be aware of the commands that are supported or not:

- **Show IOS version**: Enter the following command to show the IOS version and router's other useful information:

  ```
  Router> show version
  ```

The output generated by the `show version` command is as shown in the following screenshot:

```
Router#show version
Cisco IOS Software, C2900 Software (C2900-UNIVERSALK9-M), Version 15.1(4)M4, RELEASE SOFTWARE (fc2)
Technical Support: http://www.cisco.com/techsupport
Copyright (c) 1986-2012 by Cisco Systems, Inc.
Compiled Thurs 5-Jan-12 15:41 by pt_team

ROM: System Bootstrap, Version 15.1(4)M4, RELEASE SOFTWARE (fc1)
cisco2911 uptime is 19 seconds
System returned to ROM by power-on
System image file is "flash0:c2900-universalk9-mz.SPA.151-1.M4.bin"
Last reload type: Normal Reload

This product contains cryptographic features and is subject to United
States and local country laws governing import, export, transfer and
use. Delivery of Cisco cryptographic products does not imply
third-party authority to import, export, distribute or use encryption.
Importers, exporters, distributors and users are responsible for
compliance with U.S. and local country laws. By using this product you
agree to comply with applicable laws and regulations. If you are unable
to comply with U.S. and local laws, return this product immediately.

A summary of U.S. laws governing Cisco cryptographic products may be found at:
http://www.cisco.com/wwl/export/crypto/tool/stqrg.html

If you require further assistance please contact us by sending email to
export@cisco.com.
Cisco CISCO2911/K9 (revision 1.0) with 491520K/32768K bytes of memory.
Processor board ID FTX152400KS
3 Gigabit Ethernet interfaces
DRAM configuration is 64 bits wide with parity disabled.
255K bytes of non-volatile configuration memory.
249856K bytes of ATA System CompactFlash 0 (Read/Write)

License Info:

License UDI:

--------------------------------------------------
Device#   PID                    SN
--------------------------------------------------
*0        CISCO2911/K9           FTX15247VIV


Technology Package License Information for Module:'c2900'

-----------------------------------------------------------------
Technology   Technology-package         Technology-package
             Current      Type          Next reboot
-----------------------------------------------------------------
ipbase       ipbasek9     Permanent     ipbasek9
security     None         None          None
uc           None         None          None
data         None         None          None

Configuration register is 0x2102
```

Figure 6.6. The IOS version displayed by the show version command

Router's initial configuration

This section covers the router's initial configuration. As such, it is recommended to run it every time the router is taken out of the box, or when you have reloaded the startup configuration on a router.

Configuring basic router settings

Just as we did in the initial configuration of the switch, this configuration type is also necessary for the router. Such, a configuration primarily covers the security aspect of the device, as well as anticipating the advanced configuration of the device before it is placed in the production environment:

- **Accessing privileged EXEC mode**: Enter the following command to access the **privileged EXEC mode**:

```
Router> enable
Router#
```

- **Accessing configuration mode**: Enter the following command to access the configuration mode:

```
Router# configure terminal
Router(config)#
```

- **Naming the router:** Enter the following command to assign a name to the router:

```
Router(config)# hostname R1
R1(config)#
```

- **Preventing unwanted DNS lookups:** Enter the following command to prevent the router from trying to interpret incorrect commands:

```
Router(configure)# no ip domain-lookup
```

- **Setting up the password for privileged EXEC mode:** Enter the following commands to set up a password for privileged EXEC mode:

```
Router(config)# enable secret class
Router(config)# exit
Router#
```

- **Setting up the password for the console port:** Enter the following commands to set up a password for the console port:

```
Router(config)# line console 0
Router(config-line)# password cisco
Router(config-line)# login
Router(config-line)# exit
Router(config)#
```

- **Setting up the password for Virtual Terminal Lines (VTY):** Enter the following commands to set up a password for VTY:

```
Router(config)# line vty 0 15
Router(config-line)# password cisco
Router(config-line)# login
Router(config-line)# exit
Router(config)#
```

- **Encrypting the plain text passwords**: Enter the following commands to encrypt the plain text passwords in running configuration:

```
Router(config)# service password-encryption
Router(config)# exit
Router#
```

- **Setting up the login MOTD banner**: Enter the following commands to setup a login **Message of the Day (MOTD)**:

```
Router(config)# banner motd # Message of the Day #
Router(config)# exit
Router#
```

- **Saving the running configuration**: Enter the following command to save the running configuration to the startup configuration on NVRAM:

```
Router# copy running-config startup-config
Destination filename [startup-config]?
Building configuration... [OK]
Router#
```

- **Showing the running configuration**: Enter the following command to show the running configuration:

```
Router# show running-config
```

- **Configuring the VLAN 1:** Enter the following commands to **configure the** `vlan 1` to access the router remotely:

```
Router(config)# interface vlan 1
Router(config-if)# ip address <ip-address> <subnet-mask>
Router(config-if)# no shutdown
Router(config-if)# exit
Router(config)#
```

Configuring IPv4 and IPv6 addresses on router interfaces

Remember that a computer network needs hostnames and IP addresses so that devices can communicate either between themselves, or with other devices beyond that network. That said, just as we assign IP addresses to computer network adapters (NICs), similarly, it is required to assign IP addresses in the router interfaces too:

- **Configuring an IPv4 address**: Enter the following command to configure an IPv4 address on a router interface:

```
Router# configure terminal
Router(config)# interface <interface-ID>
Router(config-if)# description <description>
Router(config-if)# ip address <IP-address> <subnet-mask>
Router(config-if)# no shutdown
Router(config-if)# exit
Router(config)#
```

- **Configuring a global unicast IPv6 address:** Enter the following command to configure a global unicast IPv6 address on a router interface:

```
Router# configure terminal
Router(config)# interface <interface-ID>
Router(config-if)# description <description>
Router(config-if)# ipv6 address <ipv6-address>/<prefix-length>
Router(config-if)# no shutdown
Router(config-if)# exit
Router(config)#
```

- **Configuring a global unicast IPv6 address with an interface identifier** (ID):
  Enter the following command to configure a global unicast IPv6 address on a
  router interface with an interface identifier (ID) in the low-order 64 bits of the
  IPv6 address using the EUI-64 process:

```
Router# configure terminal
Router(config)# interface <interface-ID>
Router(config-if)# description <description>
Router(config-if)# ipv6 address <ipv6-prefix>/<prefix-length>
eui-64
Router(config-if)# no shutdown
Router(config-if)# exit
Router(config)#
```

- **Configuring static link-local IPv6 address:** Enter the following command to
  configure a static link-local IPv6 address on a router interface:

```
Router# configure terminal
Router(config)# interface <interface-ID>
Router(config-if)# ipv6 address <ipv6-address>/<prefix-length>
link-local
Router(config-if)# description <description>
Router(config-if)# no shutdown
Router(config-if)# exit
Router(config)#
```

- **Configuring an IPv4 loopback address:** Enter the following command to
  configure an IPv4 loopback address on a router interface:

```
Router# configure terminal
Router(config)# interface loopback <number>
Router(config-if)# ip address <IP-address> <subnet-mask>
Router(config-if)# exit
Router(config)#
```

Configuring static routes and default static routes

As you know, routers use routing tables to move packets between networks. As the name indicates, the routing table contains routes to directly connected networks and remotely connected networks. These routes are entered into the routing table manually and dynamically. The network administrator enters routes into the router's routing table *manually*, whereas dynamic routing protocols update the routes into router's routing table *dynamically*. That makes for both static routing and dynamic routing to have their pros and cons. In this section, we will learn how to configure static routes and default static routes on a Cisco router.

Configuring IPv4 static routes and default static routes

Remember the word to *educate* the router in Chapter 5, *Introduction to Routing*, that is because the router needs to know what the available routes are to forward the packets to the destination:

- **Configuring next hop static routes:** Enter the following command to configure a next hop static route on a router:

  ```
  Router(config)# ip route <network-address> <subnet-mask> <ip-
  address>
  ```

- **Configuring directly-connected static routes:** Enter the following command to configure a directly-connected static route on a router:

  ```
  Router(config)# ip route <network-address> <subnet-mask> <exit-
  interface>
  ```

- **Configuring fully-specified static routes:** Enter the following command to configure a fully-specified static route on a router:

  ```
  Router(config)# ip route <network-address> <subnet-mask> <exit-
  interface> <ip-address>
  ```

- **Configuring default static routes:** Enter the following command to configure a default static route on a router:

  ```
  Router(config)# ip route 0.0.0.0 0.0.0.0 <ip-address>
  ```

- **Configuring floating static routes:** Enter the following command to configure a floating static route on a router:

  ```
  Router(config)# ip route 0.0.0.0 0.0.0.0 <ip-address>
  <administrative-distance>
  ```

- **Configuring static host routes:** Enter the following command to configure a static host route on a router. Note that the static host route requires a destination host IP address and a 255.255.255.255/32 subnet mask:

  ```
  Router(config)# ip route <destination-host-ip-address> <subnet-
  mask> <ip-address>
  ```

- **Verifying routes:** Enter the following command to show routes on a router:

  ```
  Router# show ip route
  ```

- **Verifying static routes:** Enter the following command to show static routes on a router:

  ```
  Router# show ip route static
  ```

- **Verifying specific static IP routes:** Enter the following command to show static routes for a specific IP address on a router:

  ```
  Router# show ip route <ip-address>
  ```

- **Verifying specific static network routes:** Enter the following command to show static routes for a specific network address on a router:

  ```
  Router# show ip route <network-address>
  ```

Syntax interpretation:

- `<network-address>` is the destination network address of a remote network
- `<subnet-mask>` is the subnet mask of the remote network
- `<ip-address>` is the next hop router's IP address
- `<exit-interface>` is the outgoing router's interface
- `<administrative-distance>` is the dynamic routing protocol's administrative distance

Configuring IPv6 static routes and default static routes

Similar to the previous section, in this section you will learn the commands to configure IPv6 static routes and default static routes.

- **Enabling routers to forward IPv6 packets:** Enter the following command to enable IPv6 routing on a router:

  ```
  Router(config)# ipv6 unicast-routing
  ```

- **Configuring next hop static routes:** Enter the following command to configure a next-hop static route on a router:

  ```
  Router(config)# ipv6 route <ipv6-prefix/prefix-length> <ipv6-
  address>
  ```

- **Configuring directly-connected static routes:** Enter the following command to configure a directly-connected static route on a router:

  ```
  Router(config)# ipv6 route <ipv6-prefix/prefix-length> <exit-
  interface>
  ```

- **Configuring fully-specified static routes:** Enter the following command to configure a fully-specified static route on a router:

  ```
  Router(config)# ipv6 route <ipv6-prefix/prefix-length> <exit-
  interface> <ipv6-address>
  ```

- **Configuring default static routes:** Enter the following command to configure a default static route on a router:

  ```
  Router(config)# ipv6 route ::/0 <ipv6-address>
  ```

- **Configuring floating static routes:** Enter the following command to configure a floating static route on a router:

  ```
  Router(config)# ipv6 route ::/0 <ipv6-address> <administrative-
  distance>
  ```

- **Configuring static host routes:** Enter the following command to configure a static host route on a router. Note that the static host route requires a destination host IP address and a /128 prefix length:

  ```
  Router(config)# ipv6 route <destination-host-ipv6-address/prefix-
  length>> <ipv6-address>
  ```

- **Verifying routes:** Enter the following command to show routes on a router:

  ```
  Router# show ipv6 route
  ```

- **Verifying static routes:** Enter the following command to show static routes on a router:

  ```
  Router# show ipv6 route static
  ```

- **Verifying specific static IP routes:** Enter the following command to show static routes for a specific IP address on a router:

  ```
  Router# show ipv6 route <ipv6-address>
  ```

- **Verifying specific static network routes:** Enter the following command to show static routes for a specific network address on a router:

  ```
  Router# show ipv6 route <ipv6-prefix>
  ```

Syntax interpretation:

- <ipv6-prefix> is the destination network address of a remote network
- <prefix-length> is the prefix length of the remote network
- <ipv6-address> is the next-hop router's IP address
- <exit-interface> is the outgoing router's interface
- <administrative-distance> is the dynamic routing protocol's administrative distance

Configuring Routing Information Protocol (RIP)

Just to remind you, **RIP** is a dynamic routing protocol that enables routers to exchange routing information. RIP is IETF's oldest distance vector protocol. In every 30 seconds, RIP exchanges routing information with the other routers in a network topology based on *distance* (hop count) and *direction* (next-hop). Further, RIP is considered an IGP, because it transmits the routing information with AS. Predominantly, it is used in small to medium-sized networks. It comes in two versions, such as **RIPv1**, defined by IETF's RFC 1058, and as **RIPv2**, defined by IETF's RFC 1723. Nowadays, it is rarely used, thus it can be said that it has been replaced by OSPF; however, because of its uncomplicated routing nature, it is used a lot in education to understand basic network routing. That said, this section describes how to configure RIP on a Cisco router:

- **Enabling RIP routing:** Enter the following command to enable RIP routing on a router:

  ```
  Router(config)# router rip
  Router(config-router)#
  ```

- **Disabling RIP routing:** Enter the following command to disable RIP routing on a router:

  ```
  Router(config-router)# no router rip
  Router(config)#
  ```

- **Enabling RIPv2 routing:** Enter the following command to enable RIP version 2 routing on a router:

  ```
  Router(config)# router rip
  Router(config-router)# version 2
  Router(config-router)# end
  ```

- **Restoring RIP routing default setting:** Enter the following command to restore the default RIP routing setting on a router by sending updates over version 1, and listening for updates from version 1 and version 2:

  ```
  Router(config-router)# no version
  ```

- **Displaying RIP commands:** Enter the following command to show the RIP commands supported by the IOS version of the router:

```
Router(config-router)# ?
auto-summary           Enter Address Family command mode
default-information    Control distribution of default information
distance               Define an administrative distance
exit                   Exit from routing protocol configuration mode
network                Enable routing on an IP network
no                     Negate a command or set its defaults
passive-interface      Suppress routing updates on an interface
redistribute           Redistribute information from another routing
protocol
timers                 Adjust routing timers
version                Set routing protocol version
```

- **Advertising networks using RIP routing:** Enter the following commands to advertise a network using RIP routing on a router. Note that RIP requires classful network addresses to be entered for advertising networks:

```
Router(config)# router rip
Router(config-router)# network <network-address>
```

- **Verifying RIP routing:** Enter the following command to show the RIP settings currently configured on the router:

```
Router# show ip protocols
```

- **Disabling auto summarization in RIP routing:** Enter the following commands to disable auto summarization in RIP routing on a router. Note that RIP by default automatically summarizes networks at major network boundaries:

```
Router(config)# router rip
Router(config-router)# no auto-summary
Router(config-router)# end
```

- **Configuring passive interfaces using RIP routing:** Enter the following commands to configure passive interfaces using RIP routing on a router. Note that RIP updates are forwarded out to all RIP-enabled interfaces, thus it is required to send the RIP updates only over interfaces that are connected to other RIP enabled routers:

```
Router(config)# router rip
Router(config-router)# passive-interface <interface-id>
Router(config-router)# end
```

- **Propagating default static routes using RIP routing:** Enter the following commands to propagate the default static route using RIP routing on a router:

```
Router(config)# ip route 0.0.0.0 0.0.0.0 <ip-address>
Router(config)# router rip
Router(config-router)# default-information originate
Router(config-router)# end
```

InterVLAN configuration

In legacy interVLAN routing (see *Figure 6.7*), the router has multiple interfaces where each interface connects to a certain VLAN. After assigning IP addresses both on the PCs and router interfaces, where each one belongs to a certain subnet, the router can then perform interVLAN routing. Therefore, this section describes how to configure legacy interVLAN routing on a Cisco router:

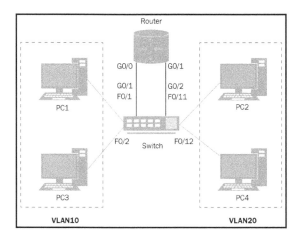

Figure 6.7. Legacy interVLAN routing

The following represents the configurations on a router, as well as displaying the routing table on a router. To configure a switch, and to verify the VLAN information on a switch, see section *Configuring legacy Inter-VLAN routing*, in `Chapter 4`, *Setting up the Switch*:

- **Router configuration**: Enter the following commands to configure interVLAN routing on a router:

```
Router(config)# interface G0/0
Router(config-if)# ip address <ip address> <subnet mask>
Router(config-if)# no shutdown
Switch(config-if)# exit
Router(config)# interface G0/1
Router(config-if)# ip address <ip address> <subnet mask>
Router(config-if)# no shutdown
Router(config-if)# exit
Router(config)# end
Router# copy running-config startup-config
```

- **Showing the routing table**: Enter the following command to show the routing table on a router:

```
Router# show ip route
```

Router-on-a-stick interVLAN configuration

Unlike legacy interVLAN routing, the **router-on-a-stick** scenario (see *Figure 6.8*) of the interVLAN routing concept uses a different approach to enable communication among VLANs. The router establishes a trunk link with the switch where the VLANs are configured. Then, on a router side, the subinterfaces are configured with an appropriate IP address in a way that each subinterface represents a separate subnet, maps a specific VLAN, and tags a frame for the VLANs. In addition, it requires assigning the IP addresses in PCs' interfaces according to the corresponding subnets of the subinterfaces where they do belong.

After all that configuration, the router can then perform communication among VLANs by traversing the trunk link. In this section, router-on-a-stick interVLAN routing on a Cisco router is explained:

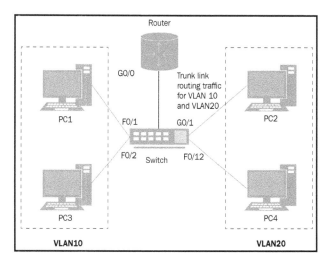

Figure 6.8. Router-in-a-stick interVLAN routing

The following represents the configurations on a router, as well as displaying the routing table on a router. To configure a switch and to verify the VLAN information on a switch, see the section *Configuring router-on-a-stick interVLAN routing,* Chapter 4, *Setting up the Switch:*

- **Router configuration**: Enter the following commands to configure router-on-a-stick interVLAN routing on a router:

```
Router(config)# interface G0/0.10
Router(config-subif)# encapsulation dot1q 10
Router(config-subif)# ip address <ip address> <subnet mask>
Switch(config-subif)# exit
Router(config)# interface G0/0.20
Router(config-subif)# encapsulation dot1q 20
Router(config-subif)# ip address <ip address> <subnet mask>
Router(config-subif)# exit
Router(config)# interface G0/0
Router(config-if)# no shutdown
Router(config-if)# end
Router# copy running-config startup-config
```

- **Showing the routing table**: Enter the following command to show the routing table on a router:

```
Router# show ip route
```

Summary

We summarize the chapter with the following points:

- Routers use LED indicators to provide a way to monitor their activity and performance.
- After connecting the router to a PC, plug in the power cable and press the power switch on to power up the router.
- To connect a router to a PC, a rollover console cable and a DB9 serial port on the PC are needed.
- A USB-to-DB9 adapter in combination with a rollover console represents an alternative solution for connecting the router to the PC.
- A terminal emulator program like PuTTY is required for establishing a connection with a router.
- User EXEC Mode [Router>] enables access to only a limited number of basic monitoring commands.
- Privileged EXEC Mode [Router#] enables access to all monitoring, configuration, and management commands.
- Global Configuration Mode [Router(config)#] provides root access to a router.
- Line Configuration Mode [Router(config-line)#] enables users to configure management features.
- Interface Configuration Mode [Router(config-if)#] enables users to configure routers' interfaces.
- It is recommended to run an initial configuration on a router when the router is taken out of the box, or when the startup configuration has been reloaded.
- The routing table contains routes to directly connected networks and remotely connected networks.
- The network administrator enters routes into the router's routing table manually.
- Dynamic routing protocols update the routes dynamically into the router's routing table.

- The Routing Information Protocol (RIP) is a dynamic routing protocol that enables routers to exchange routing information.
- RIP is IETF's oldest distance vector protocol that, in every 30 seconds, exchanges routing information with the other routers in a network topology based on distance (hop count) and direction (next-hop).
- RIP comes in two versions: **RIPv1**, defined by IETF's RFC 1058, and as **RIPv2**, defined by IETF's RFC 1723.
- Nowadays, RIP is rarely used, thus it can be said that it has been replaced by OSPF.
- In legacy interVLAN routing, the router has multiple interfaces where each interface connects to a certain VLAN.
- In router-on-a-stick interVLAN routing, the router establishes a trunk link with the switch where the VLANs are configured.

Questions

1. It is recommended to run initial configuration on a router when the router is taken out of the box. (True | False)
2. To establish connection between the PC and the switch, an emulator program such as_____ is required.
3. Which of the following commands provides access to Privileged EXEC Mode? (Choose two.)
    1. Router> **enable**
    2. Router> **en**
    3. Router> **enable EXEC**
    4. Router> **en EXEC**
4. The Routing Information Protocol (RIP) is a dynamic routing protocol that enables routers to exchange routing information. (True | False)
5. _____ enables users to configure management features. The prompt looks like `Router(config-line)#`.

6. Which of the following commands configures a static host route on a router?
   1. Router(config)# **ip route** *<destination-host-ip-address> <subnet-mask> <ip-address>*
   2. Router(config)# **ip route** *<destination-host-ip-address> <subnet-mask> <exit-interface>*
   3. Router(config)# **ip route** *<destination-host-ip-address> <subnet-mask> <administrative-distance>*
   4. Router(config)# **ip route** *<destination-host-ip-address> <subnet-mask> <source-host-ip-address>*

7. The Interface Configuration Mode prevents users from configuring the router's interfaces. The prompt looks like Switch(config-if)#. (True | False)

8. The _____ contain routes to directly connected network and remotely connected networks.

9. Which of the following commands provides access to configuration mode? (Choose two)
   1. Router# **configure global**
   2. Router# **config g**
   3. Router# **configure terminal**
   4. Router# **config t**

10. User EXEC Mode enables access to only a limited number of basic monitoring commands (Router>). (True | False)

11. Router(config)# _____ command is used to enable RIP on a router.

12. Which of the following commands is used to enable IPv6 routing on a router?
    1. Router(config)# **ipv6 unicast-routing**
    2. Router(config)# **ipv6 multicast-routing**
    3. Router(config)# **ipv6 anycast-routing**
    4. Router(config)# **ipv6 broadcast-routing**

13. The DB9 serial port on the PC and rollover console cable are needed to physically connect the PC with the router. (True | False)

14. _____ the router has multiple interfaces where each interface connects to a certain VLAN.

15. Which of the following commands are used to save running-configuration? (Choose two.)
    1. Router# **copy running-config startup-config**
    2. Router# **copy run start**
    3. Router# **copy start run**
    4. Router# **copy startup-config running-config**

7
Networking Services and Maintenance

This chapter is designed to teach you about various networking technologies. By getting to understand the important role of each and every networking technology in a computer network, as a network administrator, you will be able to orientate the network to serve the business. That said, this chapter is designed to provide you with a brief introduction to what DHCP, NAT, NTP, CDP and LLDP, and Syslog are, and step-by-step instructions for configuring them. In addition, this chapter explores device maintenance considerations, such as backing up and restoring configuration files and IOS software images. This enables you to react in a timely manner, thus consolidating networking services in an organization. Further, this chapter explains the licensing process that encompasses activities from purchasing a device to installing a license. Then, the chapter gives a clear explanation of the importance of network traffic management. Finally, the chapter concludes with a summary and chapter questions.

In this chapter, we will cover the following topics:

- DHCP overview
- NAT overview
- NTP overview
- CDP and LLDP overview
- Syslog overview
- Device maintenance
- Traffic management

Dynamic Host Configuration Protocol overview

As you know, the **Dynamic Host Configuration Protocol (DHCP)** is a protocol that dynamically assigns IP addresses to devices on a network. This makes it clear that DHCP is a network service that works in client/server architectures where clients request services, and servers respond back with services. Naturally, a DHCP service in such a networked environment is named a **DHCP server**. With that being said, this section discusses DHCP servers from the perspective of the Cisco router.

Assigning IPv4 addresses dynamically

As the name implies, a **DHCPv4 server** dynamically assigns IPv4 addresses to devices. Usually, IP addresses that are assigned to devices are located in the **DHCP pool**. Since these IP addresses have a defined period, they are named **leased IP addresses**. After the lease expires, the DHCP client must ask for another IPv4 address. It often happens that the same IP address is being reassigned. That is known as **IP address renewal**. Certainly, a DHCP server makes the IP address assignment process extremely quick and easy for the network administrator.

Discovery, Offer, Request, and Acknowledgment (DORA) explains how DHCP works. It means, and it goes as follows:

1. In a computer network, when a computer is turned on and the operating system boots up, the DHCP client service broadcasts the request for an IP address. In fact, the request known as **DHCPDISCOVER** represents an attempt to identify a DHCP server in LAN. If there is a DHCP server available, it accepts the **DHCPDISCOVER** message from the client and reserves an IP address.

2. Next, the DHCP server responds to the client's request with the **DHCPOFFER** message, which contains an IP address and associated elements, such as a subnet mask, default gateway, lease time, and the DHCP server's IP address.

3. Once this offer is received by the client, the client sends a **DHCPREQUEST** message to DHCP server confirming the interest for the offered IP address.

4. On the server side, as soon as the **DHCPREQUEST** message reaches the DHCP server, the **ACKNOWLEDGMENT** is initiated in order to respond back to the client with the **DHCPPACK** message, which contains the previously mentioned elements requested by the client. This then concludes the assignment of an IP address to a DHCP client by the DHCP server.

Configuring DHCPv4

In this section, you will learn the commands to configure DHCPv4 on a router:

- Enter the following command to exclude a single IP address on a router:

    ```
    Router(config)# ip dhcp excluded-address <ip-address>
    ```

- Enter the following command to exclude a range of IP addresses on a router:

    ```
    Router(config)# ip dhcp excluded-address <low-address> <high-address>
    ```

- Enter the following command to configure a DHCP pool on a router:

    ```
    Router(config)# ip dhcp pool <pool-name>
    Router(dhcp-config)#
    ```

- Enter the following command to configure a network for a DHCP server on a router:

    ```
    Router(dhcp-config)# network <network-address> <subnet-mask>
    ```

- Enter the following command to configure a default gateway for a DHCP server on a router:

    ```
    Router(dhcp-config)# default-router <ip-address>
    ```

- Enter the following command to configure a DNS server for a DHCP server on a router:

    ```
    Router(dhcp-config)# dns-server <dns-server-address>
    ```

- Enter the following command to configure a domain name for a DHCP server on a router:

    ```
    Router(dhcp-config)# domain-name <domain-name>
    ```

- Enter the following command to show the IP address to MAC address bindings that have been provided by the DHCP server on a router:

    ```
    Router# show ip dhcp binding
    ```

- Enter the following commands to configure an IP helper address to enable a router to forward DHCP broadcasts to the DHCP server on a router:

```
Router(config)# interface <interface-id>
Router(config-if)# ip helper-address <ip-address>
Router(config-if)# exit
```

- Enter the following commands to configure a router as a DHCP client:

```
Router(config)# interface <interface-id>
Router(config-if)# ip address dhcp
Router(config-if)# no shutdown
```

 You can learn more about DHCPv4 from `http://www.ciscopress.com/articles/article.asp?p=330807seqNum=8`.

Assigning IPv6 addresses dynamically

Just to remind you, unlike IPv4 addresses, which are 32-bits long, IPv6 addresses are 128-bits long. Can you imagine how difficult it would be to manually assign IPv6 addresses on the organization's network devices? To simplify and automate it at the same time, just as with IPv4 addresses, IPv6 global unicast addresses can be assigned dynamically too. With that in mind, the following details the methods for dynamically assigning IPv6 global unicast addresses to devices:

- **Stateless Address Autoconfiguration** (**SLAAC**) is a method that assigns IPv6 address devices without the need for a DHCPv6 server. It is based on the ICMPv6 protocol; thus, it uses **Router Solicitation** (**RS**) and **Router Advertisement** (**RA**) messages to provide addressing and other configuration information to devices. An RS message is a multicast address, FF02::2, sent by the client to routers, whereas an RA message is a multicast address, FF02::1, sent every 200 seconds by routers to clients. The RA message contains a prefix and a prefix length which are used by the client to create its own IPv6 global unicast address.
- **Stateless DHCPv6** is a hybrid method in which the client uses the information in the RA message for addressing, while configuration information is obtained from the DHCPv6 server. Usually the list of DNS server IPv6 addresses is obtained from the DHCPv6 server. It should be noted that the DHCPv6 server does not handle the list of available and allocated IPv6 addresses because the DHCPv6 server only provides configuration information to the client and not IPv6 addresses. Hence, this method is named **stateless DHCPv6**.

- **Stateful DHCPv6** is the method that is similar to the DHCPv4 server. The DHCPv6 server is responsible for assigning IPv6 global unicast addresses to clients. Thus, clients obtain both addressing information and configuration information from the DHCPv6 server. It is worth mentioning that it is the task of the RA message to inform the client not to use the information in the RA message. Therefore, it is named stateful DHCPv6 because DHCPv6 servers handle the list of available and allocated IPv6 addresses and the configuration information.

Configuring stateless DHCPv6

In this section, you will learn the commands to configure stateless DHCPv6 on a router:

- Enter the following command to configure IPv6 routing on a router:

```
Router(config)# ipv6 unicast-routing
```

- Enter the following command to configure a stateless DHCPv6 server pool on a router:

```
Router(config)# ipv6 dhcp pool <pool-name>
Router(config-dhcpv6)#
```

- Enter the following command to configure a DNS server for stateless DHCPv6 server on a router:

```
Router(config-dhcpv6)# dns-server <dns-server-address>
```

- Enter the following command to configure a domain name for stateless DHCPv6 server on a router:

```
Router(config-dhcpv6)# domain-name <domain-name>
```

- Enter the following commands to configure the stateless DHCPv6 server interface on a router:

```
Router(config)# interface <interface-id>
Router(config-if)# ipv6 dhcp pool <pool-name>
Router(config-if)# ipv6 nd other-config-flag
```

- Enter the following command to show the name of the stateless DHCPv6 server pool and its parameters on a router:

```
Router# show ipv6 dhcp pool
```

- Enter the following commands to configure a router as a stateless DHCP client:

```
Router(config)# interface <interface-id>
Router(config-if)# ipv6 enable
Router(config-if)# ipv6 address autoconfig
```

Configuring Stateful DHCPv6

In this section, you will learn the commands to configure stateful DHCPv6 on a router.

- Enter the following command to configure a stateful DHCPv6 server pool on a router:

```
Router(config)# ipv6 dhcp pool <pool-name>
```

- Enter the following commands to configure stateful pool parameters for DHCPv6 server on a router:

```
Router(config-dhcpv6)# address prefix <prefix-length> <lifetime>
Router(config-dhcpv6)# dns-server <dns-server-address>
```

- Enter the following commands to configure the stateful DHCPv6 server interface on a router:

```
Router(config)# interface <interface-id>
Router(config-if)# ipv6 dhcp pool <pool-name>
Router(config-if)# ipv6 nd managed-config-flag
```

- Enter the following command to show the automatic binding between the client's link-local address and the address assigned by the stateful DHCPv6 serve on a router:

```
Router# show ipv6 dhcp binding
```

- Enter the following commands to configure a router as a stateful DHCP client:

```
Router(config)# interface <interface-id>
Router(config-if)# ipv6 enable
Router(config-if)# ipv6 address dhcp
```

 You can learn about DHCPv6 from https://www.cisco.com/c/en/us/td/docs/ios-xml/ios/ipaddr_dhcp/configuration/xe-16/dhcp-xe-16-book/ip6-dhcp-stateless-auto.html.

Network Address Translator overview

In the *IPv4 network addresses* section of, `Chapter 2`, *Communication in Computer Networks,* it is said that the total number of IPv4 addresses is $2^{32} = 4,294,967,296$. Comparing that with the world population, it is obvious that nearly 3 billion IP addresses are missing if a single IPv4 address is assigned to every person on the planet. That was a sign that the **Internet Engineering Task Force (IETF)** should do something to overcome the problem of exhaustion of the IPv4 address space. In light of that, the **Request for Comment (RFC) 1918** document was created, which precisely specified the IP address ranges for private use. That enabled the birth of the **Network Address Translator (NAT)**. As the name suggests, NAT translates private IPv4 addresses to public IPv4 addresses. In fact, private IP addresses as specified by the document RFC 1918 cannot be routed on the internet. As such, a NAT is required so that private IPv4 addresses can be translated to IPv4 public addresses thus being able to route on the internet. This way, the NAT enables a single public address to be shared by many devices each configured with an IPv4 address. Usually, the NAT is deployed on the border of a stub network. A **stub network** is a network that has one way to enter the network and another way to exits the network. Thus, the benefits of the NAT, such as preserving public IPv4 addresses and providing network security by hiding the private network from the internet, have paid the price of performance degradation, and loss of end-to-end IP tracking. No matter how useful the NAT proved to be, it remains an interim solution until IPv6 gets in charge to roam the internet.

Although from its definition the NAT may seem easy to understand, its topology indicates that NAT can be complicated too. That is evidenced by the different names that NAT uses to refer to the addresses:

- From the perspective of the device with the translated address:
    - **Inside local address** is the address of the device that is being translated by the NAT
    - **Inside global address** is the address of the inside interface of the NAT-enabled router
- From the perspective of the device that provides the NAT:
    - **Outside local address** is the address of the NAT-enabled router that connects the LAN
    - **Outside global address** is the address of the NAT-enabled router that connects to internet

Regarding how NAT operates, the following types of translations are taking place:

- **One-to-one translation**, known also as **static address translation** (**static NAT**), translates a private IPv4 address to a public IPv4 address. This type of NAT employs a static public IPv4 address.
- **Many-to-many translation**, known also as **dynamic address translation** (**dynamic NAT**), translates multiple private IPv4 addresses to multiple public IPv4 addresses. This type of NAT employs a pool of public IPv4 addresses.
- **Many-to-one translation**, known also as **dynamic NAT with overloading**, translates multiple private IPv4 addresses to a single public IPv4 address. This type of NAT employs ports; thus, it is known as **Port Address Translation** (**PAT**).

Configuring static NAT

In this section, you will learn the commands to configure static NAT on a router:

- Enter the following commands to configure static NAT on a router:

```
Router(config)# ip nat inside source static <local-ip> <global-ip>
Router(config)# interface <interface-id>
Router(config-if)# ip nat inside
Router(config-if)# exit
Router(config)# interface <interface-id>
Router(config-if)# ip nat outside
```

- Enter the following command to show the NAT translations on a router:

```
Router# show ip nat translations
```

- Enter the following command to show the NAT statistics on a router:

```
Router# show ip nat statistics
```

Configuring dynamic NAT

In this section, you will learn the commands to configure dynamic NAT on a router. Enter the following commands to configure the dynamic NAT on a router:

```
Router(config)# ip nat pool <name> <start-ip> <end-ip> <netmask>
Router(config)# access-list <access-list-number> permit <source-
wildcard>
Router(config)# ip nat inside source list <access-list-number> pool
```

```
<name>
Router(config)# interface <interface-id>
Router(config-if)# ip nat inside
Router(config-if)# exit
Router(config)# interface <interface-id>
Router(config-if)# ip nat outside
```

Configuring PAT

In this section, you will learn the commands to configure PAT on a router. Enter the following commands to configure PAT for a single public IPv4 address on a router:

```
Router(config)# access-list <access-list-number> permit <source-wildcard>
Router(config)# ip nat inside source list <access-list-number> interface <interface-id> overload
Router(config)# interface <interface-id>
Router(config-if)# ip nat inside
Router(config-if)# exit
Router(config)# interface <interface-id>
Router(config-if)# ip nat outside
```

Configuring port forwarding

In this section, you will learn the commands to configure port forwarding on a router. Enter the following commands to configure port forwarding on a router:

```
Router(config)# ip nat inside source static <tcp-or-udp> <local-ip local-port> <global-ip global-port> [extendable]
Router(config)# interface <interface-id>
Router(config-if)# ip nat inside
Router(config-if)# exit
Router(config)# interface <interface-id>
Router(config-if)# ip nat outside
```

NAT and IPv6

Referring to the statement in the *IPv6 network addresses* section of, `Chapter 2`, *Communication in Computer Networks*, that unlike IPv4, IPv6 is a 128-bit address that in total generates 340 undecillion addresses, then instantly you think that IPv6 does not need NAT! Sure, that stands true; however, although IPv6 has been designed to remove NAT from the IP addressing stage, again there is a NAT implementation form in IPv6. Just like IPv4, IPv6 has its private address space too, known as **Unique Local Addresses (ULA)** (for more on ULA, see, *Unique local addresses* section of, `Chapter 2`, *Communication in Computer Networks*) as defined by RFC 4193 that are mainly used for communications within a local site. NAT in IPv6 does not play the role of translating private addresses into public addresses; instead, it is exclusively used for migrating from IPv4 to IPv6. One such example is NAT64, which enables a mapping between the IPv6 and the IPv4 addresses.

 You can learn more about NAT from `http://www.ciscopress.com/articles/article.asp?p=25273seqNum=4`.

Network Time Protocol overview

To understand the importance of time synchronization between networking devices, we need to think about monetary transactions, video surveillance, broadcasting shows, and other activities that are time dependent. Thus, **Network Time Protocol (NTP)** is another protocol of the TCP/IP protocol suite that enables time synchronization among networking devices. Both Cisco switches and routers are equipped with a software clock that starts when IOS boots up; however, as a network grows, it becomes difficult for the network administrator to maintain time synchronization among all networking devices in an organization's infrastructure. So, as is DHCP to clients, so NTP is to networking devices when it comes to time synchronization. Thereby, scheduled tasks, jobs, and events will get executed smoothly and in a timely manner. Usually, there are two methods to configure date and time on switches and routers:

- **Manually** by configuring each network device separately
- **Dynamically** using an NTP server locally or on the internet

When it comes to NTP server deployment, their topology is hierarchical, meaning that it is organized into levels where each level is named a **stratum** and is accompanied by a number that identifies its level. In general, levels or stratums have numbers from 0 to 16, where the largest numbers represent the lowest levels in the hierarchy of stratums, unlike small numbers, which represent the highest levels. For example, in the case of several NTP servers in a network infrastructure, stratum 0 represents the authoritative time source in the NTP topology to whom the stratum 1 devices are connected. Similarly, stratum 2 devices are connected to stratum 1 devices, then stratum 3 devices are connected to stratum 2 devices, and so on. That, however, reminds you of a distributed system. Knowing that the maximum hop count is 15, then stratum 16, the lowest stratum level, represents an unsynchronized device.

Configuring and verifying NTP

In this section, you will learn the commands to configure and verify NTP on a router:

- Enter the following commands to configure the router to use an NTP server:

```
Router(config)# ntp server <ip-address>
Router(config)# exit
```

- Enter the following commands to configure time zone on a router:

```
Router(config)# clock timezone <name-of-time-zone>
Router(config)# exit
```

- Enter the following command to show the current time on a router:

```
Router# show clock
```

- Enter the following command to show the NTP status on a router:

```
Router# show ntp status
```

- Enter the following command to show that the router is synchronized with an NTP server:

```
Router# show ntp associations
```

You can learn more about NTP from http://www.galsys.co.uk/news/what-is-ntp-time-and-how-does-it-benefit-me/.

Cisco Discovery Protocol and Link-Layer Discovery Protocol overview

It is apparent that both the **Cisco Discovery Protocol** (**CDP**) and **Link Layer Discovery Protocol** (**LLDP**) operate on OSI Layer 2 and have to do with discovering neighbor devices. However, CDP is a Cisco proprietary protocol, while LLDP is a vendor-neutral protocol. In addition, CDP is enabled by default on Cisco devices, where as LLDP is required to be enabled. This section describes how to configure both CDP and LLDP on Cisco switches.

Device discovery with CDP

Obviously, since it is developed by Cisco, CDP runs on all Cisco devices. CDP periodically sends advertisements out of all ports to connected devices. These advertisements contain information, such as the name of the neighbor device, the local port and the remote port, the type of the neighbor device, and the hardware platform of the neighbor device. That type of information is very useful for documenting the network topology:

- Enter the following commands to enable CDP globally on a switch:

```
Switch(config)# cdp run
Switch(config)# exit
Switch#
```

- Enter the following commands to disable CDP globally on a switch:

```
Switch(config)# no cdp run
Switch(config)# exit
Switch#
```

- Enter the following commands to enable CDP on a specific interface on a switch:

```
Switch(config)# interface <interface-ID>
Switch(config-if)# cdp enable
Switch(config-if)# exit
Switch(config)#
```

- Enter the following commands to disable CDP on a specific interface on a switch:

```
Switch(config)# interface <interface-ID>
Switch(config-if)# no cdp enable
Switch(config-if)# exit
Switch(config)#
```

- Enter the following command to show the status of CDP and information about CDP on a switch:

```
Switch# show cdp
```

- Enter the following command to show the status of CDP and the list of neighbors on a switch:

```
Switch# show cdp neighbors
```

- Enter the following command to show the status of CDP and the detailed list of neighbors on a switch:

```
Switch# show cdp neighbors detail
```

- Enter the following command to show the interfaces that are CDP enabled on a device on a switch:

```
Switch# show cdp interface
```

 You can learn more about CDP from `https://learningnetwork.cisco.com/docs/DOC-26872`.

Device discovery with LLDP

Although LLDP is vendor neutral, it is supported by Cisco devices. Like CDP, LLDP operates on routers, switches, and access points. Thus, in devices where LLDP is enabled, the **LLDP agent** is installed. Then, that agent sends advertisements out of all ports either at certain times or whenever changes occur:

- Enter the following commands to enable LLDP globally on a switch:

```
Switch(config)# lldp run
Switch(config)# exit
Switch#
```

- Enter the following commands to disable LLDP globally on a switch:

```
Switch(config)# no lldp run
Switch(config)# exit
Switch#
```

- Enter the following commands to enable LLDP on a specific interface on a switch:

```
Switch(config)# interface <interface-ID>
Switch(config-if)# lldp transmit
Switch(config-if)# lldp receive
Switch(config-if)# exit
Switch(config)#
```

- Enter the following commands to disable LLDP on a specific interface on a switch:

```
Switch(config)# interface <interface-ID>
Switch(config-if)# no lldp transmit
Switch(config-if)# no lldp receive
Switch(config-if)# exit
Switch(config)#
```

- Enter the following command to show the status of LLDP and information about LLDP on a switch:

```
Switch# show lldp
```

- Enter the following command to show the status of LLDP and the list of neighbors on a switch:

```
Switch# show lldp neighbors
```

- Enter the following command to show the status of LLDP and the detailed list of neighbors on a switch:

```
Switch# show lldp neighbors detail
```

 You can learn more about LLDP from https://learningnetwork.cisco.com/docs/DOC-26851.

System logging overview

From routine operations to degradation of network performance, from alerts about disruption of services to failure of device—all are events that can occur in the network infrastructure. Therefore, network administrators must have the right tools to be alerted to these events. For that reason, tools such as logs and alerts play an important role in that process. While logs are useful for detailed analysis and archiving of records, alerts enable you to be vigilant about the performance and configuration of the networking devices. With that in mind, **system logging** is a standard that records events in the network in general, and on servers, clients, and network devices in particular. Meanwhile, syslog is a protocol that enables access to system logging events as specified by the IETF's RFC 3164. Syslog operates on a client/server network architecture and uses UDP port 514 for transporting notifications about occurred events to a certain syslog server. From the severity point of view, syslog messages can be informative, alarming, and critical.

As far as Cisco equipment is concerned, both switches and routers support syslog and are capable to communicate with the syslog server. Usually, switches and routers send the system messages to the local logging process, and from there to the syslog server based on device configurations. It is up to network administrator to specify what messages are distributed where and how they are handled. In general, the collected logs in a syslog server can be used for later analysis and report generation. Regarding the syslog server, a syslog application should be installed in a workstation or a server in a network.

The syslog application can be a freeware (see Figure 7.1.) or shareware version from the internet, or an enterprise version with purchase:

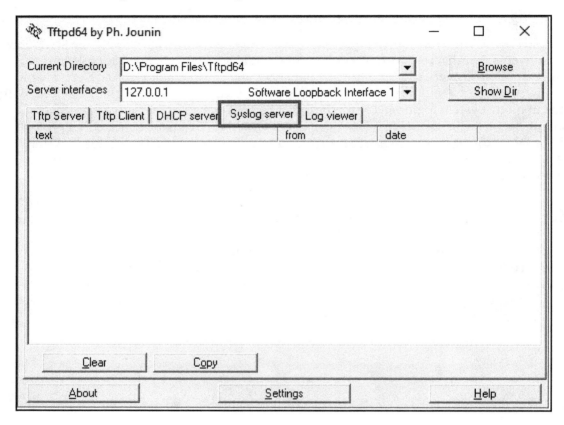

Figure 7.1. TFTPD32 is a freeware syslog app

 You can download the TFTPD32 freeware app from `http://tftpd32.jounin.net/tftpd32_download.html`.

Configuring syslog

To record an event, the time factor plays an important role. That is because most of the network services are time dependent. Therefore, depending on the complexity of the network infrastructure, many organizations prefer to have an NTP server (see Figure 7.2) in their infrastructure. That being said, the NTP server maintains the source of time synchronization with switches and routers, thus enabling networking devices to record events at due time and to send their timestamps with the logs to the **Syslog server**:

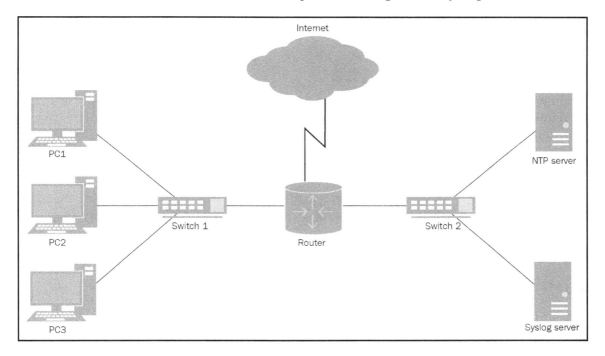

Figure 7.2. Syslog server in action

The steps required for configuring the syslog are as follows:

- Enter the following command to configure the router to use the syslog server:

    ```
    Router(config)# logging <hostname_or_IPv4>
    ```

- Enter the following command to control the messages that will be sent to the syslog server:

    ```
    Router(config)# logging trap <level>
    ```

- Enter the following command to configure the source interface on a router:

```
Router(config)# logging source-interface <interface_id>
```

- Enter the following command to configure a `loopback 0` interface on a router:

```
Router(config)# interface loopback 0
```

- Enter the following command to show messages that are logged on a router:

```
Router# show logging
```

Device maintenance

There is a saying: *prevention is better than a cure*. If you apply that to networking devices, then you will be able to understand the importance of device maintenance. **Device maintenance** is an ongoing activity that helps preventing problems from turning into costly problems, both time and business wise. As such, it requires dedication and patience from network administrators. Thus, in order to have productive device maintenance, a clear plan with the right tools is required. Hence, device maintenance includes activities such as backing up Cisco IOS images and configuration files in a safe location and keeping the IOS images up to date. In this section, file maintenance, image management, and software licensing are covered.

Router and switch file maintenance

As you know, the IOS is a CLI-based operating system. So, if you have experience with a **Disk Operating System (DOS)**, Windows PowerShell, or Linux Shells, then you will have no hurdles doing file maintenance both in routers and switches. As in the aforementioned environments, in Cisco **IOS File System (IFS)**, you can navigate to different directories and list the files in a directory. In addition, you can create subdirectories both in flash memory or on disk.

 You can learn about how to move around the Cisco IFS, how to create folders, copy files, and create/extract TAR files from `https://networklessons.com/cisco/ccna-routing-switching-icnd1-100-105/cisco-ios-filesystem/`.

Router file systems

In this section, you will learn the commands to navigate around a router's file systems:

- Enter the following command to show the amount of available and free memory, the type of file system, and its permissions on a router, as shown in *Figure 7.3*:

      Router# **show file systems**

```
Router#show file systems
File Systems:

            Size(b)        Free(b)      Type   Flags  Prefixes
  *       255744000      221896413      disk     rw   flash0: flash:#
           262136         255005        nvram    rw   nvram:
```

Figure 7.3. The output from the show file system command on a router

From *Figure 7.3*, note the rw permission both for Flash and NVRAM. It means that you can read the content from both Flash and NVRAM, as well as write on Flash and NVRAM. Other permissions to consider are ro, read only, and, wo, write only. Another important element from the *Figure 7.3* is an asterisk sign, *, which precedes the Flash file system and the pound sign, #, that is appended to the flash listing. These indicate that a bootable IOS is located in Flash and that the Flash is acting as a bootable disk.

- Enter the following command to show the content of Flash on a router, as shown in *Figure 7.4*:

      Router# **dir**

```
Router#dir
Directory of flash0:/

   3  -rw-     33591768      <no date>  c2900-universalk9-mz.SPA.151-4.M4.bin
   2  -rw-        28282      <no date>  sigdef-category.xml
   1  -rw-       227537      <no date>  sigdef-default.xml

255744000 bytes total (221896413 bytes free)
```

Figure 7.4. The output from the **dir** command on a router

From Figure 7.4, among several files that are located in Flash, it is obvious that the current Cisco IOS file image is running in RAM.

- Enter the following commands to show the content of NVRAM on a router, as shown in Figure 7.4:

```
Router# cd nvram:
Router# pwd
nvram:/
Router# dir
```

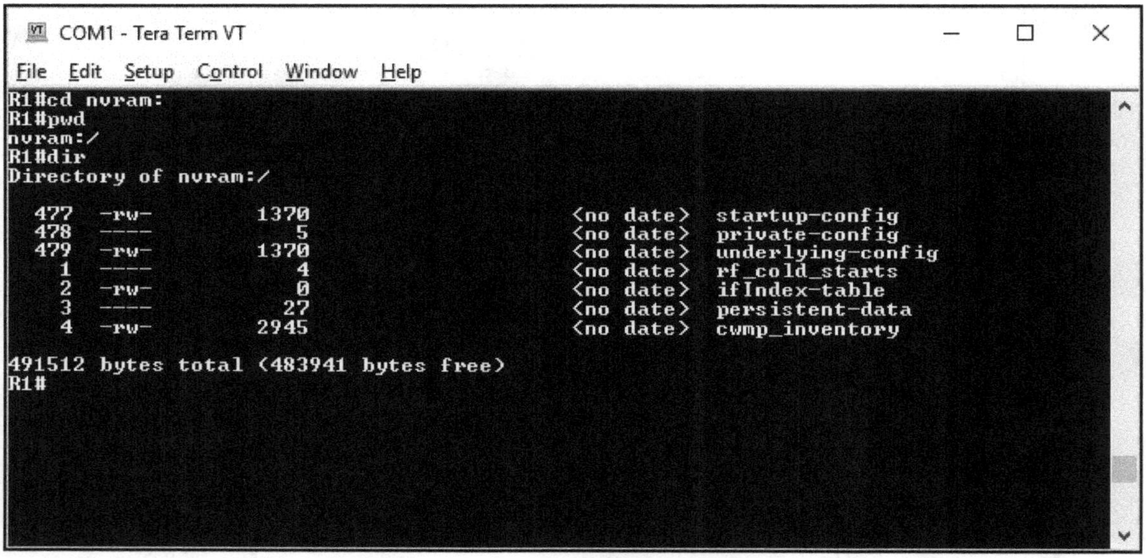

Figure 7.5. Showing the content of NVRAM on a router

Since Flash is the current default filesystem then use the change directory, `cd`, command to locate NVRAM. Next, enter the present working directory `pwd`, command to ensure that NVRAM is the directory we are viewing. Afterward, just as with the listing of Flash content, enter the `dir` command to show the content of NVRAM.

Switch file systems

In this section, you will learn the commands to navigate around a switch's filesystems:

- Enter the following command to show the amount of available and free memory, the type of filesystem, and its permissions on a switch, as shown in Figure 7.6:

    Switch# **show file systems**

```
Switch#show file systems
File Systems:

             Size(b)        Free(b)      Type    Flags   Prefixes
  *         64016384       55098373      flash     rw     flash:
              29688          23590       nvram     rw     nvram:
```

Figure 7.6. The output from the show file system command on a switch

- Enter the following command to show the content of Flash on a switch, as shown in Figure 7.7:

    Switch# **dir**

```
Switch#dir
Directory of flash:/

    3   -rw-     8662192        <no date>   c3560-advipservicesk9-mz.122-37.SE1.bin
    2   -rw-       28282        <no date>   sigdef-category.xml
    1   -rw-      227537        <no date>   sigdef-default.xml

64016384 bytes total (55098373 bytes free)
```

Figure 7.7. The output from the dir command on a switch

- Enter the following commands to show the content of NVRAM on a switch:

```
Switch# cd nvram:
Switch# pwd
nvram:/
Switch# dir
```

Backing up and restoring text files

This method of style is based on text capture using the **Tera Term** emulator, thus enabling configurations to be saved to a text file. To make such a backup, complete the following steps:

1. Connect your PC to a router over console cable.
2. Open the Tera Term emulator on your PC and establish a serial connection with a router.
3. Click on the **File** menu and select **Log...** as in Figure 7.8:

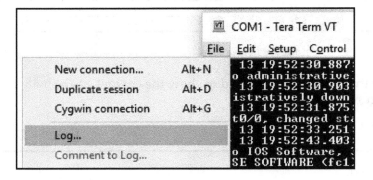

Figure 7.8. Selecting Log from the File menu

4. Specify the location where you want to save the file (see Figure 7.9). Make sure that the **Append** and **Plain text** options are selected. Next, click on the **Save** button. Soon after that, Tera Term begins capturing text:

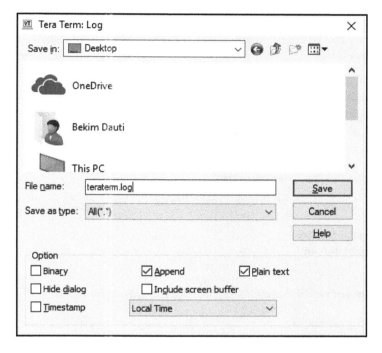

Figure 7.9. Saving the captured text

5. In the privileged EXEC prompt, enter the `show running-config` (or `show startup-config`) command and press *Enter*.

6. The Tera Term prompts through **Tera Term: Log** dialog box, as shown in Figure 7.10 when the capture is complete. Click on the **Close** button:

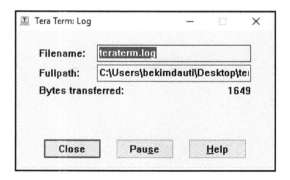

Figure 7.10. Tera Term: Log dialog box indicates that capturing text completed

7. Locate the folder where you have saved the text file and edit it with **Notepad**. Make sure to remove **--More--** and IOS messages, if any, and make sure the first row starts with `service timestamps debug datetime msec` (see Figure 7.11):

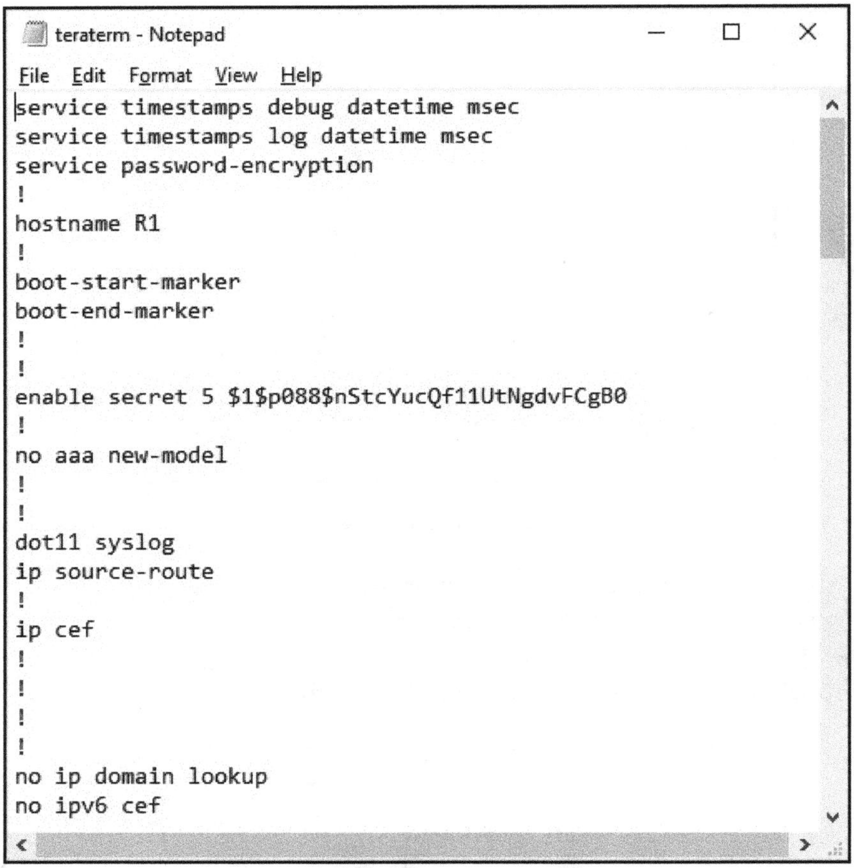

```
teraterm - Notepad                                    —    □    ×

File   Edit   Format   View   Help
service timestamps debug datetime msec
service timestamps log datetime msec
service password-encryption
!
hostname R1
!
boot-start-marker
boot-end-marker
!
!
enable secret 5 $1$p088$nStcYucQf11UtNgdvFCgB0
!
no aaa new-model
!
!
dot11 syslog
ip source-route
!
ip cef
!
!
!
!
no ip domain lookup
no ipv6 cef
```

Figure 7.11. Editing the captured text with Notepad

8. Save the edited text file with a descriptive name (for example, `R1-config-backup.txt`).

To restore the file back to a router, make sure to set it at the global configuration mode. It will enable the router to receive the commands from the text file sent by the Tera Term emulator. In addition, this is a convenient method to automate the router's basic configuration. To make such a restore, complete the following steps:

1. Click on the **File** menu and select **Send file...** as in Figure 7.12:

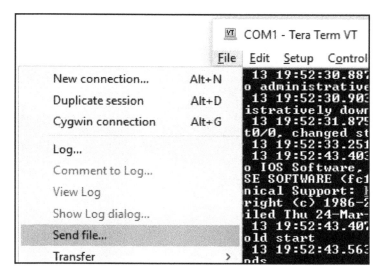

Figure 7.12. Sending commands from the text file to a router

2. Locate the folder and select the file that you want to send to a router (see Figure 7.13). Next, click on the **Open** button:

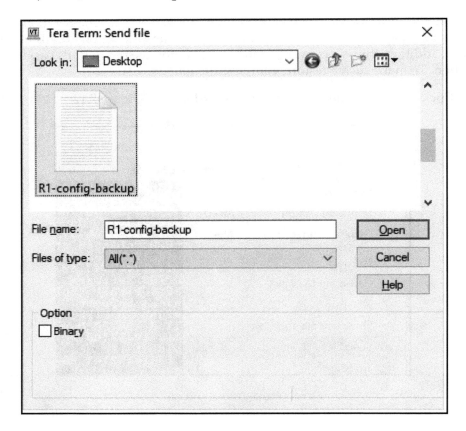

Figure 7.13. Selecting the file

3. Tera Term will display a progress bar of a transfer in a small dialog box, as shown in Figure 7.14. Next, click on the **Close** button when the transfer completes:

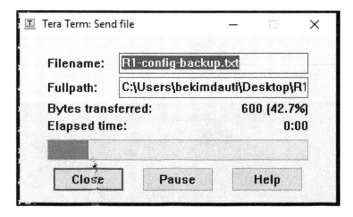

Figure 7.14. The progress bar of the file transferee

4. Enter the `copy running-config startup-config` command to save the running configuration to the startup configuration file and press *Enter*.
5. Make sure to verify the new running configuration.

Backing up and restoring to/from TFTP

To back up configuration files to a TFTP server, complete the following steps:

1. Download the TFTPD32 freeware from the internet and install it on a PC or server.
2. Connect your PC or server to a router over console cable.
3. Open **Tera Term** emulator on your PC and establish a serial connection with a router.

4. In the privileged EXEC prompt, enter the `copy running-config tftp:` (or `copy startup-config tftp:`) command (see Figure 7.15) and press *Enter*:

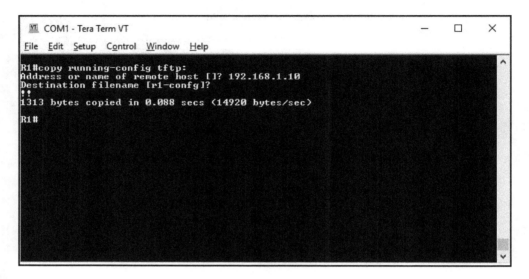

Figure 7.15. Backing up configuration files to a TFTP server

5. Provide the IP address or name of the remote host where you intend to back up the configuration files and press *Enter*.

6. Enter a descriptive name for your file backup and press *Enter*.

7. Soon after that, the configuration file gets copied to a TFTP server, as shown in Figures 7.16:

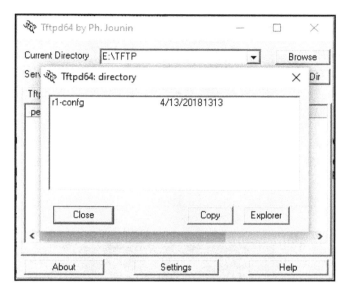

Figure 7.16. Backing up a configuration file on a TFTP server

8. Make sure to verify that a copied configuration file is stored in the right folder on the TFTP server as in Figure 7.17:

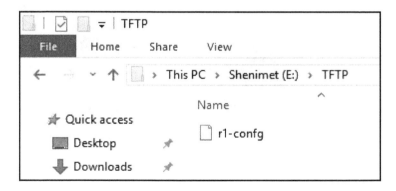

Figure 7.17. Verifying that a configuration file is stored into a folder on a TFTP server

B09348_07_17

To restore configuration files from a TFTP server, complete the following steps:

1. In the privileged EXEC prompt, enter the `copy tftp: running-config` (or `copy tftp: startup-config`) command and press *Enter*.
2. Provide the IP address or name of the remote host where the configuration files are stored and press *Enter*.
3. Enter a source file name for your backup file and press *Enter*.
4. Press *Enter* when you are asked about the destination file name.
5. Soon after that, the configuration file gets copied to a router, as shown in Figure 7.18:

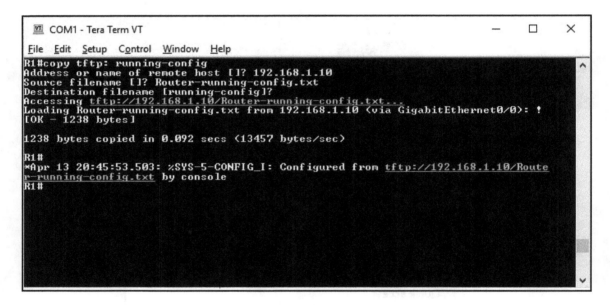

Figure 7.18. Restoring the configuration file from a TFTP server to a router

Using USB ports on a Cisco router

First things first: the USB flash drive is a secondary storage technology that can be plugged into and unplugged from the router while it is running. It is attached to a router using **Universal Serial Bus** (**USB**) ports, as shown in Figure 7.19, and can act as an additional boot device, as well as an optional secondary storage capability. That said, from IOS images to router's configurations, you can save them all on the USB flash drive:

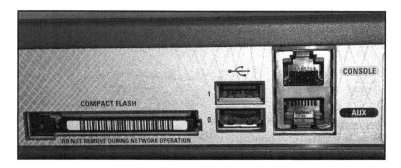

Figure 7.19. USB ports on a front panel of a router

It is important to know that before plugging the USB flash drive in a switch or router, it must be formatted with the **File Allocation Table** (**FAT**) filesystem. Otherwise, it will not be recognized. That way, when a USB flash drive is plugged, in the emulator's session window, a notification that a USB flash drive has been inserted in a device is displayed (see Figure 7.20):

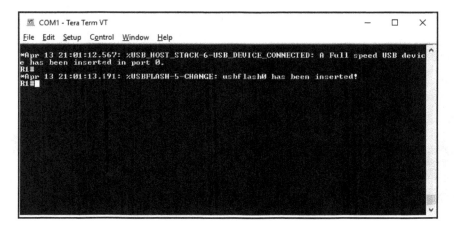

Figure 7.20. A switch or router notification upon inserting a USB flash drive

Enter the following command to list the content of USB flash drive on a router:

```
Router# dir usbflash0:
```

Backing up and restoring to/from a USB flash drive

In addition to a TFTP server, another way to back up the configuration files is to use a USB flash drive. To back up configuration files to the USB flash drive, complete the following steps:

1. Connect your PC to a router over console cable.
2. Open the Tera Term emulator on your PC and establish a serial connection with the router.
3. Format the USB flash drive with the FAT filesystem on your PC, and after removing it safely from the PC, try plugging it in the router.
4. Shortly afterwards, a message is displayed in Tera Term's session window that the USB drive has been inserted.
5. Next, in the privileged EXEC prompt, enter the show file systems command as in Figure 7.21 to verify that the USB flash drive is recognized by a router and press *Enter*:

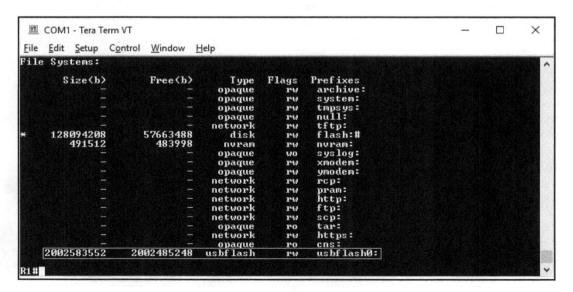

Figure 7.21. The USB flash drive is recognized by a router

6. Next, in the privileged EXEC prompt, enter the `copy running-config usbflash0:` (or `copy start-config usbflash0:`) command to save the configuration file to the USB flash drive (see Figure 7.22) and press *Enter*.

7. Enter a descriptive name (for example, `R1-running-config-backup.txt`) for the destination file and press *Enter*:

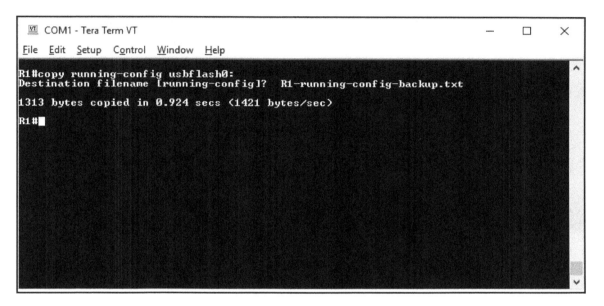

Figure 7.22. Saving the configuration file to the USB flash drive

8. Next, enter the `dir usbflash0:` command to verify that the configuration file has been copied to the USB flash drive, as shown in Figure 7.23, and press *Enter*:

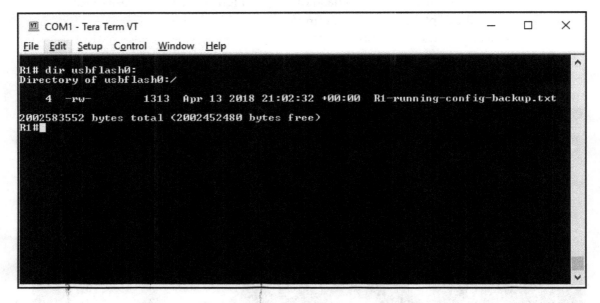

Figure 7.23. Verifying that the configuration file has been copied to the USB flash drive

To restore configuration files from the USB flash drive to a device, complete the following steps:

1. Remove the USB flash drive from a router and edit the text file with Notepad.
2. Make sure to remove the IOS messages right at the beginning of the file and add missing commands, such as no shutdown, whenever appropriate (see Figure 7.24):

Figure 7.24. Editing the configuration file with Notepad

3. Save changes and remove the USB flash drive from the PC safely.

4. Plug the USB flash drive into the router and in the privileged EXEC prompt, enter the `copy usbflash0:R1-running-config-backup.txt running-config` command to restore the configuration file from the USB flash drive to the router as shown in Figure 7.25, and press *Enter*.

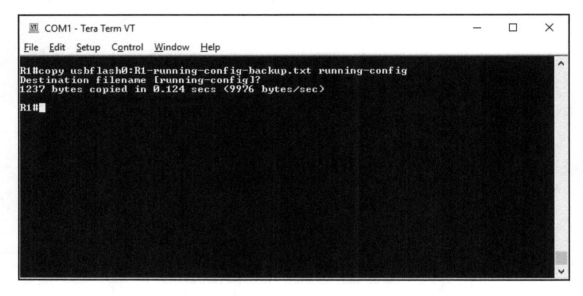

Figure 7.25. Restoring the configuration file from the USB flash drive to a router

Almost the same as the USB flash drive, you can use a compact flash card (see Figure 7.26) to back up and restore configuration files from/to a switch or router:

Figure 7.26. Compact flash card

Password recovery using ROMMON

As you might know, **ROM Monitor** (**ROMMON**) is a bootstrap program that helps initialize the processor and boot the IOS. Because it is a mini OS, it does not offer configuration options. Instead, every time you forget your password, it helps you recover it. In addition, it helps in downloading software over serial connection and upgrading the IOS on switches and routers. To recover the forgotten password, complete the following steps:

1. Connect your PC to a router over console cable.
2. Open the Tera Term emulator on your PC and establish a serial connection with the router.
3. While still consoled into the router, remove the power cord from the back of the router, and after 1 (one) minute, plug it in again.
4. As soon as you note the initialization of a router in the console session, issue a hard break (for Tera Term, press simultaneously *Alt* + *B*) to interrupt the router's normal boot process and enter ROMMON mode as in Figure 7.27:

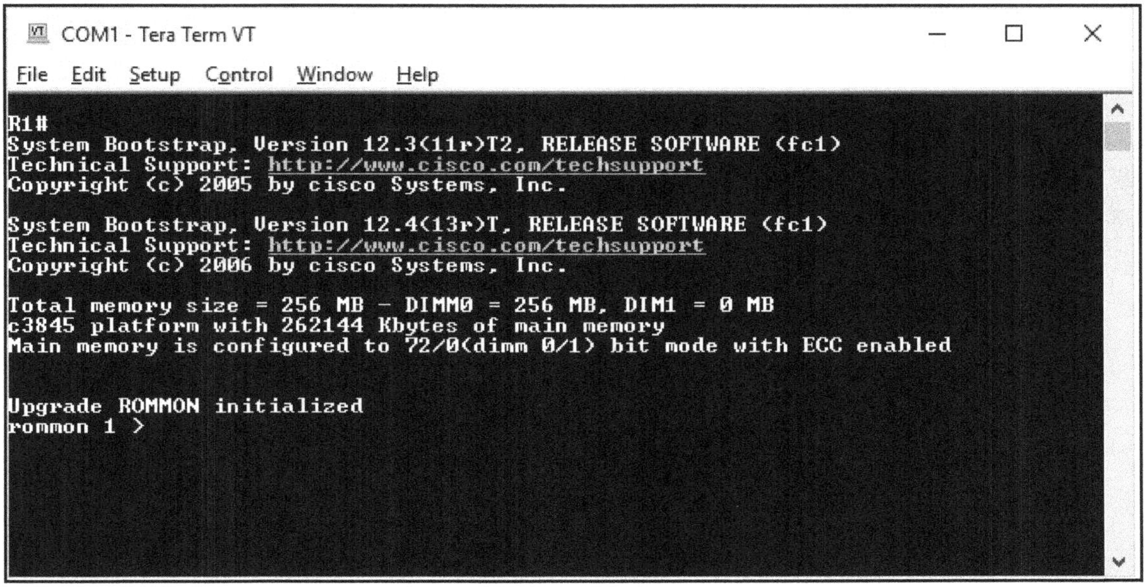

Figure 7.27. Entering ROM Monitor mode in a router

5. Type ? and press *Enter* to display a list of available ROMMON commands. Locate the `confreg` command in this list, as shown in Figure 7.28:

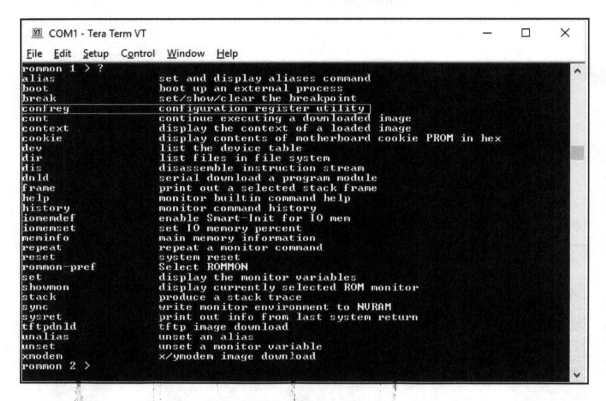

Figure 7.28. Configuration register utility command

6. Type `confreg 0x2142` and press *Enter* to tell the router not to automatically load the startup configuration when booting (see Figure 7.29).

7. Type `reset` and press *Enter* to reboot the router as in Figure 7.29:

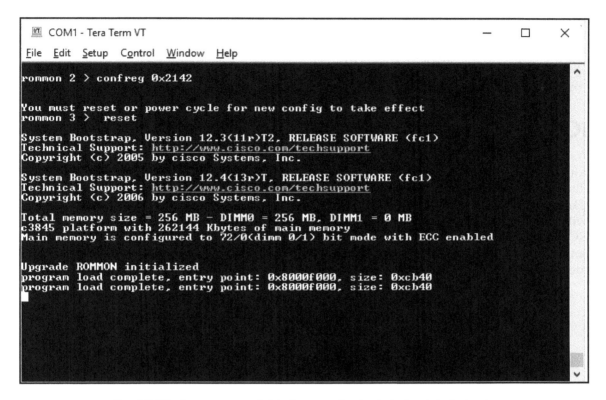

Figure 7.29. Telling the router not to automatically load the startup configuration when booting and rebooting the router

8. Once a router completes its boot process and displays the user EXEC prompt, try to enter in the privileged EXEC mode (see Figure 7.30). Note that no password is required:

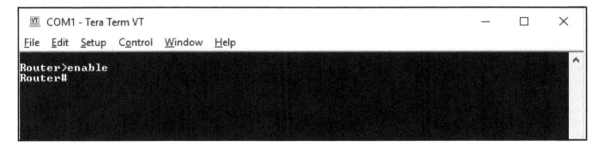

Figure 7.30. No password is required when entering in the privileged EXEC mode

You can learn more about standard break key sequence combinations for the most common operating systems and some tips on how to troubleshoot problems from `https://www.cisco.com/c/en/us/support/docs/routers/10000-series-routers/12818-61.html`.

IOS system files

As you know now, the **IOS** is the Cisco's operating system that is used in most switches and routers. That being said, exceptions include **Advanced Security Appliance (ASA)** devices that do not use Cisco IOS; instead, they use an OS derived from Linux. In addition, IOS is a CLI-based operating system that is based on modes. Thus, I guess, you are already familiar with modes such as user EXEC mode, privileged EXEC Mode, global Configuration Mode, ROM Monitor Mode, Setup mode, and many others where each mode is characterized by a set of commands. When it comes to versions, Cisco typically uses the following letters to identify the types of versions of IOS:

- *a* represents the major version number
- *b* represents the minor version number
- *c* represents the release number
- *d* represents the interim build number
- e represents the software release train, where *T* is for Technology, *E* is for Enterprise, *S* is for Service provider, and so on.

In this way, depending on what the Cisco IOS versions are aimed at, they are grouped into:

- Rebuilds, which are used to fix problems or vulnerabilities
- Interim releases, which represent the actual developments
- Maintenance releases, which include enhancements and fixes

You can learn more about the basic set of commands used to manipulate files on your routing device using the Cisco **IOS File System (IFS)** from `https://www.cisco.com/c/en/us/td/docs/ios/12_2/configfun/command/reference/ffun_r/frf006.html`.

IOS 15.0 system image packaging

It is interesting to note that Cisco IOSs are organized into packages where each package supports a certain service category, such as data, unified communication, and security which is are activated using Cisco Software Activation licensing keys. Unlike switches, routers by default include the IP Base service category. In general, there are eight new packages for routers and five packages for switches. So, starting as of Cisco **Integrated Services Routers Generation 2** (**ISR G2**), that includes product series such as 1900, 2900, and 3900; Cisco provides services on demand that are enabled through the use of licensing. To obtain a license key from Cisco, a customer must provide the product ID, the router's serial number, and the **Product Activation Key (PAK)**. This licensing method has made it possible for customers to save money using only the services that they need. Therefore, in every new order of the ISR G2 platform, along with a single universal Cisco IOS software image comes a license that enables access to the required functionalities. There are two types of universal images:

- `Universalk9` image, which offers all of the Cisco IOS software features
- `Universalk9_npe` image, which lacks any strong payload encryption

IOS image filename

Now that we know that each package contains certain feature sets, then that helps in choosing the proper IOS for our device every time that we want to purchase or upgrade. That being said, from the example given in Figure 7.31, let's identify the significance of each element of the IOS image file version 15 on an ISR G2:

```
c 2 9 0 0 - u n i v e r s a l k 9 - m z . S P A . 1 5 1 - 1 . M 4 . b i n
```

Figure 7.31. Different elements of an IOS version 15 image file

- **c2900** indicates the platform (that is, device)
- **universalk9** indicates the type of universal image
- **mz** indicates that the image file is running from RAM and is compressed
- **SPA** indicates that the image file is digitally signed by Cisco
- **151-1.M4** indicates the version of IOS
- **bin** indicates that this file is a binary executable file

IOS image management

If you take into account the fact that you cannot prevent the unexpected from happening, you can at least minimize losses if you are always prepared. Because of that, it is necessary to have the right procedures and tools in place. That helps establish a proactive approach that will greatly ease the process of bringing back the services in the case of a disaster. Thus, necessarily, IOS software images and configuration files must be backed up to a router, a workstation, or a server.

TFTP servers as a backup location

Best practices recommend setting up a **Trivial File Transfer Protocol (TFTP) server** (see, *System logging overview* section earlier in this chapter about downloading TFTP freeware from the internet) to back up IOS images files in the event of downtime.

Steps to back up an IOS image to a TFTP server

Among the activities anticipated to recover network services in the case of downtime, backing up undoubtedly backup plays an important role. To back up an IOS image to a TFTP server, complete the following steps:

1. Connect your PC to a router over console cable.
2. Open the Tera Term emulator on your PC and establish a serial connection with the router.
3. Check the connectivity with the TFTP server by pinging it.
4. Enter the `show flash:` command to verify the image size and press *Enter*.
5. Next, in the privileged EXEC mode, enter the `copy flash: tftp:` command to copy the IOS image to a TFTP server as in Figure 7.29 and press *Enter*.
6. Enter a source filename for the IOS image backup and press *Enter*.
7. Provide the IP address or name of the remote host where you intend to back up the IOS images and press *Enter*.

8. Press *Enter* when you are going to be asked about the destination filename as in Figure 7.32:

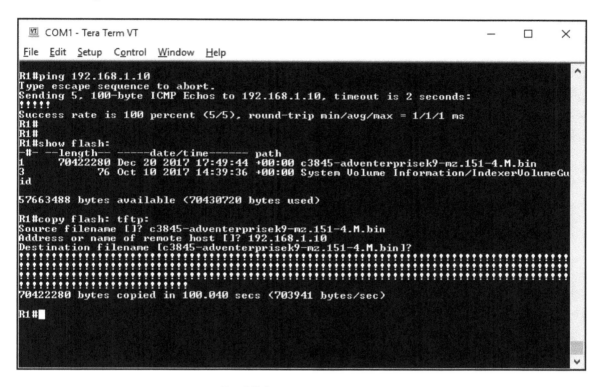

Figure 7.32. Copying IOS image to a TFTP server

9. Soon after this, the IOS image gets copied to a TFTP server, as shown in Figure 7.33:

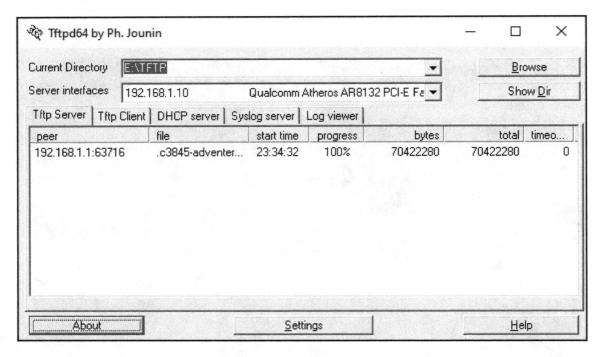

Figure 7.33. IOS image is copied to a TFTP server

Copying an IOS image to a device

Unlike backing up, a restore is the process of recovering configuration files whenever such files are damaged on switches or routers. To restore an IOS image from a TFTP server to the router, complete the following steps:

1. Check the connectivity with a TFTP server by pinging it.
2. Next, enter the `copy tftp: flash:` command to copy the IOS image from a TFTP server to the route and press *Enter*.
3. Provide the IP address or name of the remote host where the IOS images are stored and press *Enter*.
4. Enter a source filename for the IOS image that you want to restore and press *Enter*.
5. Press *Enter* when you are asked about the destination filename.

6. You will be asked to overwrite if there is a file already existing with the same name. Then, press *Enter*.

7. Soon after that, the IOS image is restored from a TFTP server to the router, as shown in Figure 7.34:

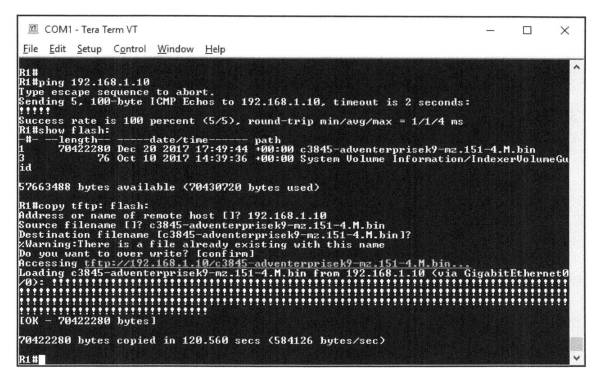

Figure 7.34. Restoring an IOS image from a TFTP server to the router

8. In the global configuration mode, enter the `boot system flash://<IOS image>` command to specify the newly added IOS image as a boot system.

9. Exit the global configuration mode and reload the router as in Figure 7.35:

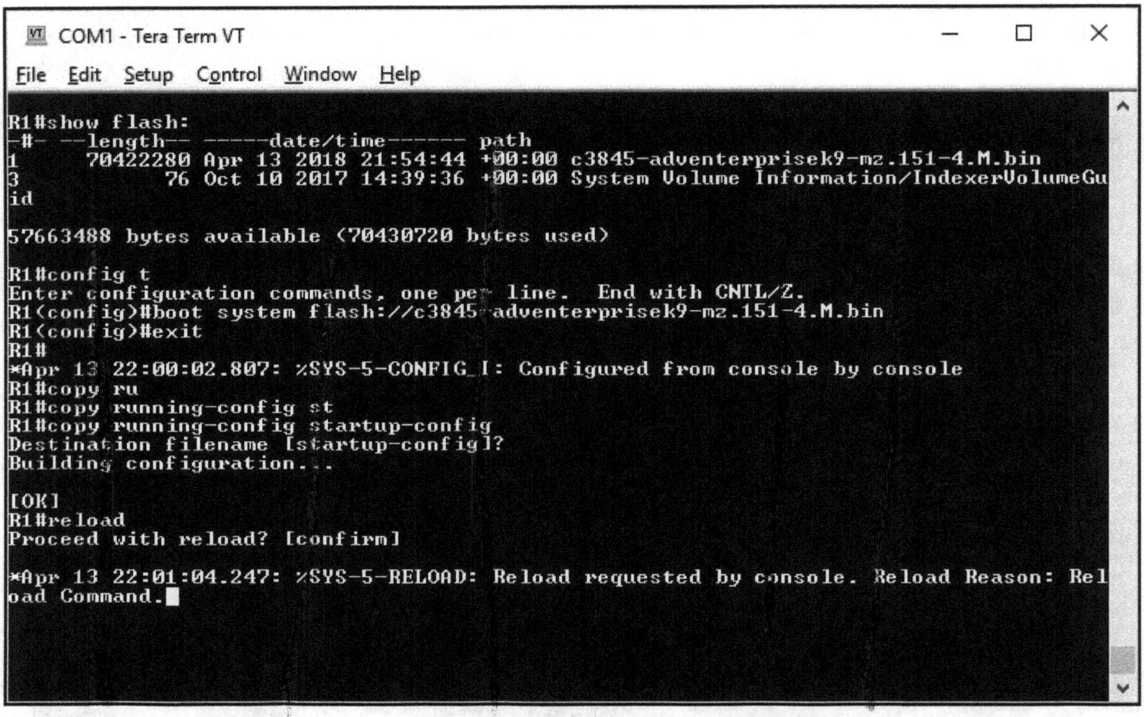

Figure 7.35. Reloading the router after specifying the newly added IOS image as a boot system

The boot system command

It is required to specify the newly upgraded or restored IOS image on the router as a boot system as in Figure 7.35. To do so, enter the following commands:

```
Router(config)# boot system flash://<IOS image>
Router(config)# exit
Router# reload
Proceed with reload? [confirm]
```

Software licensing

As mentioned earlier, as of IOS version 15.0, Cisco has modified the licensing methodology. This approach has made it possible to enable new technologies within the IOS feature sets without administrative overhead. That is achieved using universal image on any new device. Thus, using CSA licensing keys, the customer fairly easily enables technology packages in the universal image.

Licensing overview

Likewise, technology packages were also mentioned earlier. The eight new packages for routers mentioned in the, *IOS 15.0 system image packaging* section of this chapter, are: IP Base, IP Voice, Enterprise Base, Advanced Security, SP Services, Advanced IP Services, Enterprise Services, and Advanced Enterprise Services. Knowing that the packages are meant to satisfy the requirements of four service categories, it is important to understand what these service categories offer:

- IP Base is included by default in the routers, and as such it is a prerequisite for installing the data, security, and unified communications licenses. It offers features found in the IP Base package.
- Data offers data features found in the SP Services and Enterprise Services packages.
- **Unified Communications** (**UC**) offers unified communications features found in IP Voice package.
- **Security** (**SEC**) offers security features found in the Advanced Security package.

Enter the following command to view the technology package licenses and feature licenses supported on a router:

```
Router# show license feature
```

Licensing process

When a new router is purchased, it includes a preinstalled IOS software image, a temporary license, and a permanent license. A temporary license, often known as an evaluation license, enables the customer to try out most of the packages and features supported on the newly purchased router, whereas a permanent license enables activation of the customer-specified packages and features. For any future packages or features that the customer wants to activate, they must get a new software license. Licensing is a process in itself. As such, it consists of the following steps:

- **Purchasing the software package or feature to install** is the first step in the licensing process. Assuming that the customer wants to add Security to an existing IP Base service category, then the Software Claim Certificate is provided by Cisco or Cisco sales channel at the time of purchase. The Software Claim Certificate provides the **PAK**, an 11-digit alphanumeric key that is used to obtain a license.

- **Obtaining a license** is the second step in the licensing process. In order for the customer to acquire a license file, they must associate the PAK with a **Unique Device Identifier (UDI)**. UDI combines the **Product ID (PID)**, **Serial Number (SN)**, and the hardware version. All that information is entered into the **Cisco License Manager (CLM)** or Cisco License Registration Portal. The customer then receives an email that contains the information to install the license and an XML attachment that represents the license file:

  ```
  Router# show license udi
  ```

- **Installing the license** is the third step in the licensing process. After the license file has been obtained, the customer can install the license on a router by entering the commands shown here. Once the license is installed and the router has been reloaded, the license duration is as much as the life of the router across the IOS versions:

  ```
  Router# license install <stored-location-url>
  Router# reload
  ```

  The URL for CLM is https://www.cisco.com/c/en/us/products/cloud-systems-management/license-manager/index.html, while the URL for the Cisco License Registration Portal is https://cloudsso.cisco.com/sp/startSSO.ping?SpSessionAuthnAdapterId=standardnomfa TargetResource=https://sso.cisco.com/autho/login/loginaction.html.

License verification and management

In this section, you will learn the commands to verify the installed license on a router.

License verification

As explained earlier, the router must be rebooted using the `reload` command so that the license is activated.

Enter the following command to verify that the license has been installed on the router:

```
Router# show version
```

Activating an evaluation right-to-use license

In general, as mentioned earlier, Cisco provides the following types of licenses that can be ordered on purchasing networking devices:

- **Permanent licenses** are bundled for the lifespan of the device and as such have no expiration date
- **Evaluation licenses** are temporarily preinstalled on switches and routers and are valid from 60 to 90 days

However, as of IOS 15.0, Cisco has introduced the **Right-to-Use** (**RTU**) license. RTU is an honor-based model for licensing, meaning that after 60 days of an evaluation period, the *Evaluation license* automatically converts into an RTU license. These licenses do not use Cisco Software Activation. Hence, they require the acceptance of an **End User License Agreement** (**EULA**) by a customer. The EULA is only accepted once, and it is automatically applied to all Cisco IOS software licenses on a device:

- Enter the following command to determine which license is running on a router:

```
Router# show license
```

- Enter the following command to configure a one-time acceptance of the EULA on a router:

```
Router(config)# license accept end user agreement
```

Backing up the license

Usually, a directory or a URL that points to a filesystem is used as the location for storing licenses.

- Enter the following command to back up a copy of the licenses on a router:

  ```
  Router# license save <file-sys>://<lic-location>
  ```

- Enter the following command to show that the licenses have been saved on a router:

  ```
  Router# show flash0:
  ```

Uninstalling the license

The following commands for uninstalling licenses are applicable on 1900 series, 2900 series, and 3900 series Cisco routers.

- Enter the following commands to disable the technology package on a router:

  ```
  Router(config)# license boot module <module-name> technology-
  package <package-name> disable
  Router(config)# exit
  Router# reload
  ```

- Enter the following command to clear the technology package license from license storage on a router:

  ```
  Router# license clear <feature-name>
  ```

- Enter the following commands to clear the license boot module command in order to disable the active license on a router:

  ```
  Router(config)# no license boot module <module-name> technology-
  package <package-name> disable
  Router(config)# exit
  Router# reload
  ```

Traffic management

Traffic is the data that moves through a computer network at a given time. Specifically, there is voice data, text, graphics, and videos making up the computer network traffic. In addition, it leads to further categorization of traffic into realtime (voice and video) and non realtime traffic (text and graphics). This certainly represents different types of traffic and as such their handling requires appropriate skills and tools. In that regard, an important role in traffic management. This implies that all components of the computer network, including passive and active devices, must be in the service of network traffic. In this way, a well-designed network will enable the network administrators to classify traffic carefully according to priority. Therefore, regardless of whether it is a small, medium, or large network, all of these should be consistent with good network design standards so that computer network traffic serves the right purpose. Ultimately, well-managed network traffic increases employee productivity and minimizes downtime for the network.

Summary

We summarize the chapter with the following points:

- DHCP is a protocol that dynamically assigns IP addresses to devices on a network.
- IP addresses that are assigned to devices are located in the DHCP pool.
- DORA is the acronym that explains how DHCP works.
- NAT translates private IPv4 addresses to public IPv4 addresses.
- A stub network is a network that has one way to enter into the network and another way to exit the network:
    - Inside the local address is the address of the device that is being translated by NAT.
    - Inside the global address is the address of the inside interface of the NAT-enabled router.
    - Outside the local address is the address of the NAT-enabled router that connects the LAN.
    - Outside the global address is the address of the NAT-enabled router that connects to internet.
    - One-to-one translation, known also as static address translation (static NAT), translates a private IPv4 address to a public IPv4 address.

- Many-to-many translation, known also as dynamic address translation (dynamic NAT), translates multiple private IPv4 addresses toa multiple public IPv4 addresses.
- Many-to-one translation, known also as dynamic NAT with overloading, translates multiple private IPv4 addresses to single public IPv4 address.
- NTP is another protocol of the TCP/IP Protocol Suite that enables time synchronization among networking devices:
  - Manually by configuring each network device separately.
  - Dynamically using NTP server locally or on the internet.
- NTP topology is hierarchical, meaning that it is organized into levels where each level is called a stratum and is accompanied by a number to identify its level.
- Both CDP and LLDP operate on OSI Layer 2 and are to do with discovering neighbor devices:
  - CDP is a Cisco proprietary protocol
  - LLDP is a vendor-neutral protocol
- System logging is a standard that records events in the network in general, and on servers, clients, and network devices in particular.
- Syslog is a protocol that enables access to system logging events.
  - Device maintenance is an ongoing activity that helps prevent problems from turning into costly problems, both time- and business-wise.
- In Cisco IFS, you can navigate to different directories and list the files in a directory.
- ROMMON means ROM Monitor and is a bootstrap program that helps to initialize the processor and boot IOS.
- Cisco IOSs are organized into packages where each package supports a certain service category, such as data, unified communication, and security, which are activated using Cisco Software Activation licensing keys.
  - IP Base is included by default in the routers and as such it is a pre-requisite for installing the data, security, and unified communications licenses. It offers features found in IP Base package.
  - Data offers data features found in the SP Services and Enterprise Services packages.

- UC offers unified communications features found in the IP Voice package.
- SEC offers security features found in Advanced Security package.

- A temporary license, often known as an evaluation license, enables the customer to try out most of the packages and features supported on the newly purchased router.

- A permanent license enables the activation of the customer-specified packages and features.

- An RTU license is an honor-based model for licensing, meaning that after 60 days of an evaluation period, the evaluation license automatically converts into RTU license.

- Ultimately, a well-managed network traffic increases employee productivity and minimizes downtime for the network.

Questions

1. ROMMON means ROM Monitor and is a bootstrap program that helps initialize the processor and boot the IOS. (True | False)
2. _____ enables activation of the customer-specified packages and features.
3. Which of the following protocols operate on OSI Layer 2 and are used for discovering neighbor devices? (Choose two)
   1. CDP
   2. LLDP
   3. NTP
   4. DHCP
4. A stub network is a network that has two ways to enter into the network and another two ways to exit the network. (True | False)
5. _____ is an ongoing activity that helps prevent problems from turning into costly problems, both time- and business-wise.
6. Which of the following activities are part of the DORA in DHCP? (Choose three)
   1. Discovery
   2. Provide
   3. Request
   4. Acknowledgment

7. NTP topology is hierarchical meaning that it is organized into levels where each level is called an orbital and is accompanied by a number to identify its level. (True | False)

8. _____ is a standard that records events in the network in general, and on servers, clients, and network devices in particular.

9. Which of the following are steps of the licensing process? (Choose two)
   1. Assigning a license
   2. Obtaining a license
   3. Archiving the license
   4. Installing the license

10. Network Address Translator (NAT) converts private IPv4 addresses to public IPv4 addresses. (True | False)

11. _____ is a protocol that dynamically assigns IP addresses to devices on a network.

12. Which of the following terms is used by NAT? (Choose two)
    1. Inside regional address
    2. Outside local address
    3. Inside regional address
    4. Outside global address

13. Right-to-use (RTU) license is an honor-based model for licensing, meaning that after 60 days of an evaluation period the Evaluation license automatically converts into RTU license. (True | False)

14. IP addresses that are being assigned to devices are located in _____ .

15. Which of the following command configures a one-time acceptance of EULA in a router?
    1. `Router(config)# license accept end user agreement`
    2. `Router(config)# license accept EULA`

16. Which of the following command configures a loopback 0 interface on a router
    1. `Router(config)# interface loopback 0`
    2. `Router(config)# interface loopback 127.0.0.1`

17. Which of the following command disables CDP globally on a switch?
    1. `Switch(config)# disable cdp run`
    2. `Switch(config)# no cdp run`

18. Which of the following command enables LLDP globally on a switch?
    1. `Switch(config)# lldp run`
    2. `Switch(config)# enable lldp`

19. Which of the following command configures a stateful DHCPv6 server pool on a router?
    1. `Router(config)# ipv6 dhcp pool <pool-name>`
    2. `Router(config)# ipv6 dhcp pool <ip-address>`

20. Which of the following command configures the router to use an NTP server?
    1. `Router(config)# ntp server <ip-address>`
    2. `Router(config)# ntp server <host-name>`

Network Troubleshooting

8

This chapter is designed to teach you about the hardest part of working with computer networks. Yes, that is true! And trust me, troubleshooting is not an easy job. However, if you are willing to learn and practice at the same time, then no work is difficult. Thus, by understanding the importance of troubleshooting methodology, updating, and maintaining networking devices, you can increase the potential of a high standard of business continuity. Along the same lines, this chapter teaches you the different aspects of troubleshooting various networking devices and technologies. That being said, troubleshooting cables and interfaces, switches, routers, VLANs, ACLs, DHCP, and NAT are the topics discussed in regard to troubleshooting. In addition, this chapter discusses the tools for assessing basic network performance, as well as security threats and vulnerabilities. Finally, the chapter concludes with a summary and questions.

In this chapter, we will cover the following topics:

- Troubleshooting methodologies
- Troubleshooting scenarios
- Troubleshooting cables and interfaces
- Troubleshooting switches
- Troubleshooting routers
- Troubleshooting VLANs
- Troubleshooting ACLs
- Troubleshooting DHCP
- Troubleshooting NAT
- Basic network performance
- Network security

Troubleshooting methodologies

Troubleshooting in **Information Technology (IT)** is a skill that you are going to master with time, meaning each time you solve a problem, you gain more confidence, become more experienced, and you establish a knowledge base. That is why learning and practicing means a lot in IT, because while learning how to troubleshoot, you practice troubleshooting at the same time. With that in mind, the more you refine your mastery, the bigger the chances that you will solve problems and overcome issues.

Basic approaches

The ability to troubleshoot network issues is a very useful skill for a network administrator. With that in mind, no matter how skillful you are, know that troubleshooting is a skill that relies on certain procedures. This requires a logical and organized approach to problems with switches and routers in particular and computer networks in general. The procedures that you may want to consider in the troubleshooting process are as follows:

- You may want to consider checking the documentation to see if the problem has happened in the past
- You may want to check any available logs in a Syslog server
- You may want to consider searching the Cisco Knowledge Base articles
- You may want to consider running diagnostics programs
- You may want to consider discussing the issue with senior colleagues

Another approach to problem solving is the application of best practices. Best practices, known also as well-defined methods, are based on past practices when a certain method happened to be successful in solving similar problems. However, the word *best* is relative, as all problems are unique. This means that, while the same problem can be solved by the same method in a particular infrastructure, that necessarily might not work in another infrastructure. For that reason, in establishing good practices, practices are subject to a process that consists of a number of significant steps that are intended to filter the practices in such a way as to ascertain that they fulfill the criteria to be called best practices.

Among dozens of available troubleshooting methodologies, Cisco uses CompTIA's A+ six-step troubleshooting process. The steps are as follows:

1. **Identify the problem**: Gather as much technical information as possible.
2. **Establish a theory of probable cause**: Ask questions to determine whether changes were made recently.

3. **Test the theory to determine the cause:** Isolate the problem through removing or disabling components and services.

4. **Establish a plan of action to resolve the problem and implement the solution**: Test solution.

5. **Verify full-system functionality and, if applicable, implement preventative measures**: If the problem is not solved, go back to step three.

6. **Document findings, actions, and outcomes**: Document changes that you have made during troubleshooting.

Finally, know that the troubleshooting process and problem-solving techniques recognize two methods:

1. **Systematic approach**: Regardless of the type of problem, this is an effective troubleshooting methodology that is based on structured steps in solving the problem.

2. **Specific approach**: This is primarily based on knowledge and preliminary experience of solving the same/similar problems. In this approach, guesswork comes into play.

Resolve or escalate?

Experience has proved that sometimes problems are not solved immediately. That is because in the process of solving the problem, there may be situations when the network administrator does not have sufficient access rights, or an additional specific expertise is required, or that the implementation of the solution might need a manager's approval. Regardless of what the additional requirements may be, one thing is known for sure: in such situations, the problem shall be escalated. As a network administrator, prior to escalating the problem, you'd better consult your organization's policy.

Verifying and monitoring solutions

When the solution is implemented and the problem is resolved, according to the six-step troubleshooting process, you must document the changes that are made during the troubleshooting of the problem, including the implemented solution. However, the component part of the documenting step is also verifying the system operation. With regards to that, in the world of computer networks, there are tools that appear to be very simple, but their contribution is extraordinary in testing the functionality of the system. They are simply commands that are supported by Cisco IOS. That being said, the verification tools are as follows:

- The `ping` command verifies physical connectivity between hosts on the same network or hosts on different networks.
- The `traceroute` command defines the path from a local computer to a remote computer.
- The `show` command displays and narrows down information about the configurations preinstalled or made by you.

 The Cisco Knowledge Base can be accessed from `https://sbkb.cisco.com`.

Troubleshooting scenarios

In this section, you will get acquainted with some of the possible scenarios of problems that may occur with end devices, network devices, default gateways, and DNS.

IP addressing issues on networking devices

Network devices that exclusively use IP addresses for communications are routers and servers. There may be situations when on these devices, IP addresses are assigned by DHCP; however, that is rare. Usually, these devices have static IP addresses and are assigned by the network administrator. From that, if a router does not have assigned IP addresses on its network interfaces, then two or more networks cannot communicate with each other.

Similarly, if the server does not have an IP address, then the services provided are not accessible by the clients. Obviously, these situations cause a breakdown of network services. That being said, to overcome these issues, the network administrator should be vigilant with routers and servers. Thus, the following commands are a good way of overcoming the problems of that nature:

```
Router# show ip interface brief
C:\> ipconfig /all
```

You can learn more about the `show` command from `https://www.computernetworkingnotes.com/ccna-study-guide/cisco-router-show-command-explained-with-examples.html`.

IP addressing issues on end devices

As you know, IP addresses in end devices are assigned from three sources:

- The network administrator assigning IP addresses manually
- DHCP assigning IP addresses dynamically
- Windows OS assigning APIPA addresses to end devices that have not received an IP address from the network administrator or DHCP

Naturally, when a device does not have an IP address, it will be impossible to communicate on the network. Therefore, to verify that the device has an IP address, try using the following command:

```
C:\> ipconfig
```

You can learn more about the `ipconfig` command from `https://www.lifewire.com/ip-config-818377`.

Default gateway issues

The simplest definition of a **default gateway** (**DG**) is that it is a port to route packets to other networks or the internet. Then, if a DG is not functional, there is no communication of hosts in a LAN with hosts on other networks or the internet. Usually, the IP address in a DG is static, and as such it should be verified by the network administrator as to whether it belongs to the LAN's network. However, there are situations when the DG receives the IP address from DHCP. In those cases, it is necessary for the network administrator to verify that the IP address is successfully assigned by DHCP. The following command helps verify that the DG has been set:

```
Router# show ip route
```

Troubleshooting DNS issues

The **Domain Name Service** (**DNS**) is a service that translates hostnames to IP addresses. As such, DNS resolution directly serves users because it is easier to remember a name than an IP address. For example, if the DNS is down on a particular network, then it means that communication with hostnames cannot be accomplished because the resolution function is missing. However, communication over IP address communication continues to work smoothly. Thus, it is network administrator's responsibility to make sure that the DNS server IP addresses are set correctly on each and every host on a network. Among the commands that can be used to verify DNS functionality on a network are:

```
C:\> ipconfig /all
C:\> nslookup
```

 You can learn more about configuring and troubleshooting DNS on Cisco routers from https://www.cisco.com/c/en/us/support/docs/ip/domain-name-system-dns/24182-reversedns.html.

Troubleshooting cables and interfaces

In this section, you will get acquainted with some of the possible scenarios of problems that may occur on cables and interfaces.

Cable problems

As explained in the *Network medium* section of `Chapter 1`, *Introduction to Computer Networks*, usually there are three type of medium for data transferring: metallic, glass, and air. As the media are different, the problems are also different. Because of that, it is not at all strange if you experience situations when:

- **There is no connection between devices**: Recommendations are to first look at the two terminated ends to verify that the cables are properly placed in the connectors and then to carry on with cable tests. You may end up replacing connectors and reorganizing wiring too.
- **The connection goes on and off**: Recommendations are to do cable testing, as it may be that the cable is damaged or broken. You may end up replacing the whole cable.
- **There is connection, but the transfer speed is slow**: Recommendations are to have a look at both ends of the communication segment, as there might be issues with interfaces or configurations. You may end up updating interface drivers or reviewing the configurations about interfaces on switches or routers.

Duplex operation

In the *Types of communication channels* section of, `Chapter 2`, *Communication in Computer Networks*, three types of communication channel are mentioned: simplex, half-duplex, and full-duplex. It is recommended that both ends of the communication segment must operate in the same mode; otherwise, communication issues might occur. From the previous section, in the situation when there is a connection but the transfer speed is slow, it might be that **duplex mismatch** has occurred. To overcome these issues and increase performance along the communication channel, autonegotiation (see the following screenshot) was designed. Interestingly, the devices at both ends of the communication segment, at the beginning of the communication, declare the modes supported by them. Therefore, depending on the common mode supported by the interfaces of both devices, they will agree to use the highest performance mode. Another consideration to avoid duplex mismatch is that the two connected devices must operate on the same communication mode:

```
CD2#show interface gigabitEthernet 0/1 status
Port         Name              Status       Vlan     Duplex  Speed Type
Gig0/1                         connected    10       auto    auto  10/100BaseTX
```

Figure 8.1. Autonegotiation in a switch port

Duplex mismatch

When it comes to troubleshooting duplex mismatch, be prepared to be patient and focused. That is because these problems are characterized by the fact that the communication between the devices occurs at slower speeds. However, to solve this problem, the network administrator needs the appropriate tools. In that regard, the **Cisco Discovery Protocol (CDP)** as in Figure 8.2 is considered an adequate tool to detect a duplex mismatch between two Cisco devices. CDP works in such a way that whenever it detects duplex mismatch between the two ends of the communicating channel, it will immediately display log messages. For the benefit of the network administrator, those messages contain the device names and ports. This facilitates the process of identifying and fixing the duplex mismatch problems:

```
CD2#show cdp neighbors detail

Device ID: Acc3
Entry address(es):
Platform: cisco 2960, Capabilities: Switch
Interface: FastEthernet0/21, Port ID (outgoing port): FastEthernet0/21
Holdtime: 176

Version :
Cisco IOS Software, C2960 Software (C2960-LANBASE-M), Version 12.2(25)FX, RELEASE SOFTWARE (fc1)
Copyright (c) 1986-2005 by Cisco Systems, Inc.
Compiled Wed 12-Oct-05 22:05 by pt_team

advertisement version: 2
Duplex: full
------------------------
```

Figure 8.2. CDP in action

 You can learn more about troubleshooting interface errors, speed, and duplex mismatch from `https://www.ictshore.com/free-ccna-course/troubleshooting-interface-errors/`.

Switch troubleshooting

In this section, you will get acquainted with some of the possible scenarios of problems that may occur in switches.

Recovering from a system crash

If Cisco IOS is missing or damaged, you have an option to use a bootloader. It has a command line that provides access to the Flash memory. In addition, the bootloader enables you to format the Flash memory, reinstall the IOS, and recover a lost or forgotten password. You can access the bootloader in the following way:

1. Connect your PC to a switchover console cable.
2. Open the Tera Term emulator on your PC and establish a serial connection with a switch.
3. While still consoled into the switch, remove the power cord from the back of the switch, and after one minute, plug it in again.
4. As soon as you note the initialization of the switch in the console session, press and hold down the Mode button while the System LED is still flashing green.
5. When the System LED turns briefly amber and then to solid green, release the Mode button.
6. Shortly, the Tera Term window on your PC will display the bootloader prompt.

Network access layer issues

Obviously, the first impression is that the problems at the network access layer of the TCP/IP Protocol Model are mainly physical, and sure they are. However, we can benefit from Cisco IOS commands to identify those issues. For example, when running the `show interfaces` command, we get the status information for the interface and the line protocol. These are two very important parameters that help identify problems in the network access layer, because the first refers to physical medium, whereas the latter refers to the logical communication. Let's look at the following situations:

- **Interface is up, Line protocol is down**: This indicates an encapsulation type mismatch.
- **Interface is down, Line protocol is down**: This indicates that a cable is not attached.
- **Interface is administratively down**: This indicates that it has been manually disabled.

In addition to the earlier problems, which cause interruption of communications, there are problems that do not interrupt communications but do cause network performance issues. In general, that type of problem is categorized in two groups (see Figure 8.3):

1. **Input errors**: As the name suggests, these are incoming errors in frames that were received on the interface being examined. Included here are runt frames, giant frames, and **cyclic redundancy check (CRC)** errors.

2. **Output errors**: As the name implies, these are outgoing errors that prevent the final transmission of frames out the interface that is being examined. Included here are collisions and late collisions errors:

```
CD2#show interface gigabitEthernet 0/1
GigabitEthernet0/1 is up, line protocol is up (connected)
  Hardware is Lance, address is 0002.1690.e019 (bia 0002.1690.e019)
  BW 1000000 Kbit, DLY 1000 usec,
     reliability 255/255, txload 1/255, rxload 1/255
  Encapsulation ARPA, loopback not set
  Keepalive set (10 sec)
  Full-duplex, 1000Mb/s
  input flow-control is off, output flow-control is off
  ARP type: ARPA, ARP Timeout 04:00:00
  Last input 00:00:08, output 00:00:05, output hang never
  Last clearing of "show interface" counters never
  Input queue: 0/75/0/0 (size/max/drops/flushes); Total output drops: 0
  Queueing strategy: fifo
  Output queue :0/40 (size/max)
  5 minute input rate 0 bits/sec, 0 packets/sec
  5 minute output rate 0 bits/sec, 0 packets/sec
     956 packets input, 193351 bytes, 0 no buffer
     Received 956 broadcasts, 0 runts, 0 giants, 0 throttles
     0 input errors, 0 CRC, 0 frame, 0 overrun, 0 ignored, 0 abort
     0 watchdog, 0 multicast, 0 pause input
     0 input packets with dribble condition detected
     2357 packets output, 263570 bytes, 0 underruns
     0 output errors, 0 collisions, 10 interface resets
     0 babbles, 0 late collision, 0 deferred
     0 lost carrier, 0 no carrier
     0 output buffer failures, 0 output buffers swapped out
```

Figure 8.3. Where to look for input and output errors in a switch

Troubleshooting network access layer issues

As mentioned in the *Troubleshooting methodologies* section of this chapter, troubleshooting is a process that has certain procedures. As such, it requires constant vigilance from the network administrator. That is because every time a new device (say, a switch) is added to the network, new connections will necessarily be added too.

However, even though the newly added device can perform well from the infrastructure point of view, cabling might get damaged and configurations will change. This results in ongoing maintenance activities and network infrastructure troubleshooting.

As in the case of identifying problems in the network layer, so does the `show interfaces` command come in handy in the case of troubleshooting the same problems. Then, whenever there is no connection or the communication speed is not performing at the expected level, use the aforementioned command to check the following statuses of the interfaces:

- **When interface is down**: Check that the proper cables are used, the connectors are not damaged, and that duplex mismatch is not occurring
- **When interface is up, but connectivity issues exist**: Check for input errors and output errors

Ports in error-disabled state

Interestingly, whenever the security (see Figure 8.4) of a switch port is violated, whether intentionally or not, a violation can cause the port to become **error disabled**. An error-disabled port means that it is in a shutdown state and no traffic is coming or going to/from that port. Similarly, here too you can use the `show interfaces` command to identify the port status as `err-disabled`. Then, take your time to determine what caused the security violation. After you have done that and you are assured that there is no other potential for port security violation, you can go ahead and re-enable the switch port. To re-enable the port, first enter the `shutdown` command and then execute the `no shutdown` command:

```
CD2#show port-security interface gigabitEthernet 0/1
Port Security               : Enabled
Port Status                 : Secure-up
Violation Mode              : Shutdown
Aging Time                  : 0 mins
Aging Type                  : Absolute
SecureStatic Address Aging  : Disabled
Maximum MAC Addresses       : 1
Total MAC Addresses         : 1
Configured MAC Addresses    : 0
Sticky MAC Addresses        : 0
Last Source Address:Vlan    : 0001.6470.2502:10
Security Violation Count    : 0
```

Figure 8.4. Port security enabled on a switch interface

You can learn more about troubleshooting LAN switching environments from `https://www.cisco.com/c/en/us/support/docs/lan-switching/ethernet/12006-chapter22.html`.

Router troubleshooting

In this section, you will get acquainted with some of the possible scenarios of problems that may occur in routers.

Verifying IPv4 interface settings

So far, we have seen that the `show` command accompanied by its relevant options is quite handy in identifying various issues on switch interfaces. In that line of discussion, we are interested to know how handy the `show` command would be in identifying issues on router interfaces. The following lists some of the `show` command variations that can be used to verify IPv4 interface settings:

- The `show ip interface brief` command shows some brief information about all the router's interfaces, including their IPv4 addresses (see Figure 8.5):

```
Router# show ip interface brief
Interface              IP-Address      OK? Method Status                Protocol
GigabitEthernet0/0     203.0.113.5     YES manual up                    up
GigabitEthernet0/1     203.0.113.10    YES manual up                    up
GigabitEthernet0/2     unassigned      YES unset  administratively down down
Vlan1                  unassigned      YES unset  administratively down down
```

Figure 8.5. The show ip interface brief command in action

- The `show ip route` command shows the content of the IPv4 routing table stored in RAM (see Figure 8.6):

```
Router# show ip route
Codes: L - local, C - connected, S - static, R - RIP, M - mobile, B - BGP
       D - EIGRP, EX - EIGRP external, O - OSPF, IA - OSPF inter area
       N1 - OSPF NSSA external type 1, N2 - OSPF NSSA external type 2
       E1 - OSPF external type 1, E2 - OSPF external type 2, E - EGP
       i - IS-IS, L1 - IS-IS level-1, L2 - IS-IS level-2, ia - IS-IS inter area
       * - candidate default, U - per-user static route, o - ODR
       P - periodic downloaded static route

Gateway of last resort is not set

     10.0.0.0/16 is subnetted, 1 subnets
S       10.10.0.0/16 [1/0] via 203.0.113.6
     203.0.113.0/24 is variably subnetted, 5 subnets, 2 masks
S       203.0.113.0/30 [1/0] via 203.0.113.9
C       203.0.113.4/30 is directly connected, GigabitEthernet0/0
L       203.0.113.5/32 is directly connected, GigabitEthernet0/0
C       203.0.113.8/30 is directly connected, GigabitEthernet0/1
L       203.0.113.10/32 is directly connected, GigabitEthernet0/1
```

Figure 8.6. The show ip route command in action

- The `show running-config interface <interface-id>` command shows the commands configured on the specified interface
- The `show interfaces` command shows interface information and the packet flow count for all interfaces
- The `show ip interface` command shows the IPv4-related information for all interfaces

Verifying IPv6 interface settings

When it comes to verifying IPv6 settings on the router interfaces, the commands are almost identical to those for IPv4, with the only difference being that you should associate the `ipv6` tag with commands. The following lists some of the commands that can be used to verify IPv6 interface settings:

- The `show ipv6 interface brief` command shows brief information about all the router's interfaces, including their IPv6 addresses
- The `show ipv6 route` command shows the routing table of the IPv6 networks stored in RAM
- The `ping <IPv6-address>` command tests connectivity between devices that have been assigned IPv6 addresses on their interfaces

The show history command

Like any other work with computers, including network devices, activities are often repeated. That is also the case with Cisco IOS commands, where the network administrator enters the same commands in order to verify configuration settings. In this context, the show history command is of great benefit to the network administrator. As such, it is enabled by default both on switches and routers, and it temporarily stores the last 10 commands in its history buffer. You can use the *Ctrl + P* key combination or the Up arrow key to recall the commands. To view the content of the history buffer, use the following command (see Figure 8.7):

```
Router# show history
```

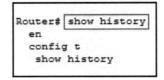

Figure 8.7. The show history command in action

Troubleshooting a missing route

Depending on the size of the network infrastructure, the complexity of the problems occurring on the network can vary. In addition, the very nature of networks is such that unpredictability is always present. That being said, issues such as interfaces failing, disruption of services, and executing wrong configuration are omnipresent in computer networks. Undoubtedly, the responsibility for solving all of these problems falls on the shoulders of the network administrator. To be able to identify and solve the issues, a network administrator must be equipped with the appropriate skills and adequate tools. The following lists some of the very useful tools in making the front run in identifying issues:

- ping
- traceroute
- show ip route
- show ip interface brief
- show cdp neighbors detail

Solving a connectivity problem

Whenever there are reports that users cannot access certain services, it is obvious that those are related to connectivity issues. However, we should not overlook the fact that in such situations, there might be a misconfigured route too. To tackle these network issues, a network administrator can rely on the following tools:

- `ping`
- `traceroute`

After the results of the tests are taken and conclusions are drawn that there is no connectivity between the networks, the next step is to investigate the routing table on the routers that connect these networks. Usually, in these situations, incorrectly configured routes are identified and removed, and the correct routes are then entered. This concludes the solution to connectivity issues.

 You can learn more about troubleshooting router crashes from `https:// www.cisco.com/c/en/us/support/docs/universal-gateways-access- servers/90-series-customer-premises-equipment/7900-crashes- router-troubleshooting.html`.

Troubleshooting VLANs

In this section, you will get acquainted with some of the possible scenarios of problems that may occur in VLANs.

IP addressing issues with VLANs

VLANs have taught us that every VLAN is characterized by a **unique IP subnet**. Thus, if two devices in the same VLAN have different subnet addresses, then they cannot communicate. These are common problems and their solutions require that incorrect configurations should be identified and replaced by correct configurations. In the aforementioned situation, the incorrect subnet address must be replaced with a correct subnet address. Next, the `ping` command confirms the solution you implemented.

You can learn more about VLANs and troubleshooting VLANs from `http://www.ciscopress.com/articles/article.asp?p=2181837 seqNum=9`.

Troubleshooting Access Control Lists

As we've said before and now, the beauty of technology in general and computer networks in particular is that everything is self-explanatory. From there, an **Access Control List** (**ACL**) is a configuration in the router consisting of several commands that control whether a router forwards or drops packets based on information found in the packet header. Thus, ACLs enable the following tasks:

- Limiting network traffic to increase network performance
- Providing traffic flow control
- Providing a basic level of security for network access
- Filtering traffic based on traffic type
- Screening hosts to permit or deny access to network services

In this section, other than discussing ACL concepts, the possible scenarios of problems that may occur with ACLs are covered too.

Processing packets with ACLs

Based on given filtering criteria on a switch or router, the following scenarios of ACL configurations can be done:

- **Implicit deny any**: A single-entry ACL with only one deny entry has the effect of denying all traffic. Recommendations are to configure at least one permit **Application Control Engine** (**ACE**) in order to avoid a situation where all traffic is blocked.
- **Order of ACEs in an ACL**: An ACL is an ordered list of actions, and each action is defined by an ACE. Thus, ACL performance is influenced by a decision specified by an ACE. Per Cisco IOS internal logic, ACEs are processed sequentially. Therefore, the order in which ACEs are entered is important.

- **Cisco IOS standard ACLs**: The `show running-config` command is used to verify the ACL configuration, whereas the `show access-lists` command displays ACEs and their sequence numbers. It is interesting that the statements are listed in a different order to that they were entered in. That being said, the order in which the standard ACEs are listed is the sequence used by the IOS to process the list. In this way, the statements are grouped into host statements and range statements.
- **Routing processes and ACLs**: The packet that arrives at the router interface is examined to verify that the MAC address destination matches the MAC address of the router's inbound interface. If it does, the frame information is removed and the packet is checked by an ACL. If permitted, the packet is then examined by the router to determine the destination interface. Next, the packet is switched to the outbound interface and checked by an ACL at the outgoing interface. If the packet is permitted, then it is encapsulated in the new layer 2 protocol and forwarded out of the interface to the next device.

Common IPv4 standard ACL errors

The most common errors in IPv4 standard ACLs are the wrong orders in which ACEs are entered. Other common errors related to IPv4 standard ACL errors include applying the ACL using the wrong direction, the wrong interface, or the wrong source address. That being said, network administrator can benefit from using the `show` command in order to reveal most of the more common ACL errors.

 You can learn more about troubleshooting IP ACLs from `https://www.cisco.com/c/en/us/td/docs/storage/san_switches/mds9000/sw/rel_3_x/troubleshooting/guide/trblgd/ts_acl.pdf`.

Troubleshooting DHCP

In this section, you will get acquainted with some of the possible scenarios of problems that may occur in DHCP.

Troubleshooting DHCPv4

To troubleshoot DHCPv4, use the `show` and `debug` commands to determine and correct the network connectivity issues:

```
Router# show run interface <interface-ID>
Router# debug ip dhcp server events
```

Troubleshooting DHCPv6

It is important to understand IPv6 address groups and how they are used when troubleshooting a network. In that regard, to troubleshoot DHCPv6, use the `service ipv6` command to determine and correct the network connectivity issues:

```
Router(config)# service dhcpv6
```

 You can learn more about understanding and troubleshooting DHCP in Catalyst Switch or Enterprise Networks from `https://www.cisco.com/c/en/us/support/docs/ip/dynamic-address-allocation-resolution/27470-100.html`.

Troubleshooting NAT

In this section, you will get acquainted with some of the possible scenarios of problems that may occur in NAT.

The show ip NAT commands

From the beginning of this chapter, it has been obvious that the contribution of the `show` command in identifying network problems in general and the connectivity issues in particular cannot be overstated. The same applies to identifying connectivity issues in an NAT scenario. So, in one way or another, it is about applying best practices in identifying and solving problems in computer networks. Therefore, the fact that the troubleshooting process begins with the verification of connectivity issues between the two devices speaks of such a standard. Then, always according to good practices, the following steps represent the activities that need to be carried out to solve the connectivity problems in NAT:

- Clearly define what NAT is supposed to achieve in your organization's infrastructure
- Use the `show ip nat` command, verifying that the correct translations exist in the translation table
- Use the `clear` and `debug` commands to verify that NAT is operating as expected
- Examine the routing information in the routers and analyze where the packet is being forwarded

The aforementioned activities include the use of the following commands:

- `show ip nat statistics`
- `show ip nat translations`
- `clear ip nat statistics`
- `clear ip nat translation *`

The debug ip NAT command

To understand whether NAT is functional, use the `debug ip nat` command to display every packet that is translated by the router. In addition to that, the `debug ip nat detailed` command generates a description of each packet considered for translation. Other than that, the `debug ip nat detailed` command provides information about certain errors, such as the failure to allocate a global address. However, note that in contrast to the `debug ip nat` command, the `debug ip nat detailed` command generates more overhead. Recommendations are that once the troubleshooting of NAT problems are finished, debugging must be turned off because enabling any debug commands on a production router may cause serious problems. Thus, the recommendations indicate that the network administrator needs to know more about using the `debug` command before using it (see the *The debug command* section later in this chapter).

 You can learn more about verifying NAT operation and basic NAT troubleshooting from `https://www.cisco.com/c/en/us/support/docs/ip/network-address-translation-nat/8605-13.html`.

Basic network performance

In this section, you will get acquainted with the use of the tools that will help in assessing basic network performance.

The ping command

In the *Verifying and monitoring solutions* section of this chapter, the definition for the `ping` command is given. Therefore, besides that, it is useful to know that the `ping` command relies on **Internet Control Message Protocol (ICMP) Echo messages** to determine the following:

- Is the remote host active or inactive?
- Are there time delays in communicating with the host?
- Is there packet loss in communicating with the host?

As an analogy, the `ping` command works a man is in a valley and is calling his friend. The voice reflected by the valley's mountains enables his friend to hear the echo of the man's voice. This is the case with the `ping` command, by sending an echo request packet to an address and then waiting for a reply. So, that being said, it is concluded that the ping is successful when the echo request packet reaches the destination and then the destination replies to the source with an echo reply packet. The echo reply packet includes and element known as a **timeout**, which represents the predetermined time of a reply. In Cisco routers, the default value of the timeout is two seconds, as shown in the following screenshot:

```
Router#ping 10.10.10.11

Type escape sequence to abort.
Sending 5, 100-byte ICMP Echos to 10.10.10.11, timeout is 2 seconds:
!!!!!
Success rate is 100 percent (5/5), round-trip min/avg/max = 0/2/10 ms
```

Figure 8.8. The ping command in action

The traceroute and tracert commands

Although they may look the same from the perspective of appearance and purpose, their implementation makes them different. Also, `tracert` is a Windows OS variation, whereas `traceroute` is Cisco variation used in its IOS. As was the case with the `ping` command definition, the definition for `traceroute` has also been covered in the *Verifying and monitoring solutions* section of this chapter. So, this enables us to discuss how both `tracert` and `traceroute` work.

Similar to the `ping` command, the `tracert` command on Windows relies in ICMP Echo Request packets. However, in contrast to the `ping` command, in the `tracert` command, the first IPv4 packet has a **Time-To-Live** (**TTL**) value of one ms, as in the following screenshot. Along the path that the ICMP Echo Request packet is traveling, it will necessarily go through routers, then the TTL value gets decremented by one before the routers forward the packet. Like this, if the TTL value is decremented to zero, the router drops the packet and returns an ICMP Time Exceeded message back to the source. On the other hand, once the source receives the ICMP Time Exceeded message from a router that just dropped the packet, it displays the source IPv4 address of the ICMP Time Exceeded message, increments the TTL by one, and sends another ICMP Echo Request. This communication cycle runs until the remote host is reached:

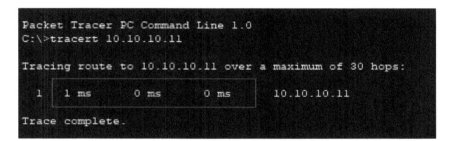

Figure 8.9. The tracert command in action

Unlike the `tracert` command, the `traceroute` command uses a sequence of UDP datagrams instead of ICMP Echo Request packets. Each of the sequences of UDP datagrams includes incrementing TTL values and destination port numbers. Cisco uses port `33434`, which is an invalid port number, and it is incremented along with the TTL. As in the case of Windows implementation, when a router decrements the TTL to zero, an ICMP Time Exceeded message is returned to the source (see Figure 8.10). Each of these returned messages displays information about another router of the path to the destination host. On reaching the destination host, the host responds with an ICMP type 3 message. Because the invalid port `33434` is used to reach the destination host, the code 3 message that indicates that the port was unreachable. However, the whole communication cycle of `traceroute` indicates to the source that the destination host has been reached:

```
Router# traceroute 10.10.10.11
Type escape sequence to abort.
Tracing the route to 10.10.10.11

1    10.10.10.11    1 msec    11 msec    0 msec
```

Figure 8.10. The traceroute command in action

The show commands

Throughout the chapter, the `show` command has been the topmost discussed topic. Following that line of discussion, this section lists some of the `show` command variations that are used by network administrators in troubleshooting routines:

- `show running-config`
- `show interfaces`
- `show arp`

```
Router# show arp
Protocol   Address        Age (min)   Hardware Addr    Type   Interface
Internet   10.10.10.1            14   0000.0C07.AC01   ARPA   GigabitEthernet0/1
Internet   10.10.10.2            -    00D0.FFEB.2D02   ARPA   GigabitEthernet0/1
Internet   10.10.10.11           14   0001.6310.5D05   ARPA   GigabitEthernet0/1
Internet   10.10.20.1            -    00D0.FFEB.2D03   ARPA   GigabitEthernet0/2
Internet   203.0.113.2           -    00D0.FFEB.2D01   ARPA   GigabitEthernet0/0
```

Figure 8.11. The show arp command in action

- `show ip route`
- `show protocols`

```
Router# show protocols
Global values:
  Internet Protocol routing is enabled
GigabitEthernet0/0 is up, line protocol is up
  Internet address is 203.0.113.2/30
GigabitEthernet0/1 is up, line protocol is up
  Internet address is 10.10.10.2/24
GigabitEthernet0/2 is up, line protocol is up
  Internet address is 10.10.20.1/30
Vlan1 is administratively down, line protocol is down
```

Figure 8.12. The show protocols command in action

- `show version`

Command syntax

The **command syntax** is an arrangement of keywords and arguments in order to create well-formed commands in Cisco IOS. As such, the syntax becomes a written standard that must be used when entering a command. The following lists the anatomy of the command syntax in Cisco IOS:

- Example: the `ping` command

  ```
  Router# ping ip-address
  ```

- Bold text indicates keywords (that is, commands)
- Italic text indicates arguments

In addition to bold and italic text, the Cisco IOS command syntax often includes optional elements represented by square brackets [ ], required elements represented by braces { }, and required choices within optional elements represented by braces and vertical lines within square brackets [{ | }].

The debug command

As mentioned before, the `show` command is much used by network administrators. That is because, if it can be said, it is favored by Cisco IOS, as it has much less overhead than the `debug` command. Another reason is that the output of the `show` command usually displays static information, compared with the output generated by the `debug` command, which displays dynamic information. That in itself means that `show` commands are mostly used for viewing configuration files, checking the status of device interfaces and processes, and verifying the device operational status, whereas `debug` commands are mainly used for monitoring events on a Cisco IOS device in real time.

Like `show` commands, `debug` commands are entered in privileged EXEC mode. However, network administrator should be very cautious when using `debug` commands. That is because `debug` commands have a higher CPU utilization and overhead compared with `show` commands. For that reason, the recommendations are that `debug` commands must only be used in troubleshooting specific problems.

The `debug` commands are more specific-oriented commands. Hence, prior to executing `debug` commands for your troubleshooting routines, make sure that you enter the command as in Figure 8.13.

```
Router#debug ?
  aaa           AAA Authentication, Authorization and Accounting
  custom-queue  Custom output queueing
  eigrp         EIGRP Protocol information
  frame-relay   Frame Relay
  ip            IP information
  ipv6          IPv6 information
  ntp           NTP information
  ppp           PPP (Point to Point Protocol) information
  standby       Hot Standby Router Protocol (HSRP)
```

Figure 8.13. The debug command in action

- Enter the following command to enable all system diagnostics on a router:

      Router# **debug all**

- Enter the following command to turn off all active debug commands at once on a router:

      Router# **undebug all**

You can learn more about using the `debug` command from `https://www.cisco.com/c/en/us/td/docs/ios/12_2/debug/command/reference/122debug/dbfintro.html`.

Network security

In this section, you will get to know the security threats and vulnerabilities and be aware of the importance of network security for business continuity.

Security threats and vulnerabilities

Many years ago, in one of the courses at Cisco Networking Academy, there was a statement that *no computer is safe except a non-connected computer*.

When we make the decision to establish security in a given computer network, the first thing to do is assess the potential threats against the given network. Identifying potential threats increases the chances of choosing the best possible solution and securing the network. Obviously, to achieve that, the adequate knowledge and experience in that area are required. That being said, nowadays, various technologies are used by businesses to provide security to their computer networks. However, the following question arises: *Is the threat to computer network services always coming from outside a network or is there something else to that?* Reports from the internet say that in addition to organized attacks coming from outside the perimeter of the organization's computer network, there are more organized attacks coming from the inside the network. From an employee inadvertently violating the security of a corporate network to a bug in application software that has caused the disruption of services, all are related to computer network security, because all that can result in loss of time and money for the business. Thus, threats can be grouped as follows:

- **Hardware threats** indicate the physical damage to every hardware component of the computer network.
- **Environmental threats** indicate the external factors that indirectly affect the computer network.
- **Electrical threats** indicate the supply voltage that directly affects the networking devices.
- **Maintenance threats** indicate the lack of activities to maintain the *health* of the computer network.

In computer security, an intruder is a person who gains access to a network without authorization. Unlike an intruder, a hacker is a person who gains access to a network with the intent of stealing data or damaging systems. In contrast to both intruders and hackers, a **vulnerability** is a weak point in a system that enables a security compromise for a network. Then, there is the question of how to protect the computer network from all these threats. Best practices recommend that awareness of employees is the point from where the process of building a network security must start. The rest is just technology.

Network attacks

If Microsoft Word enables me to write this book, a malware would definitely damage the data on my computer, including the Microsoft Word document. That being said, unlike the majority of software that generates a useful result, **malware (or malicious code)** is any software that generates a bad result, such as damaging, disrupting, or stealing data. The following lists types of malware:

- A **virus** is a type of malware that when executed modifies other computer programs
- A **worm** is a type of malware that replicates itself in order to spread to other computers
- A **trojan horse** is a type of malware that pretends to be a legitimate software, when in fact it is not

Other than malware, there exists other potential for attacking networks. The following are three major categories of network attacks:

- A **reconnaissance attack** is an attack that enables an attacker to gain unauthorized access to certain machine in a corporate network and try to explore the vulnerabilities in the network
- An **access attack** is an attack that enables an attacker to gain unauthorized access to a corporate network
- **Denial of service** is an attack that aims to make the service unavailable

Network attack mitigation

An old saying says that *the more knowledgeable you are, the less fearless you become.* In my opinion, everything has to do with the education about the huge potential of the harm that threats, vulnerabilities, and attacks have. That being said, the more aware employees are about the consequences of malware and cyber attacks, the more secure the computer network will be. In addition, maintaining regular system and device updates can lead to a more effective defense against network attacks. The following are several best practices to protect corporate networks from threats and attacks:

- Keeping OSes up to date
- Setting up a central patch server or a WSUS server in Windows-based networks
- Establishing a triple A (Authentication, Authorization, and Accounting) framework to set up access control on a network device
- Setting up a defense-in-depth topology with firewalls on the frontline
- Securing and keeping up-to-date endpoints

Device security

In general, the security of the computer network is organized in securing network devices and servers and securing the endpoint devices. Unlike networking devices and servers, endpoint devices are more likely to have OS installation in regular basis, thus the following list represents the best practices that should be taken into consideration in regard to most OSes:

- Change default usernames and passwords immediately
- Enable access to resources for only authorized users
- Disable unnecessary services and applications

As corporations make bulky purchases of endpoint devices, it is natural for these systems to have preinstalled OSes that do not have the most up-to-date patches installed. That is because manufacturers have been keeping the endpoint devices sitting in a warehouse for a period of time. The following guidelines must be followed to enable security on endpoint devices:

- Use a password length of at least 8 characters
- Make passwords complex
- Avoid using passwords that are easy to guess
- Deliberately misspell passwords

- Change passwords often
- Do not write down passwords and leave them under keyboards or near computers

When it comes to securing network devices, the following needs to be taken into consideration:

- Enter the following command to block login attempts for 120 seconds if there are three failed login attempts within 60 seconds on a router:

```
Router(config)# login block-for 120 attempts 3 within 60
```

- Enter the following commands to disconnect idle users after 10 minutes on a router:

```
Router(config)# line vty 0 4
Router(config-line)# exec-timeout 10
Router(config-line)# exit
```

Other security considerations in regard to network devices relate to enabling SSH as Telnet is not secure. Use the following steps to enable SSH on a Cisco device:

- Ensure that the router has a unique hostname
- One-way secret keys must be generated for a router to encrypt SSH traffic
- Create a local database username entry
- Enable inbound SSH sessions

 You can learn more about Cisco Router Security Solutions from `https://www.cisco.com/c/dam/en/us/products/collateral/security/router-security/routersec_tdm.pdf`.

Summary

We summarize the chapter with the following points:

- The ability to troubleshoot network issues is a very useful skill for a network administrator.
- Best practices, known also as well-defined methods, are based on past practices where a certain method happened to be successful in solving similar problems.

- Cisco uses CompTIA's A+ six-step troubleshooting process.
- A systematic approach is an effective troubleshooting methodology that is based on structured steps in solving the problem.
- A specific approach is primarily based on knowledge and preliminary experience of solving the same/similar problems.
- When the network administrator does not have sufficient access rights, or an additional specific expertise is required, or the implementation of the solution might need a manager's approval, the problem shall be escalated.
- The `ping` command verifies physical connectivity between hosts on the same network or hosts on different networks.
- The `traceroute` command defines the path from a local computer to a remote computer.
- The `show` command displays and narrows down information about the configurations preinstalled or made by you.
- IP addresses in end devices are assigned from three sources:
  - The network administrator assigning IP addresses manually
  - DHCP assigning IP addresses dynamically
  - Windows OS assigning APIPA addresses to end devices that have not received an IP address from the network administrator or DHCP
- The simplest definition for DG is that it is a port to route packets to other networks or the internet.
- DNS is a service that translates hostnames to IP addresses.
- Usually, there are three type of medium for data transferring: metallic, glass, and air.
- There are three types of communication channel: simplex, half-duplex, and full-duplex.
- Input errors, as the name suggests, are incoming errors in frames that were received on the interface being examined.
- Output errors, as the name implies, are outgoing errors that prevented the final transmission of frames out of the interface that is being examined.
- Whenever the security of a switch port is violated, whether intentionally or not, a violation can cause the port to become error disabled.
- The `history` command is enabled by default both on switches and routers, and it temporarily stores the last 10 commands in its history buffer.
- VLANs have taught us that every VLAN is characterized by a unique IP subnet.

- An ACL is a configuration in the router consisting of several commands that control whether a router forwards or drops packets based on information found in the packet header.
- The most common errors in IPv4 standard ACLs are wrong orders in which ACEs are entered.
- The `tracert` command is a Windows OS variation, whereas `traceroute` is a Cisco variation used in IOS.
- The command syntax is an arrangement of keywords and arguments in order to create well-formed commands in Cisco IOS.
- An intruder is a person who gains access to a network without authorization.
- A hacker is a person who gains access to a network with the intent of stealing data or damaging systems.
- A vulnerability is a weak point in system that enables a security compromise for a network.
- Malware is a software that generates a bad result, such as damaging, disrupting, or stealing data.

Questions

1. Best practices, known differently as well-defined methods, are based on past practices when a certain method happened to be successful in solving similar problems. (True | False)
2. _____ is a configuration in the router consisting of several commands that control whether a router forwards or drops packets based on information found in the packet header.
3. Which of the following are media for data transferring?
    1. Metallic
    2. Glass
    3. Air
    4. All of the above
4. A vulnerability is a strong point in system that enables a security compromise for a network. (True | False)
5. _____ are incoming errors in frames that were received on the interface being examined.

6. Which of the following are types of communication channel?
   1. Simplex
   2. Half-duplex
   3. Full-duplex
   4. All of the above
7. The `traceroute` command is a Windows OS variation, whereas `tracert` is a Cisco variation used in IOS. (True | False)
8. The _____ command is enabled by default both on switches and routers, and it temporarily stores the last 10 commands in its history buffer.
9. Which of the following tools help in identifying connectivity issues? (Choose two)
   1. `ping`
   2. `traceroute`
   3. `ipconfig`
   4. `flushdns`
10. The simplest definition for DG is that it is a port to route packets to other networks or the internet. (True | False)
11. _____ is a software that generates a bad result, such as damaging, disrupting, or stealing data.
12. Which of the following are network attacks? (Choose two)
    1. Reconnaissance attack
    2. Access attack
    3. Trojan horse
    4. Worm
13. Cisco uses CompTIA's A+ six-step troubleshooting process. (True | False)
14. _____ is primarily based on knowledge and preliminary experience of solving the same/similar problems.
15. Which of the following is part of the six-step troubleshooting process?
    1. Identify the problem
    2. Establish a theory of probable cause
    3. Document findings, actions, and outcomes
    4. All of the above

Studying and Preparing for ICND 1 (100-105) Exam

9

This chapter is designed to provide you with an overview of the **Interconnecting Cisco Networking Devices** (**ICND 1**) exam (100-105) exam objectives. In addition, this chapter contains explanations as to what the ICDN 1 (100-105) exam is, and how to register for the exam. Also, this chapter contains suggestions on how to prepare for the exam and considerations that need to be taken into account with regard to the exam. The beauty of this chapter is that it provides you with the detailed topics of the ICND 1 (100-105) exam, as well as the chapter references for each and every objective so that you can find more explanations in the book concerning the respective objectives. Last but not least, learn and practice as much as you can with computer networks in general, and Cisco switches and routers in particular, because only by doing so will you be able to get the skills to become a network administrator and pass the examination without hurdles.

In this chapter, we will cover the following topics:

- What is the ICND 1 (100-105) exam?
- What are the ICND 1 (100-105) exam topics?
- What to expect in the ICND 1 (100-105) exam?
- How to prepare for the ICDN 1 (100-105) exam?
- How to register for the ICND 1 (100-105) exam?
- On the day of the ICND 1 (100-105) exam
- Post-ICND 1 (100-105) exam certification path

What is the ICND 1 (100-105) exam?

The acronym **ICND** stands for **Interconnecting Cisco Networking Devices**, then number **one** (1) means that this is the first part of the two parts that the **Cisco Certified Network Associate** (**CCNA**) exam has (ICND 1 + ICND 2 = CCNA), and the digits **100-105** represent the exam code issued and standardized by Cisco all over the world. In one sentence, ICND 1 (100-105) exam tests a candidate's knowledge and skills related to network fundamentals, LAN switching technologies, routing technologies, infrastructure services, and infrastructure maintenance.

 You can learn more about CCENT certification from https://www.cisco.com/c/en/us/training-events/training-certifications/certifications/entry/ccent.html.

What are the ICND 1 (100-105) exam topics?

In general, it is an unwritten standard that is practiced by the IT industry when it comes to **certification exams**. Usually, **exam objectives** or **topics** represent general guidelines for a certain certification exam issued by the exam client (in this case, Cisco) that are likely to be included in the exam. At the same time, as Cisco updates exam questions from time to time without prior notice, it will necessarily update exam topics so as to better reflect the content of the exam. From what was said, you will find ICND 1 (100-105) exam topics in the following sections.

Topic 1.0–Network fundamentals (20%)

To accomplish this objective, the candidate should have a good understanding of the network fundamentals. This exam topic may include, but is not limited to: know what is computer network and how to build a computer network, identify network components, recognize network architectures, know what is NOS, describe TCP/IP and OSI, select the appropriate cabling for data transmission, describe hostnames and IP addresses, have good understanding of IPv4 and IPv6 addressing, and apply troubleshooting methodologies in resolving problems. When you feel confident that you have all the skills that are required on this exam topic, feel free to move on to the next topic:

- 1.1 Compare and contrast OSI and TCP/IP models
- 1.2 Compare and contrast TCP and UDP protocols

- 1.3 Describe the impact of infrastructure components in an enterprise network
  - 1.3.a Firewalls
  - 1.3.b Access points
  - 1.3.c Wireless controllers
- 1.4 Compare and contrast collapsed core and three-tier architectures
- 1.5 Compare and contrast network topologies
  - 1.5.a Star
  - 1.5.b Mesh
  - 1.5.c Hybrid
- 1.6 Select the appropriate cabling type based on implementation requirements
- 1.7 Apply troubleshooting methodologies to resolve problems
  - 1.7.a Perform fault isolation and document
  - 1.7.b Resolve or escalate
  - 1.7.c Verify and monitor resolution
- 1.8 Configure, verify, and troubleshoot IPv4 addressing and subnetting
- 1.9 Compare and contrast IPv4 address types
  - 1.9.a Unicast
  - 1.9.b Broadcast
  - 1.9.c Multicast
- 1.10 Describe the need for private IPv4 addressing
- 1.11 Identify the appropriate IPv6 addressing scheme to satisfy addressing requirements in a LAN/WAN environment
- 1.12 Configure, verify, and troubleshoot IPv6 addressing
- 1.13 Configure and verify IPv6 Stateless Address Autoconfiguration
- 1.14 Compare and contrast IPv6 address types
  - 1.14.a Global unicast
  - 1.14.b Unique local
  - 1.14.c Link local
  - 1.14.d Multicast
  - 1.14.e Modified EUI 64
  - 1.14.f Autoconfiguration
  - 1.14.g Anycast

Topic 2.0 - LAN switching fundamentals (26%)

To accomplish this objective, the candidate should have a good understanding of the LAN switching fundamentals. This exam topic may include, but is not limited to: describe switching concepts, explain Ethernet frame format, being able to troubleshoot interface and cable problems, know what VLAN is? and being able to troubleshoot it, to have a good understanding of interswitch connectivity and port security including configuration and troubleshooting. When you feel confident that you have all the skills that are required on this exam topic, feel free to move on to the next topic:

- 2.1 Describe and verify switching concepts
    - 2.1.a MAC learning and aging
    - 2.1.b Frame switching
    - 2.1.c Frame flooding
    - 2.1.d MAC address table
- 2.2 Interpret Ethernet frame format
- 2.3 Troubleshoot interface and cable issues (collisions, errors, duplex, and speed)
- 2.4 Configure, verify, and troubleshoot VLANs (normal range) spanning multiple switches
    - 2.4.a Access ports (data and voice)
    - 2.4.b Default VLAN
- 2.5 Configure, verify, and troubleshoot interswitch connectivity
    - 2.5.a Trunk ports
    - 2.5.b 802.1Q
    - 2.5.c Native VLAN
    - 2.6 Configure and verify Layer 2 protocols
    - 2.6.a Cisco Discovery Protocol
    - 2.6.b LLDP
- 2.7 Configure, verify, and troubleshoot port security
    - 2.7.a Static
    - 2.7.b Dynamic
    - 2.7.c Sticky
    - 2.7.d Max MAC addresses
    - 2.7.e Violation actions
    - 2.7.f Err-disable recovery

Topic 3.0 - Routing fundamentals (25%)

To accomplish this objective, the candidate should have a good understanding of the routing fundamentals. This exam topic may include, but is not limited to: describe routing concepts, have good understanding of routing table components, know how routing table is populated and updated, recognize and compare static routing with dynamic routing, being able to configure and troubleshoot inter-VLAN routing and router on a stick, and being able to configure and troubleshoot IPv4 and IPv6 static routing. When you feel confident that you have all the skills that are required on this exam topic, feel free to move on to the next topic:

- 3.1 Describe the routing concepts
    - 3.1.a Packet handling along the path through a network
    - 3.1.b Forwarding decision based on route lookup
    - 3.1.c Frame rewrite
- 3.2 Interpret the components of routing table
    - 3.2.a Prefix
    - 3.2.b Network mask
    - 3.2.c Next hop
    - 3.2.d Routing protocol code
    - 3.2.e Administrative distance
    - 3.2.f Metric
    - 3.2.g Gateway of last resort
- 3.3 Describe how a routing table is populated by different routing information sources
    - 3.3.a Admin distance
- 3.4 Configure, verify, and troubleshoot inter-VLAN routing
- 3.4.a Router on a stick
- 3.5 Compare and contrast static routing and dynamic routing
- 3.6 Configure, verify, and troubleshoot IPv4 and IPv6 static routing
    - 3.6.a Default route
    - 3.6.b Network route
    - 3.6.c Host route
    - 3.6.d Floating static
    - 3.7 Configure, verify, and troubleshoot RIPv2 for IPv4 (excluding authentication, filtering, manual summarization, and redistribution)

Topic 4.0 - Infrastructure services (15%)

To accomplish this objective, the candidate should have a good understanding of the infrastructure services. This exam topic may include, but is not limited to: describe DNS and its lookup operation, being able to troubleshoot end devices connectivity, being able to identify DHCP problems and troubleshoot them both on clients and routers, know what is NAT and being able to configure and troubleshoot NTA, know what is NTP and being able to configure and troubleshoot NTP, and know what is access list and be able to configure and troubleshoot. When you feel confident that you have all the skills that are required on this exam topic, feel free to move on to the next topic:

- 4.1 Describe DNS lookup operation
- 4.2 Troubleshoot client connectivity issues involving DNS
- 4.3 Configure and verify DHCP on a router (excluding static reservations)
  - 4.3.a Server
  - 4.3.b Relay
  - 4.3.c Client
- 4.3.d TFTP, DNS, and gateway options
- 4.4 Troubleshoot client- and router-based DHCP connectivity issues
- 4.5 Configure and verify NTP operating in client/server mode
- 4.6 Configure, verify, and troubleshoot IPv4 standard numbered and named access list for routed interfaces
- 4.7 Configure, verify, and troubleshoot inside source NAT
  - 4.7.a Static
  - 4.7.b Pool
  - 4.7.c PAT

Topic 5.0 – Infrastructure maintenance (14%)

To accomplish this objective, the candidate should have a good understanding of the general concepts of the troubleshooting methodology. This exam topic may include, but is not limited to: know what is syslog and being able to configure and troubleshoot syslog, being able to configure and verify device configuration and management, being able to configure and verify switch and router initial configurations, recognize the importance of device maintenance, recognize the importance of device security, and identify the proper network troubleshooting commands and tools. When you feel confident that you have all the skills that are required on this exam topic, feel free to move on to the next topic:

- 5.1 Configure and verify device-monitoring using syslog
- 5.2 Configure and verify device management
    - 5.2.a Backup and restore device configuration
    - 5.2.b Using Cisco Discovery Protocol and LLDP for device discovery
    - 5.2.c Licensing
    - 5.2.d Logging
    - 5.2.e Timezone
    - 5.2.f Loopback
- 5.3 Configure and verify initial device configuration
- 5.4 Configure, verify, and troubleshoot basic device hardening
    - 5.4.a Local authentication
    - 5.4.b Secure password
    - 5.4.c Access to device
        - 5.4.c. [i] Source address
        - 5.4.c. [ii] Telnet/SSH
    - 5.4.d Login banner
- 5.5 Perform device maintenance
    - 5.5.a Cisco IOS upgrades and recovery (SCP, FTP, TFTP, and MD5 verify)
    - 5.5.b Password recovery and configuration register
    - 5.5.c filesystem management
- 5.6 Use Cisco IOS tools to troubleshoot and resolve problems
    - 5.6.a Ping and traceroute with extended option
    - 5.6.b Terminal monitor
    - 5.6.c Log events

 You can learn about the exam topics of the ICND 1 (100-105) exam from `https://learningnetwork.cisco.com/community/certifications/ccna/icnd1/exam-topics`.

What to expect in the ICND 1 (100-105) exam

Usually, exam have **45-55 questions** for your ICND 1 (100-105) exam. The exam duration is **90 minutes**, but if you are a non-native English speaker, then you will be given an additional *30 minutes*. Cisco does not publish passing scores for their exams, however, expect passing scores to be **800-850** for your ICND 1 (100-105) exam. Questions do not have a *mark for review* or *flag for review later*, which means that you **cannot go back** to a previous question.

How to prepare for the ICDN 1 (100-105) exam

In general, there is no written standard on how to prepare for the certification exams, and ICND 1 (100-105) exam in particular. In fact, it has more to do with the best practices in a process of an exam preparation. In the case of the ICND 1 (100-105) exam, they are as follows:

- **Active work experience** in the ICT industry for 1-2 years
- Attending a **CCNA training** at Cisco Networking Academy
- Reading **CCENT/CCNA books**
- **Practicing** with routers and switches, or Packet Tracer and GNS3
- It helps a lot if you are certified with **CompTIA Network+**
- Taking **practice tests** so that you become familiarized with the ICND 1 (100-105) exam format
- Review the **exam topics** carefully to identify the points where you have weakness
- **Meet with friends** who have passed the certification exam and learn from their experiences

 You can help yourself preparing for the CCENT exam by exploring the content at `https://www.internetworktraining.com/`.

How to register for the ICND 1 (100-105) exam?

In general, all Cisco exams are provided by PearsonVUE. There are two types of exams:

- **Proctored exams** delivered at a test center
- **Self-administered** online exams

ICND 1 (100-105) is a proctored exam that is delivered at a test center. The test center is a facility that is authorized by PearsonVUE to deliver certification exams. So, when you feel that you are ready to take the ICND 1 (100-105) exam, go ahead and schedule your exam in the following ways:

- **Online** through PearsonVUE website (requires a web account) or
- Contacting a nearby **test center** (requires visiting a test center)

 You can schedule your ICND 1 (100-105) exam online through `http://www.vue.com/cisco/`.

On the day of the ICND 1 (100-105) exam

Make sure that you have **slept well** the night before the exam. **Do not stress yourself** in trying to remind the things that you have learned while preparing for the exam. Make sure to **arrive at the testing center 30 minutes before the exam is scheduled** and that you are carrying with you the required IDs. On entering the testing center, **be polite** with the test center administrator and read carefully the Pearson VUE **Candidate Rules Agreement**. When sitting in front of the workstation exam delivery, **say a prayer** because it will build up your self-confidence, **read the exam instructions** carefully, and **begin the exam**. Read each question very carefully and do not rush answering the questions before reading each answer carefully too. Remember that you **cannot go back to review the answer**, so try to do the best you can by **selecting the correct answers**. At the same time, **be rational with the exam time** because, even though there is **enough time at your disposal**, if you do not adequately manage it, then it may not suffice you. At any point, **do not let panic get in your way**; instead, **enjoy the exam** to its fullest by **having fun** with the exam questions. And like that, **question after question,** you will complete your ICND 1 (100-105) exam. At the end, you **will get the exam score**. Believe me, it is a **joyful feeling** when you realize that you **have passed** the exam.

However, if the exam result is not the one you hoped for, then **do not let the exam test you**. Instead, **accept the result** as such, and as of the next day, begin preparing to retake the exam by **identifying the points** at which you **performed insufficiently**. Remember that now you have the exam experience and that will greatly help you prepare for the exam and successfully pass it. **Good luck with your exam!**

You can familiarize yourself with the Pearson VUE Candidate Rules Agreement by visiting `http://www.pearsonvue.com/fl/doh/PVTC_Rules.pdf`.

Post-ICND 1 (100-105) exam certification path

Having passed the ICND 1 (100-105) exam, the candidate automatically obtains **Cisco Certified Entry Networking Technician (CCENT)** certification. **Congratulations on obtaining the CCENT certification!** CCENT is an entry-level networking credential from Cisco. In addition, the CCENT certification is the first step toward obtaining the CCNA certification. To do so, the candidate must pass the ICND 2 (200–105) exam. **Good luck with your upcoming Cisco exams, and I wish you a successful career as a network administrator!**

You can learn more about Cisco certifications from `https://www.cisco.com/c/en/us/training-events/training-certifications/certifications.html`.

Appendix A: Answers to Chapter Questions

As you have noted, each chapter is accompanied by a considerable number of questions to help you reinforce the concepts and definitions gained from the book. That said, in the following sections, you can find the answers to chapter questions, so you can compare your answers with those in the book.

Chapter 1–Answers

1. True
2. **Metropolitan Area Network (MAN)**
3. (1) Access, (4) Core
4. False
5. Twisted pairs
6. (1) Single, (4) Multi
7. True
8. Routers
9. (1) PAN, (4) LAN
10. True
11. Star
12. All of the above
13. False
14. **Personal Area Network (PAN)**
15. (1) Peer-to-Peer, (2) Client/Server
16. True
17. Internet
18. All of the above

Chapter 2—Answers

1. True
2. Multicast delivery
3. (1) Access method, (2) Flow control, (3) Response timeout
4. False
5. Subnetting
6. (1) EtherType, (2) **Frame Check Sequence (FCS)**
7. True
8. Application Layer
9. (1) Network Access, (2) Internet
10. False
11. IPv6
12. (1) **Logical Link Control (LLC)**, (2) **Media Access Control (MAC)**
13. True
14. **Spanning Tree Protocol (STP)**
15. (1) **Hypertext Transfer Protocol (HTTP)**, (2) **User Datagram Protocol (UDP)**
16. True
17. Classless subnetting
18. (1) **Stateless Address Autoconfiguration (SLAAC)**, (2) Stateful DHCPv6

Chapter 3—Answers

1. True
2. Network congestion
3. (1) Half-duplex, (4) Full-duplex
4. False
5. Modular Configuration Switches
6. (3) Telnet, (4) SSH
7. False
8. Frame filtering
9. (2) Source MAC Address, (3) Destination MAC Address, (5) EtherType, (6) FCS
10. True
11. Static secure MAC addresses

12. (1) Legacy inter-VLAN routing, (2) Router-on-a-stick
13. True
14. Fast-forward switching
15. (1) Number of ports, (2) Storing frames, (3) PoE

Chapter 4—Answers

1. False
2. Emulator
3. (1) `Switch> enable`, (2) `Switch> en`
4. True
5. Line Configuration Mode
6. `Switch(config-if)# switchport port-security`
7. False
8. bootloader
9. (3) `Switch# configure terminal`, (4) `Switch# config t`
10. True
11. vlan <vlan-ID>
12. `Switch(config-if)# mdix auto`
13. True
14. **Power-on self-test** (**POST**)
15. (1) `Switch# copy running-config startup-config`, (2) `Switch# copy run start`

Chapter 5—Answers

1. False
2. Distance vector
3. (1) Routing algorithm, (2) Metric, (3) Administrative distance
4. True
5. The **Routing Information Base** (**RIB**)
6. (1) Data structures, (2) Routing protocol messages, (3) Routing algorithms
7. False

8. Forwarding process
9. (1) Manually, (2) Dynamically
10. True
11. Routing
12. (1) Hostname, (2) IP address
13. True
14. Level 1 routes
15. (1) Classful routing protocols, (2) Classless routing protocols
16. False
17. Summary static routes
18. (3) **Enhanced Interior Gateway Routing Protocol (EIGRP)**, (4) **Open Shortest Path First (OSPF)**

Chapter 6—Answers

1. True
2. Putty
3. (1) `Router> enable`, (2) `Router> en`
4. True
5. Line Configuration Mode
6. `Router(config)# ip route <destination-host-ip-address> <subnet-mask> <ip-address>`
7. False
8. Routing table
9. (3) `Router# configure terminal`, (4) `Router# config t`
10. True
11. Router rip
12. `Router(config)# ipv6 unicast-routing`
13. True
14. In legacy inter-VLAN routing
15. (1) `Router# copy running-config startup-config`, (2) `Router# copy run start`

Chapter 7—Answers

1. True
2. A permanent license
3. (1) **Cisco Discovery Protocol (CDP)**, (2) **Link Layer Discovery Protocol (LLDP)**
4. False
5. Device maintenance
6. (1) Discovery, (2) Request, (4) Acknowledgement
7. False
8. System logging
9. (2) Obtain a license, (4) Install the license
10. False
11. **Dynamic Host Configuration Protocol (DHCP)**
12. (2) Outside local address, (4) Outside global address
13. True
14. DHCP pool
15. `Router(config)# license accept end user agreement`
16. `Router(config)# interface loopback 0`
17. `Switch(config)# no cdp run`
18. `Switch(config)# lldp run`
19. `Router(config)# ipv6 dhcp pool <pool-name>`
20. `Router(config)# ntp server <ip-address>`

Chapter 8 — Answers

1. True
2. **Access Control Lists** (**ACL**)
3. All of the above
4. False
5. Input errors
6. All of the above
7. False
8. History
9. (1) Ping, (2) Traceroute
10. True
11. Malware
12. (1) Reconnaissance attack, (2) Access attack
13. True
14. Specific approach
15. All of the above

Appendix B: Cisco Device Icons

The network administrator's task is not just to administer the organization's computer network. On the contrary, one of the important responsibilities is planning and designing network. This implies that sketches and projections must be made, so the network administrator should know what symbol represents what in the so-called Cisco Network Topology icons.

Cisco network topology icons

The following are a few of the Cisco device icons:

- **100Base-T**:

- **Access point**:

- **Broadband router:**

- **Cloud:**

- **Database:**

- Firewall:

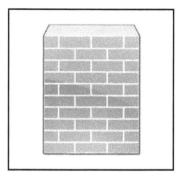

- Building:

- Hub:

- **Laptop**:

- **Layer 3 switch**:

- **Modem**:

- **Router**:

- **Switch**:

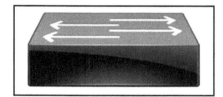

- **Wireless router**:

 You can download Cisco network topology icons from `https://www.` `cisco.com/c/en/us/about/brand-center/network-topology-icons.` `html.`

Appendix C: Numbering Systems and Conversions

We are taught to use the decimal numbering system, and we can say that we feel comfortable every time we have to play with the numbers in that system. However, in addition to the decimal numbering system, there are also other numerical systems that have found application in certain technological areas. Some of these numerical systems are: binary, octal, and hexadecimal.

Binary numbering system

Unlike the **decimal numbering system** that has base 10 and uses ten digits, the **binary numbering system** is the base 2 and uses two digits, that is, 0 and 1. As such, the binary numbering system has had a number of applications in technology, especially in the field of electronics.

Table C.1 represents the both decimal and binary numbering systems:

Decimal	Binary
0	0000
1	0001
2	0010
3	0011
4	0100
5	0101
6	0110
7	0111
8	1000
9	1001
10	1010

11	1011
12	1100
13	1101
14	1110
15	1111

Decimal to binary conversion

For me, the simplest conversion method for decimal to binary conversion is by using the following table:

2^7	2^6	2^5	2^4	2^3	2^2	2^1	2^0
128	64	32	16	8	4	2	1

Table C.2. Decimal to binary conversion

Example: Conversion of decimal number 196_{10} to binary number $?_2$

To convert decimal number 196 to binary, in table C.2 from left to right, begin placing 0s and 1s until you reach decimal number 196. You will enter 1s for numbers that are part of the calculation, and 0s for the numbers that are not part of the calculation. In that way, you will get the numbers 128 + 64 + 4 = 196. Finally, the string made up of 0s and 1s represents the result of the decimal to binary conversion. That being said, 196 in decimal is equal to 11000100 in binary (see *Table C.3*).

2^7	2^6	2^5	2^4	2^3	2^2	2^1	2^0
128	64	32	16	8	4	2	1
1	1	0	0	0	1	0	0

Table C.3. Converting decimal number 196 to binary number 11000100

Binary to decimal conversion

As it was the case with decimal to binary conversion, table C.2. will be used for converting numbers from binary to decimal. In this case, 0s and 1s are placed from right to left, as shown in *Table C.4*.

Example: Conversion of binary number 10101100_2 to decimal number $?_{10}$

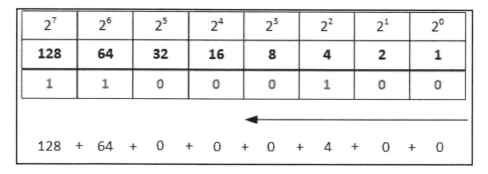

Table C.4. Converting the binary number 11000100 to decimal number 196

Like that, 11000100 in binary is equal to 196 in decimal.

Octal numbering system

The **Octal numbering system** is an old numbering system used in computers. It is a base eight numbering system that consists of eight digits: 0, 1, 2, 3, 4, 5, 6, 7. To convert from decimal to octal, you need to use binary in between. Binary serves as a bridge to facilitate the conversion between decimal and octal.

Table C.5. Represents both the octal and binary numbering systems.

Octal	Binary
0	0000
1	0001
2	0010
3	0011
4	0100

5	0101
6	0110
7	0111

Decimal to octal conversion

As explained earlier, to convert a decimal number to hexadecimal number, binary comes handy. First, the decimal number must be converted into binary. Next, the binary number gets divided into sets of three bits each and then from that gets computed the octal number.

Example: The conversion of decimal number 196_{10} to octal $?_8$

Because we have already completed the conversion of the decimal number 196 to binary number 11000100, let's divide the binary number into sets of three bits each, as follows:

```
011| 000| 100 - binary number 11000100 divided in two sets of four bits
each
 3 | 0 |  4  - result in octal referring to numbering representation in
Table C.5
```

Note that we have added a zero on the left side of the binary number 11000100. The reason for that is to be able to have three sets of three bits each. Adding a zero on the right side of the number not changes its value. However, avoid adding zeros on the right side of number in any numbering system. In that way, the decimal number 196 in octal is 304.

Hexadecimal numbering system

Unlike the octal numbering system, **hexadecimal numbering system** is used a lot in mathematics and computing. It is a base sixteen (16) numbering system that consists of sixteen digits, that is, 0 to 9 and A to F. Similarly to decimal to octal conversion, you need to use binary in between whenever you are converting from decimal to hexadecimal.

Table C.6. Represents decimal, binary, and hexadecimal numbering systems.

Decimal	Binary	Octal	Hexadecimal
0	0000	0	0
1	0001	1	1
2	0010	2	2
3	0011	3	3
4	0100	4	4
5	0101	5	5
6	0110	6	6
7	0111	7	7
8	1000	10	8
9	1001	11	9
10	1010	12	A
11	1011	13	B
12	1100	14	C
13	1101	15	D
14	1110	16	E
15	1111	17	F

Decimal to hexadecimal conversion

As explained earlier, to convert a decimal number to hexadecimal number, binary comes into play. First, the decimal number must be converted into binary. Next, the binary number gets divided into groups of four bits (a nibble) and then from that, gets converted to a hexadecimal number.

Example: The conversion of the decimal number 196_{10} to hexadecimal $?_{16}$

As we have already completed conversion of the decimal number 196 to the binary number 11000100, let's divide the binary number into two sets of four bits each, as follows:

```
1100 | 0100 - binary number 11000100 divided in two sets of four bits each
   C |  4   - result in hexadecimal referring to numbering representation
in Table C.6
```

In this way, the decimal number 196 in hexadecimal is C4.

 You can learn more about numbering conversions at `http://fourier.eng.hmc.edu/e85_old/lectures/arithmetic/node3.html`.

Appendix D: Boolean Algebra

Boolean algebra is a mathematical structure that has found a major application in electronics. That is because the two values of Boolean algebra, that is, true and false, can describe the best possible way the operation within logical circuit comprised two states, that is, on and off. That has given the Boolean algebra a very important role in designing integrated circuits and computer chips.

AND operation

The result of the **AND** operation is based on the common elements of 0s and 1s. The following is the AND operation:

AND	0	1
0	0	0
1	0	1

OR operation

The result of the **OR operation** is based on the combination of the two values of Boolean algebra. The following is the OR operation:

OR	0	1
0	0	1
1	1	1

NOT operation

The result of the **NOT operation** is based on the inversion of the two values of Boolean Algebra. The following is the NOT operation:

Binary value	0	1
NOT	1	0

 You can learn more about Boolean Algebra at `http://www.ee.surrey.ac.uk/Projects/Labview/boolalgebra/`.

Appendix E: Subnetting

In the *Subnetting* section in Chapter 2, *Communication in Computer Networks*, **subnetting** is explained, but no example has been provided showing how subnetting is performed. Therefore, in the following sections, an example of how subnetting is performed will be provided for each class of IP address.

Example—Class A subnetting

The 10.10.150.0/27 network is given. How many subnets and hosts are on this network?

```
11111111.11111111.11111111.11100000 - the subnet mask 255.255.255.224
represented in bits
11100000 - is the fourth octet in subnet mask 255.255.255.224
111 - is the network portion in the fourth octet 2³ = 8 subnets
00000 - is the host portion in the fourth octet 2⁵ - 2 = 32 - 2 = 30 hosts
0 to 31 - is the first subnet with 1 to 30 representing the range of
available IP addresses for hosts
32 to 63 - is the second subnet with 33 to 62 representing the range of
available IP addresses for hosts
........
224 to 255 - is the eighth subnet with 225 to 254 representing the range of
available IP addresses for hosts
The first IP address on each subnet is reserved for network, and the last
IP address on each subnet is reserved for broadcast.
```

Example—Class B subnetting

The 172.16.150.0/28 network is given. How many subnets and hosts are on this network?

```
11111111.11111111.11111111.11110000 - the subnet mask 255.255.255.240
represented in bits
11110000 - is the fourth octet in subnet mask 255.255.255.240
1111 - is the network portion in the fourth octet 2⁴ = 16 subnets
0000 - is the host portion in the fourth octet 2⁴ - 2 = 16 - 2 = 14 hosts
0 to 15 - is the first subnet with 1 to 14 representing the range of
available IP addresses for hosts
16 to 31 - is the second subnet with 17 to 30 representing the range of
available IP addresses for hosts
........
240 to 255 - is the eighth subnet with 241 to 254 representing the range of
available IP addresses for hosts
The first IP address on each subnet is reserved for network, and the last
IP address on each subnet is reserved for broadcast.
```

Example—Class C subnetting

The 192.168.150.0/29 network is given. How many subnets and hosts are on this network?

```
11111111.11111111.11111111.11111000 - the subnet mask 255.255.255.248
represented in bits
11111000 - is the fourth octet in subnet mask 255.255.255.248
11111 - is the network portion in the fourth octet 2⁵ = 32 subnets
000 - is the host portion in the fourth octet 2³ - 2 = 8 - 2 = 6 hosts
0 to 7 - is the first subnet with 1 to 6 representing the range of
available IP addresses for hosts
8 to 15 - is the second subnet with 9 to 14 representing the range of
available IP addresses for hosts
........
248 to 255 - is the eighth subnet with 249 to 254 representing the range of
available IP addresses for hosts
The first IP address on each subnet is reserved for network, and the last
IP address on each subnet is reserved for broadcast.
```

Appendix F: Cisco Packet Tracer

Cisco Packet Tracer is an application that simulates a computer network on your computer. The fact that it is a simulator means that there may be situations when any Cisco IOS command or functionality on switches or routers is not supported. So, with all its benefits and shortcomings, it is a required application for any administration network.

Downloading Packet Tracer

Cisco **Packet Tracer** is a simulator dedicated to Cisco Networking Academy students. However, with the changes made in recent years, Cisco Networking Academy has enabled the public to sign up free of charge for the Introduction to Packet Tracer 0318 course, where participants can learn about Packet Tracer and at the same time have an option to download it. So, if you want to benefit from learning about Packet Tracer, and at the same time download it, then navigate to `https://www.netacad.com/courses/packet-tracer/introduction-packet-tracer`.

Installing Packet Tracer

After you download Packet Tracer to your computer, all you have to do is begin the installation. To do so, follow the following steps:

1. Locate the downloaded file **Packet Tracer 7.1.1 for Windows 64Bit** and double-click on it.
2. In Windows 10, click on **Yes** to let the app make changes to your device.
3. Check *I accept the agreement* and then click on **Next**, as shown in *Figure F.1*:

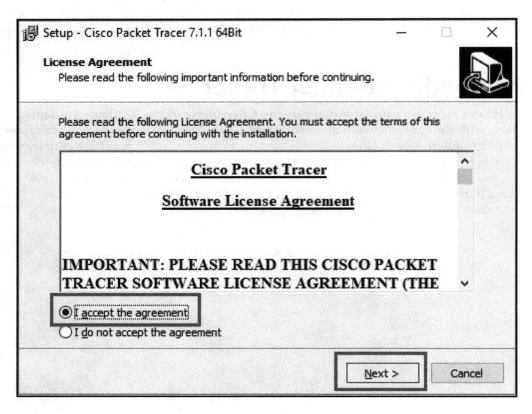

Figure F.1. Accept agreement and click Next

4. Either check or don't check the **Additional shortcuts** and then click on **Next**.
5. Click on **Install** to begin the installation of Packet Tracer on your computer.
6. Shortly, the Packet Tracer installation will be complete, as shown in *Figure F.2*:

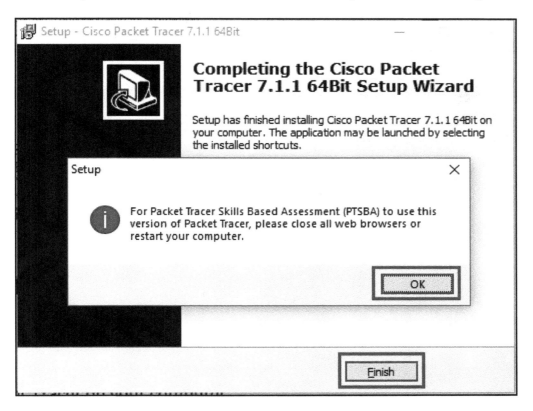

Figure F.2. Packet Tracer installation is complete

7. Click on **OK** to confirm closing all web browsers or restarting your computer, and then click on **Finish**.
8. The first time you launch the Packet Tracer, it will ask you to log in by providing your Netacad credentials.
9. After successful login, **Cisco Packet Tracer** is at your disposal (see *Figure F.3*):

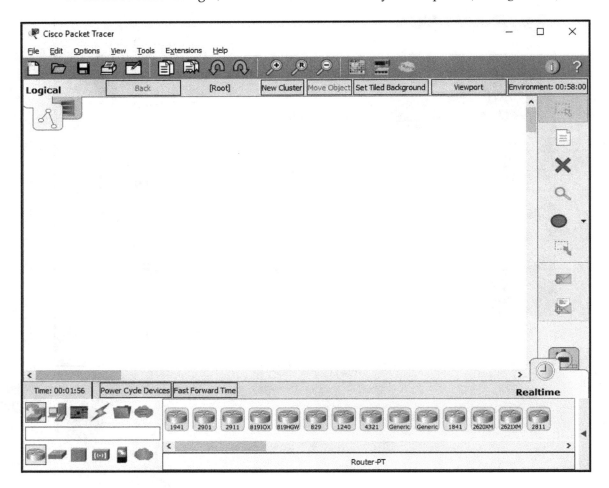

Figure F.3. Cisco Packet Tracer user interface

 You can download and learn more about Cisco Packet Tracer at https:// www.netacad.com/courses/packet-tracer.

Appendix G: Graphical Network Simulator-3 (GNS3)

Unlike Cisco Packet Tracer, **Graphical Network Simulator-3**, or better known as **GNS3**, is an application that emulates a computer network on your computer. The fact that it is an emulator means that you are simulating the Cisco IOS. Actually, you play with devices such as switches and routers as if they were physical devices. Compared to Cisco Packet Tracer, this means that any functionality and command that works on physical switches and routers will work in GNS3. With all its benefits, for an administrator network, GNS3 is an application that must be owned.

Downloading GNS3

In contrast to Packet Tracer, **GNS3** is an emulator dedicated to anyone involved in computer networks. From students to network professionals, everyone can use GNS3 because it offers an easy way to design and build networks of any size without the need for hardware. And the best part is it is free!

However, you need to sign up (see Figure G.1) if you want to download it. To do so, navigate to `https://gns3.com/software`:

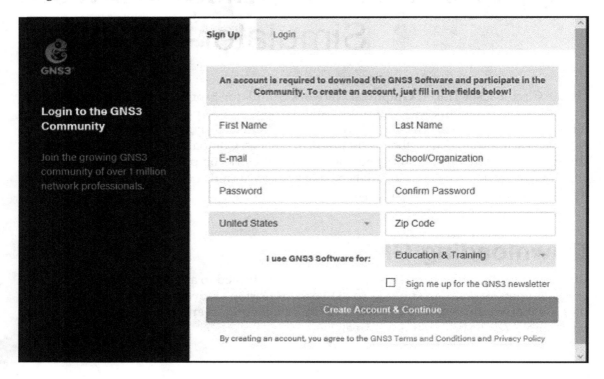

Figure G.1. Signing up for GNS3 download

Once you complete your signup and log in for the first time, you will be shown the download window, as shown in *Figure G.2*. Select your desired platform by clicking on the **DOWNLOAD** button.

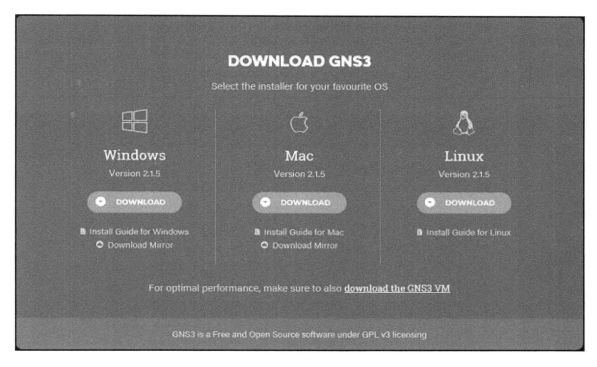

Figure G.2. Downloading GNS3

Installing GNS3

After you download the GNS3, all you need to do is double-click on the **GNS3-2.1.5-all-in-one** file to begin installing it on your computer. Unlike Cisco Packet Tracer, GNS3 installation is a bit complex because several components are part of the installation process, and the majority of them are mandatory for GNS3 to run smoothly. Because of that, I recommend you follow the installation instructions carefully: `https://www.technig.com/install-gns3-network-simulator/`.

When you are done with the GNS3 installation on your computer, then it is at your disposal. Note that GNS3 user interface (as shown in *Figure G.3*) is completely different from its counterpart Cisco Packet Tracer. Another thing to consider is that you need to have **Cisco IOS images**, so you can work with switches and routers on GNS3.

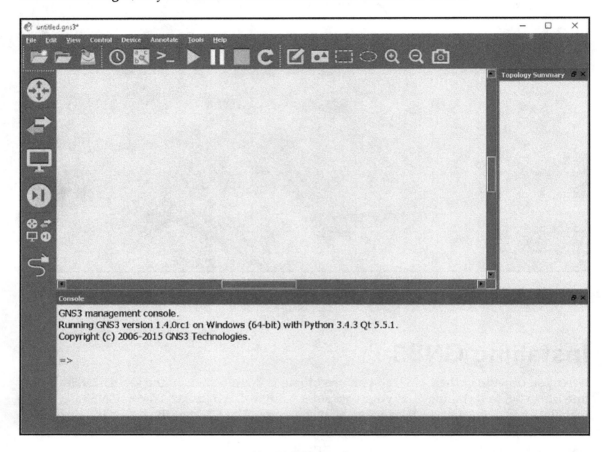

Figure G.3. GNS3 user interface

 You can download Cisco IOS images for GNS3 from `http://docs.gns3.com/1-kBrTplBltp9P3P-AigoMzlDO-ISyL1h3bYpOl5Q8mQ/`.

Other Books you may enjoy

Implementing Cisco UCS Solutions Second Edition
Anuj Modi, Farhan Nadeem, Prasanjit Sarkar

ISBN: 978-1-78646-440-8

- Set up your Lab using Cisco UCS Emulator
- Configure Cisco UCS, LAN, and SAN connectivity
- Create and manage Service profiles
- Perform various tasks using UCS
- Backup and restore Cisco UCS configuration
- Test various Cisco UCS scenarios
- Manage and automate multiple domains

Cisco ACI Cookbook

Stuart Fordham

ISBN: 978-1-78712-921-4

- Master the Cisco ACI architecture
- Discover the ACI fabric with easy-to-follow steps
- Set up Quality of Service within ACI
- Configure external networks with Cisco ACI
- Integrate with VMware and track VMware virtual machines
- Configure apply and verify access policies
- Extend or migrate a VMware virtual-machine LAN inside the ACI fabric
- Monitor ACI with third party tools and troubleshoot issues

Index

www.ingramcontent.com/pod-product-compliance
Lightning Source LLC
Chambersburg PA
CBHW080615060326
40690CB00021B/4706